VOYAGE INTO LANGUAGE

Voyage into Language

Space and the Linguistic Encounter, 1500–1800

DAVID B. PAXMAN
Brigham Young University, USA

ASHGATE

Published by
Ashgate Publishing Limited
Gower House
Croft Road
Aldershot
Hampshire GU11 3HR
England

Ashgate Publishing Company
Suite 420
101 Cherry Street
Burlington, VT 05401-4405
USA

Ashgate website: http://www.ashgate.com

British Library Cataloguing in Publication Data
Paxman, David B.
  Voyage into language : space and the linguistic encounter,
  1500–1800
  1. Linguistics – Europe – History – 16th century
  2. Linguistics – Europe – History – 17th century
  3. Linguistics – Europe – History – 18th century 4. Space and
  time in language 5. Cognitive maps (Pyschology) 6. Voyages
  and travels – Psychological aspects 7. Cartography –
  Psychological aspects
  I. Title
  410.9'4'0903

Library of Congress Cataloging-in-Publication Data
Paxman, David B., 1946-
    Voyage into language : space and the linguistic encounter, 1500–1800 /
    David B. Paxman.
        p. cm.
    Includes bibliographical references and index.
    ISBN 0-7546-0697-X (hardback)
      1. Space and time in language–History. 2. Language and languages–
    Philosophy. I. Title.

P37.5.S65 P39 2003
410–dc21

2002036808

ISBN 0 7546 0697 X

Printed and bound in Great Britain by MPG Books Ltd, Bodmin, Cornwall

Contents

List of Figures

Acknowledgments

Hans Aarsleff at Princeton University first introduced me to the study of language at a National Endowment for the Humanities summer seminar in 1988. I am indebted to him and the NEH for what has become a continuing exploration. I also thank my wife and family, who will find here a more complete answer to their questions about what I am working on. I am grateful to Brigham Young University's College of Humanities and the Department of English for time and resources to undertake this project and for their patience as I mentally traveled three centuries and four continents. I also thank students who, at one stage or another, helped me with the research. These students include Robert Bennett, Ed Cutler, John Duffy, Michael Hansen, Dan Peck, and Heidi Gassman Yates. I express gratitude to Emily Gigger and April Robinson Maughan for their excellent help in production. I greatly appreciate the contributions of Linda Hunter Adams to this volume.

Introduction

Developments in European language thought from 1500 to 1800 have generally been attributed to two factors, the refinement of tools in phonetics, grammar, and linguistic genealogy and the increasing exposure to diverse languages from around the world. To these forces I add another, spatial exploration and the novel application of spatial concepts. My title, Voyage into Language, suggests that language was an unfamiliar space that Europe entered and navigated, posing challenges similar to those encountered in terrestrial navigation. Spatial experience influenced linguistic thought in two ways. First, ordinary spatial experience—terrain and boundaries, near and far, journeys and paths, locations, and perspectives—provided conceptual structures, both conventional and novel, that guided those who investigated the properties of language. Second, these conceptual structures themselves underwent change. Expanding horizons, the sense of terrestrial space, and recognition of the difficulties of representing and navigating a spherical earth contributed to language thought by offering conceptual structures applicable to a different and equally challenging domain.

In the last two decades, cognitive science, or the contemporary study of how the mind thinks and processes information to achieve knowledge and make decisions, has shown that metaphorical mappings are not just verbal decoration and surface expression but a deeply rooted procedure for thinking. Much of our thinking involves conceiving one thing in terms of another. George Lakoff and Mark Johnson convey the point in the title of their book *Metaphors We Live By*.[1] Some topics, such as life, time, the mind, and language, pose a special problem to our intellect. Even though we experience many such ideas immediately, they have minimal intrinsic structure. Of such ideas, Lakoff has observed: "In domains where there is no clearly discernible prnceptual structure, we import such structure via metaphor. . . . A great many of our domains of experience are like this. Comprehending experience via metaphor is one of the great imaginative triumphs of the human mind."[2]

Thus we discuss the mind as a container, life as a journey, and time as a river. We think in this manner because our minds are modular. That is, they have multiple functions and corresponding inputs that are not entirely compatible. This principle has become foundational in cognitive science and has been advocated in various forms by Jerry Fodor, Noam Chomsky, John

Tooby and Leda Cosmides, Ray Jackendoff, Steven Pinker, and others.[3] Pinker says, "The mind is organized into modules or mental organs, each with a specialized design that makes it an expert in one arena of interaction with the world."[4] Jackendoff elaborates:

> Seeing, speaking a language, thinking, and remembering, for example, are not simply diverse uses of a single general psychological mechanism (be it associationism, stimulus-response connections, generalized problem-solving, or whatever). Rather they are specialized mechanisms, or modules, that subserve each function, each with its own task-relevant adaptations.[5]

The brain has specialized sites or networks of sites for each sensory input: language, different types of memory, our awareness of our limbs and the state of our bodies, movement in space, the recognition of other people as having minds of their own, and other functions. Even an apparently single sense like sight is assembled from different functions and processes, with different brain sites responsible for motion, size, color, distance, and shape. When we want to grasp an idea holistically, we do so by combining in patchwork fashion multiple images, associations, sensory data, contexts, hierarchies, purposes, and applications. Our minds work by assembling multiple yet different data streams into patchy, not seamless, gestalts. The process of knowing something shifts considerably in this paradigm. Knowledge results from the incomplete, partially redundant, multimodal representations we achieve through the cooperation of varied inputs and neural regions, each on contract to provide its resources to the functioning of the whole.

In approaching language study through space, I am paying homage to modularity. We know language by many means because our minds require it and because language, reflecting our mental structures, is also multi-modal and manifold in nature. It is like a varied terrain we travel in by different means. We might argue, as did Wittgenstein, that language is more like a patchwork of devices, structures, games, and strategies than like a unified pattern for thinking and communicating.

Space provides only a limited number of avenues into language, but they are important for two reasons. Many early moderns thought about language by means of the conceptual figure of space. More broadly, language's manifold nature prevents us from seeing it for itself. Instead we must see it *as*. To know language is to think about it in terms of something else.

Space is already deeply embedded in semantics. To translate means to move from one location to another. To convey ideas is to carry them from one position or container to another. To comprehend is to enclose or contain. To understand is to step beneath. To analyze is to unloose, to criticize to separate. To articulate is to divide into parts. Etymologies also offer intersections of space with other types of experience. The words *travel* and *travail* come from the same root. In the Middle Ages to *travel* was to *travail*, to labor with discomfort and inconvenience. History shaped the semantics. As new means of transportation and more accurate maps made journeying easier, the word *travel* shed its connotations of hard work. In the sixteenth and seventeenth centuries people also applied the word *travail* to a similarly arduous process—and one directly connected with travel—the learning of new languages. Vocabularies and grammars—the maps of the language student—were written to lessen the travail, but language learning still required effort.

Ernst Cassirer holds that the forms by which we apprehend less concrete phenomena derive from perceptions such as space. Explicating Wilhelm von Humboldt via Kant, Cassirer observes that "since all our knowledge of phenomena ultimately dissolves into a knowledge of temporal and spatial relations, [form] constitutes the truly objectifying principle of knowledge."[6] I take him to be saying that our perceptions of space and time generate much of what we call form; thus a study of form will yield more fruit if we recognize the ways in which a fundamental concept such as space appears in different guises.

The great age of discovery threw up many challenges as new phenomena required new objectifying principles. Discovery itself provided some of these principles and triggered a revolution in spatial relations as fragments of the earth's terrain and oceans became an increasingly wondrous and varied yet coherent sphere. Discovery also required revolutions in the intellectual sphere. Sir Francis Bacon referred to the new learning as a New Atlantis or a "new continent of learning," and to a philosophical grammar particularly as one of the "coasts of the new intellectual world."[7] The discipline of rhetoric was reconfigured in the seventeenth century when the finite world of topoi, or the places of invention and discovery, fell before more complex and less stable concepts of space and place. Locke, reaching for an explanation of how our minds fashion ideas that have no counterpart in nature, called his new theory the "way of ideas," which in some respects resembles a path across an infinite and centerless mental space, which in turn corresponds to the absolute space of Newton.

Space and movement through space also provide us with fundamental conceptual structures for collecting, comparing, and classifying linguistic information. Almost all early modern linguistic collections are organized geographically, for good reasons. Geography is the quickest way to place a language in relation to others, and since we expect similar languages to exist in close proximity to each other, geography is the quickest way to confirm or surprise our expectation. Early modern collections of languages resemble the cabinet of curiosities, random displays of surprising and anomalous objects, but both linguistic collections and cabinets gave way to displays organized by more rigorous classification schemes which, I urge, map objects onto space in new ways. Grammars entail space in the sense that features of a language must be segregated, as if placed in different sites, when placed under analysis. The writing of a grammar further entails spatial thinking because language elements must be arranged in a literal space, that offered by sheets of paper. Grammar exists to extract the constitutive aspects of speech, which is oral and temporal, and transfer them into fewer dimensions so they can be approached singly and their mutual influences be traced one at a time. Even the word *aspect* here derives from space: aspect is what we see of an object from a certain perspective.

This book will study what Europe learned about language from mapping space onto it and, reciprocally, mapping language onto space. Chapter 1 examines the general importance of cognitive mappings and the particular relevance of spatial concepts in language study. Chapter 2 provides evidence that spatial schemes of organization and developments in the abstract conceptualization of space influenced attempts to conceptualize language systematically. I will argue in particular that the writing of grammars is a spatialization of language. Chapter 3, under the heading "barriers," explores ways in which language differences separate peoples. It also investigates attitudes toward the separation between words and nature that some saw as the great obstacle, and some as the great key, to knowledge. Chapter 4 demonstrates something of a paradox, that as colonizers tried to contain the contamination they perceived in other languages, they discovered that those languages contained their beauties and efficacies. Chapter 5 treats philosophical language, showing that it assumes a static, rather than dynamic and perspectival, view of knowledge. In Chapter 6, Europe's changing ideas of space and its ongoing terrestrial discoveries are shown to be disruptive for some systems of learning, notably rhetoric. Chapter 7 considers Locke's revolutionary study of human understanding, which, I think for the first time, explained how sense perceptions, language, and reason could cooperate in such a way as to make truly different ideas occur from one population to another. I try to show that these advances came from Locke's wide reading in travel literature and that his treatment of ideas incorporates spatial models. Chapter 8 discusses the work of Johann Gottfried Herder and Wilhelm von Humboldt, arguing that their investigations of the effects of linguistic diversity on cognition and culture are conditioned by the image of the journey, which in turn places the linguist as the scout or navigator in humanity's joint, open-ended exploration of the possibilities inherent in human nature, language, and the physical world. Herder and Humboldt in one sense bring us back to the journey into language, but they represent an important shift. They wrote when humanity had mapped and navigated much of the earth and had also vastly increased understanding of the range of linguistic diversity. That sense of near completion pointed them toward new frontiers of an intellectual, spiritual, and cultural nature.

Notes

1 George Lakoff and Mark Johnson, *Metaphors We Live By* (Chicago: University of Chicago Press, 1980).
2 George Lakoff, *Women, Fire, and Dangerous Things: What Categories Reveal about the Mind* (Chicago: University of Chicago Press, 1987), 303.
3 Jerry Fodor, *The Modularity of Mind* (Cambridge: MIT Press, 1983) and *The Mind Doesn't Work That Way: The Scope and Limits of Computational Psychology* (Cambridge: MIT Press, 2000); Noam Chomsky, *Modular Approaches to the Study of the Mind* (San Diego: San Diego State University Press, 1984). For a recent collection of work on modularity, see Lawrence Hirschfield and Susan Gelman, *Mapping the Mind: Domain Specificity in Cognition and Culture* (New York: Cambridge University Press, 1994).
4 Steven Pinker, *How the Mind Works* (New York: Norton, 1997), 21.
5 Ray Jackendoff, *Consciousness and the Computational Mind* (Cambridge: MIT Press, 1987), 260.
6 Ernst Cassirer, *The Philosophy of Symbolic Forms* (New Haven: Yale University Press, 1953–1957), 1:161.
7 Sir Francis Bacon, "Advancement of Learning," in *Advancement of Learning and Novum Organum* (New York: Colonial, 1899), 304.

I Space and Language: Language in Space

All theory may be regarded as a kind of map extended over space and time.

—Michael Polanyi[1]

Linguistic research has focused on the structure of the signal itself rather than on the nonlinguistic constructions to which the signal is connected.

—Gilles Fauconnier[2]

Language is one of the givens of human existence. We are born into a world of language, and we experience it each day as we speak, listen, read, and write. Yet the big questions, of how words mean, how ideas are selected and linked to words in different contexts, how languages originated and diversified, how language influences thinking, and how language interfaces with culture are still more the realm of theory than of knowledge. When we enter an unknown realm, whether it be an unfamiliar building or a new region of the earth, we map by anticipation, registering the strange by reference to the familiar. We apply the same process when we think about language. Modern linguistics was born when tools specific to language study—comparative grammars, phonology, the study of syntax—began to be applied. Until then, the study of language was very much a search for appropriate tropes.

Even today's linguistic tools, however, lend themselves to tropes. Cognitive linguists rely heavily on terms such as blended space, mapping, domains, and frames.[3] More deeply, cognitive linguists use spatial terms not as metaphors but as descriptions of how language structures ideas so that we can communicate as clearly as we do. Leonard Talmy, for example, argues that grammar has a semantics that includes topology, perspective, viewpoint, figure and ground, location, and motion.[4] Language does not merely name or refer to these concepts in words; they are built into the structures of language so that our utterances orient us and our listeners to space, objects, and events in such a way as to be coherent to speaker and listener. The problem posed by a study such as mine is never that spatial concepts become inappropriate, but that we have two domains, language and space, both of which humans have learned to understand in very different ways over the centuries. In that process, the two have histories of dynamic influence on each other. We want to grasp how new aspects of spatial experience offered themselves as models for investigative thought.

Try thinking about language—not French, Swahili, or Korean, but language in general—and you will probably have to do so by means of other types of experience. One reason for that is that language is not a thing at all, but a complex, abstract idea assembled from the existence of many particular experiences of communicating by sounds. When we create such a useful concept, we have to use the materials that lie at hand in our mental inventory. One of those domains will be space. Think of language as communication and you may picture ideas being conveyed from one person to another across space. If you think about the variety of languages, you may picture a map showing areas in which different languages are spoken. If you think about the descent of languages, you may do so by means of a family tree with branches. Descent itself, by the way, is a spatial concept that converts a temporal and biological event into motion downward. If you think of syntax, the way words are ordered, you may picture a string of boxes or objects representing how a language orders different types of words to perform their functions in a complete utterance. In these instances, space plays a role in thinking about language.

I want to investigate the use of spatial concepts in language thought partly because they give us one of the most important means by which to think about language. As another of the givens of human nature, space is simultaneously immediate and unexplainable. Graham Nerlich captures this fact: space is "perceptually remote: we can neither see it nor touch it"; it "seems elusive to the point of eeriness."[5] Henri Lefebvre observes, "Space 'in itself' is ungraspable, unthinkable, unknowable." Just as I am doing with language, Lefebvre sought something yet more primitive and universal by which to approach it.[6] He found that something in the Marxist idea of production. But how can production be more fundamental than space? Space is so fundamental to being that Heidegger, in "Building, Dwelling, Thinking," said that it cannot be adequately conceived as something other than ourselves:

> When we speak of man and space, it sounds as though man stood on one side, space on the other. Yet space is not something that faces man. It is neither an external object nor an inner experience. . . . To say that mortals are is to say that in dwelling they persist through spaces by virtue of their stay among things and locations. And only because mortals pervade, persist through, spaces by their very nature are they able to go through spaces.[7]

Heidegger asserts that as we think about space, we do so as if space is apart and separate from us, yet lived experience cannot sustain that view. I want to accomplish something akin to his point, showing that language—arguably something separate from us—is also so integral that we know it and think about it at the expense of putting what is integral and internal, something by virtue of which we exist, at a distance. I follow Lefebvre and Heidegger in thinking that space is elusive and that we have difficulty separating it from our sense of existence. However, even in that inseparability our experience of space provides models or structures we use constantly and coherently to think about other things.

Language, in a complementary move, also maps space. Every language has lexical and grammatical methods for encoding space. Lexically, we distinguish here and there, front and back, inside and outside, north and south. Grammatically, particles, prepositions, and inflections locate speakers and orient them to others and to space.[8] It has been argued that our spatial experience exceeds the capacity of language structures to encode it, so we find other ways to signal what cannot be expressed structurally. Just as important to this study, language imposes its own tyranny over many types of experience, such as space, that are more fluid and continuous than language can express. Charles Hampden-Turner points out that "we map with words." However, "because words come in bits and pieces many people have assumed that the world is in bits and pieces too, with bits corresponding to words." While I urge that the world does indeed contain bits and pieces that often correspond to words, Hampden-Turner is right that maps are not the territories they represent and that

> word maps have a fragmentary structure that derives from language itself, not necessarily from what language describes. The idea of linear cause and effect, for example, is inherent in the structure of a sentence, where a subject acts by way of a verb upon an object, but this may be a very inadequate rendering of what is happening, especially of mutual influences.[9]

Physical space and the less tangible but equally real social terrain are both continuous and lend themselves to various schemes that divide them up. Words name, and therefore fix, the divisions in those spaces, the objects or inhabitants therein, and the relations among them. A room, with its structure of floor, walls, ceiling, and windows lends itself so easily to analysis of structure that it becomes a map of space that can be transferred to social or cultural spheres (as in the famous Chinese room thought experiment of John Searle that attempts to answer the question, Can computers think?). Sky, horizon, and foreground provide a similar transportable structure, but in reality open space lends structure partly because words create divisions in what are more properly continuities divided conceptually, as in the difference between foreground, middle ground, and background. No clear line divides them. Take another example. When we talk of the Western mind, the Middle East, or the Orient, we apply directional terms to regions of a sphere. Strictly speaking, a sphere has no eastern region except in an arbitrary sense. We apply directions such as east and west only after we have oriented the sphere in relation to ourselves and a larger, mentally charted space. Our sense of north being upward on a map and south being downward is also strictly conventional. Such concepts allow us to share meaning, but they do not describe geometric reality.

Because of its power to reify structure in other domains of experience, language gives a false sense of mental and rhetorical control over nonlinguistic reality. A term such as "barbarian," used by the Greeks to refer to those who couldn't speak their language, consolidates in one term a cluster of ideas and thus makes it possible to make statements about barbarians, incorporating a string of connotations that accumulate in a society, in the illusion that one is making statements about a real component of the world, when in fact the term's greatest utility lies precisely in the rhetorical control of ideas, things, people. What is the reality to which "barbarians" refers? One might say, "Barbarians lack intellectual sophistication; Greeks represent the epitome of it in the ancient world." Only by appreciating the complexity of other languages and the intellectual, rhetorical, and aesthetic accomplishments all languages make possible (even these terms fail as much as does "barbarian" in naming the most salient and discrete aspects of a complex reality), does one begin to see the illusory comfort the term "barbarian," not to mention "rhetorical and aesthetic accomplishment," offers. In sum, language is an indispensable but not utterly congruent means of mapping space.

The temptation is to call language entirely conventional and space natural or immediate, but the fact is that both language and space have been conceived in wholly conventional as well as natural terms. Some go so far as to deny that there is such a thing as space at all: only objects exist, and space is an invention of the mind in which to relate them. Leibniz fairly denied that space was even a feature of existence. For him, only monads existed, each with relations to other monads, and no external frame or condition was necessary for those relations to occur. Kant also denied the reality of space except as an intuition of the mind necessary for us to comprehend nature. It was a mode of perception built into our minds but not necessarily corresponding to the external world. Others, notably Graham Nerlich in our day, advance the realist position, that space exists and has properties of its own that are necessary for objects and entities to exist also, and that one of those properties is a shape and a metric, or system of orientation and measurement (not a given ruler, but a making possible of rulers). What if, in language and space, we have interlocking systems that are partly conventional but which seem to have some qualities and structures about them, even though we can't always specify them, that are so fundamental to experience that we can't have such experience without them, something immediate that not only makes experience possible but in some sense merges with and becomes experience? Nerlich puts it this way:

> I argue that our intellectual imagination—our capacity to invent explanatory ideas, to understand them and exploit them—soars higher above a perceptual grounding than most of the philosophers who have probed the area think it can. Of course space would hold little interest for us if it did not provide a unity and system for what we perceive. There is no doubt that the perceptual imagination does help to fortify and even expand the intellectual imagination, as I hope to show. But, I argue, it is the prior grasp of spatial concepts which enables us to perform the feats of perceptual fancy, and not the other way around.[10]

Language is of a similar nature, working with the perceptual grounding to allow other "feats of perceptual fancy" and giving the intellectual imagination its freedom because there is more than an endless chain of signifiers on which to build.

Importance of Cognitive Blends

Applying structures from one type of experience to concepts in another domain is fundamental to knowledge. The act is not simply crucial to imagination, it is foundational to cognition. *Metaphor* is one term we use for it. Metaphor works by taking an input domain and mapping it onto a target domain. The input, or source domain, can be taken from just about any realm of experience: core experience of space, objects, number, body, and movement; categories whether particular or general; or processes. In the sentence *He drank in her glance*, the input domain of drinking is mapped onto the experience of a man seeing a woman look at him. In cases like these we map structures of ideas. Drinking has a structure of a prototype with radial elements: swallowing a potable liquid is at center; other elements such as thirst, necessity for life, nutritive versus poisonous attributes, taste, the drinking vessel, and the precise liquid (water, wine, chocolate, soda pop) and temperature (cold, room temperature, hot) can be applied as appropriate.

Because domains like drinking have structures, metaphors derived from them have entailments. That is, a metaphor entails, or brings along with it, other ideas. What determines the relevance of the radial elements—those that, from all the possibilities, will be recruited to illuminate the other domain—is the target. George Lakoff calls this the invariance principle: only those elements consistent with the target will be recruited.[11] Some targets have structure of their own. In the example *He drank in her glance*, the target domain—a man admiring a woman—has its own structure. Other concepts, such as mind, time, or life have little or no structure of their own; they borrow their structure from the metaphor's source domain. That is why we can hardly think about some topics at all without doing so by means of a different source domain. In these cases the borrowed structure of the source domain may determine meaning as much as the target, but the invariance principle still applies: source elements incompatible with the target will remain inert. In most cases, the target determines which elements in the input structure will be held as relevant.

Some people, including many literary critics, think of metaphor as a surface device of expression, something that happens mostly in language. They are mistaken. Metaphor is often expressed in language, but it precedes it. It is a fundamental strategy of the mind. Ronald Langacker assures us that figurative language is no peripheral matter. Although many linguists ignore this topic, "it would be hard to find anything more pervasive and fundamental in language, even (I maintain) in the domain of grammatical structure; if figurative language were eliminated from our data base, little if any data would remain."[12] Understanding its pervasiveness, Mark Turner has stated that the mind is literary: it uses what we often categorize as literary devices to think about the most ordinary problems.[13] He recognizes, as one of the most basic building blocks of cognition, what he calls "spatial stories," minimal scripts such as an object's motion through space; an arrow flying from a bow, across a field, and to a target; a bird flying left to right across the horizon; or a leaf falling from a tree to the ground. These involve a space, objects in motion, and a trajectory. They also imply an observer oriented to and within that space. Pushing an object to move it or walking around it to avoid it are actions that involve agents who are also observers. Ignoring a language is walking around it. Acting to eradicate it is to push it out of the way.

Philip Johnson-Laird has studied the way in which many kinds of thinking, including the rigorous kinds that go into solving problems, assessing probabilities, and making plans, require us to make mental models of a situation. Such models can use imagery, but they differ from vivid pictures in that they are skeletal. Only those features deemed important to the situation need show up in its schematic representation. Scientific models are examples of mental models, but mental models also include ordinary thinking about mundane problems as well. As models, they often have a strong or even definitive spatial component. In spatial reasoning, that is, reasoning that directly involves spatial relations, mental models "are functionally organized on spatial axes," and "information in them can be accessed by way of these axes." When it comes to other types of thinking, Johnson-Laird deems it highly likely that "inferences that hinge on nonspatial matters may be made by manipulating models that are functionally organized in the same way as those representing spatial relations."[14] He demonstrates by showing that mental models can guide us in thinking about temporal relations more surely than logic.

George Lakoff and Mark Johnson offer a model of metaphorical mapping and blending. This model includes two cognitive domains, called source and target, that are blended or mapped onto each other.[15] In the metaphor *To some, the self has the sweetest taste*, the source domain of eating food is mapped onto the target domain of one's experience of the self. Mark Turner and Gilles Fauconnier have more recently proposed a more elaborate model which loses some of the parsimony of the two-domain model but gains in being able to account for more of the structure and effects of blending. This model includes

- two input spaces: source and target
- a generic space: a skeletal structure that applies to both input spaces
- a blended space: a rich space integrating, in partial fashion, specific structure from both input spaces, often including structure not projected to it from either, and supporting inferences from that integration.

An example will clarify the usefulness of the four spaces in analyzing blended spaces. Here is a thinking problem: "A Buddhist monk begins at dawn to walk up a mountain. He stops and varies his pace as he pleases and reaches the mountaintop at sunset. There he meditates overnight. At dawn, he begins to walk back down, again moving as he pleases. He reaches the foot of the mountain at sunset. Prove that there is a place on the path that he occupies at the same hour of the day on the two separate journeys."[16] By imagining a scenario in which two monks set out on the same day, one heading up and the other down, we can prove that, regardless of their pace, they will meet. The point at which the two monks meet is the place the monk occupied at the same hour of the day on two separate journeys. This type of analysis helps us see that blended spaces combine and struc-ture information in such a way as to ground conclusions or projections not available in the input domains separately. In the monk example, the blended space of two simultaneous journeys yields a clear answer that neither individual journey could provide.

The generic space clarifies the structure in terms of which the logic of the blend works. The model also clarifies that the target influences meaning, so it, too, is considered an "input" along with source domain.[17] Applied to our study of language thought, the many-space model allows us to separate the strands in spatial thinking about language. It keeps us from making the mistake of many metaphor-based interpretations of thought, the assertion that those who think in metaphor (all of us) don't know the difference between the two input domains, source and target.

Although I will not be explicit about applying this many-spaces model (my study is not about a particular model of analysis but about the effect of thinking about language through spatial concepts), I want to show how the analysis will be used to reveal those effects. Sir Francis Bacon, directing his contemporaries to a new type of language study unfettered by scholastic and rhetorical errors, says that "if the great masters of them would but have gone a form lower, and looked but into the observations of Grammar and syntax . . . they might have found out more and better footsteps of common reason, help of disputation, and advantages of cavillation, than many of these which they have propounded."[18] Bacon creates several blended spaces. The one of interest here involves grammar as a help finding better footsteps of reason. This blended space is actually a complex of several blends, which I outline as follows:

- source input spaces: paths, walking, difficult terrain and the possibility of getting lost, reason as agent, footsteps as guide
- target input spaces: grammar, thinking correctly, finding out how we think
- generic space: finding or revealing the proper path through a terrain
- blended space: studying grammar helps reveal and improve thinking as footsteps show a path.

Note here that the target input space, language or grammar, influences the blend. It reacts on the source input domains just as these react on the target. In this blend Bacon is attempting to change the target (language study) by blending it with the idea of pathways. The interpretation rests on properly recruiting the elements, structures, and functions of the different domains and projecting them onto the current situation to encourage a more mundane yet more fruitful type of language study.

The four-space model provides a richer, more robust way to think about whether language generally and metaphors specifically determine our thought, or whether they provide only tentative and provisional maps of thoughts that exist separately from language. This topic has occupied whole books, and I don't pretend to give an exhaustive treatment.[19] But I do want to argue both sides. On one hand, metaphors and blended spaces have entailments: the structures they utilize emphasize certain features of the target concept. That is their function, and this means that our metaphors condition the outcome of our thinking. Lakoff notes in *Women, Fire, and Dangerous Things* that conceptual metaphors differ from people to people and serve to structure thought about the world.[20] On the other hand, the determining function of linguistic encoding is severely limited by other factors. The structures that create a blended space are not solely linguistic; rather, the language provides a framing structure in which other concepts can come into play. To talk to someone about tasting the self or drinking in someone's glance, one must have schemas and scripts full of structured information, including actors and actions, substances, observers, effects, and purposes. Words activate these schemas and scripts, but while the schemas and scripts may include language, they are more aptly understood as hierarchically ordered clusters of images, contexts, and feelings that exist apart from language and can be selectively activated in response to the specific situation the language encodes.

Language must also be severely limited in its role in determining thought because we recognize that the target concept in metaphorical thinking so heavily determines how we import information from source input domains. According to the "invariance principle" proposed by Lakoff, the target determines which features of a source domain will be activated as it is applied. Additionally, alternative metaphors are always available. Then we must recognize, as Dedre Gentner and Eric Dietrich have demonstrated,[21] that analogies and metaphors actually change knowledge. That is, they produce concepts that are not latent in the structure of either source domain or target until the analogy is produced. The fact that we make and interpret metaphors and analogies constantly and on the fly with only occasional and slight problems leads to the conclusion that our minds know before we pause to think which aspects of a blend are relevant. Then we immediately move on because discourse continues. Finally, the great limit on the determining force of conceptual metaphors comes from the world itself. Objects condition our sense perceptions of them and the thoughts we think about them.

Therefore, in studying the application of spatial concepts to language I will strive not to err on either side. We must remember that the people who used spatial terms always knew they were talking about language. Spatial figures helped them foreground particular qualities, entities, and functions in language, but no one in my reading believed he could think himself literally to another location or take a walk by stepping on words. On the other side, we must not conclude that the persistent use of spatial concepts never mattered much. What we must do is show that there is a middle area in which students of language could learn about language by applying conventional spatial concepts in novel ways or by applying changing spatial concepts to understand an elusive concept, language. And they could be aware that language differed from space as a hawk from a handsaw.

Some Entailments of Spatial Thinking

As knowledge of space underwent change in Western culture, so ideas of language evolved. People's understanding of the scope, the layout, and the physical and human topography of the world changed radically. Techniques for locating position and mapping areas developed so that the magnitude, complexity, and diversity of the earth's oceans and terrain could be comprehended and navigated. As these processes unfolded, spatial metaphors provided developing structural features to convey the essentials of language. People continued to think about language in spatial terms (and do so today). What changed was the types and intentionality of the spatial terms. From more primitive spatial concepts, cognitive models of language eventually emerged. Some of these models reflected merely the novel use of standard spatial concepts, such as horizons, movement, and containers. Other models reflected the changed spatial concepts that resulted from the mixture of long voyages, navigation problems, and abstract conventions for mapping and finding direction.

Standard spatial concepts, used in novel ways, had important analogs in language thought. Among these are ideas of barriers, containers, maps, and journeys. These terms will all figure importantly in the chapters that follow. Other ideas keep showing up in language thought: oceanic navigation and terrestrial way-finding, the change of perspective that new location brings, horizons, close and far, and filled or empty terrain all play a part in the history of language thought. Languages were conceived both as routes across space and as barriers to movement. Sampling a language put one figuratively in a new space from which the distance to—and often criticism of—one's own culture resulted. Language study proceeded as a mode of getting close to a terrain feature, with the attendant attitudes of wonder mixed with fear.

In spatial experience we can differentiate place from space. We experience a personal, immediate sense of place in any location we occupy and in which we can orient ourselves, whether it is a room, a field, a village, town, hill, or valley. Beyond that, we experience what we might call regional place, the broader expanse that will normally take us to the farthest reaches of our daily lives. Regional place might be the town or county we live in, perhaps a region of a state or province. For the globetrotter, regional place might span several continents. In a larger frame, we have a global sense of place in terms of the earth and sky. This frame is, of course, a modern one and has still not spread to all the earth's peoples.

Beyond the global place we can move to the planetary and interstellar, but this merely extends the divisions linked to place. We could continue adding senses of place/space or divide them up differently. What matters is not the number of divisions within that category but the leap to the next type of spatial experience, which is not that of place in space but of space itself: the concept of three-dimensional, unfilled space occupied by everything that exists. This kind of space is a necessary condition for place—and for existence. It, too, can be divided differently, but for my purposes the most meaningful division includes abstract relational space, that is, the space in which objects, whether pencil erasers or planets, are at a certain distance from each other in a three-dimensional continuum. This is the concept that makes it possible to map the seas and impose a grid system that can be used to navigate or measure miles from a point of origin to a destination. Abstract relational space can be further differentiated from absolute infinite space, which is the great void that is continuous from the molecular to the interstellar levels. No matter what the level, it is all of one continuous nature, stretching from any point within it to the farthest reaches of the universe, if "far reaches" makes any sense at all in this category of space. Absolute infinite space is the concept of space itself.

Turning to language, we can make similar divisions between language as phenomenon and as concept. Most immediately, we know language as my language or our language, the language of a family or community. Next, we know languages, much as in spatial terms we know that the places around us cohere in as a region. This level leads to an awareness of linguistic difference and makes possible the study of one's own vocabulary and grammar. Finally, we can think of all the languages spoken and written on this earth, even if we can name only a few. But experiencing languages doesn't necessarily include the idea of language itself, the verbal sign system by which people communicate. This concept has two divisions. The first of these we will call abstract relational language, which includes many of the systems we use to think about language as a single phenomena or entity—comparative grammar and phonology and genealogies and theories of origin and development. The second, absolute language, is language as a topic of philosophical investigation. It includes semiotics, or language as a sign system, cognitive linguistics, which investigates language as an instrument that conditions or reflects thinking, and theories of meaning.

Another particularly important facet of spatial experience maps onto language. We can think of location in two very different frames, as fixed position that doesn't change, such as grid coordinates on a map or a street number for a house, or as here and there. The latter locations depend on context; they move with the speaker and situation. I will be examining an era when humans were on the move as never before. It makes sense that their experience of space would spill over into other facets of experience, especially those that were also being explored and discovered. The history of language study shows a tension between the recognition of context-dependent features of language and those that are context-free. The recognition by missionaries that newly encountered languages were saturated with the figures, myths, and beliefs of their speakers can be likened to language that incorporates perspective and therefore moving position. The search by students of language for Adamic roots, universal grammars, and typologies can be likened to the search for fixed positions.

Spatial concepts are so varied that we can't exhaust them or the structures they entail. Space involves both two- and three-dimensional metrics, types of terrain, distances close and far, direction, the orientation of the subject in space, open and enclosed areas, boundaries of different types, containers and contents, movement down a path and across an area, modes of movement, objects in the terrain and their location and relative locations, occlusion of some zones and objects by others, geographical features, as well as sub-surface, surface, and above-surface layers, just to mention a few. Each item lends a structure that can be mapped onto other types of ideas. However, the variety of available figures prevents us from concluding that spatial thinking will necessarily lead to a specific result or conceptual limitation. If one person thinks of language as a barrier or container, the figures lend themselves to rival interpretations and novel applications. One need only change perspective on the figure and new knowledge results. If, for example, language constitutes a barrier, can one stand within the barrier, as one does with language? If language is a container, what kind of container is it and what does it hold, and what holds it? By pursuing questions such as these, early modern students of language constantly tried to achieve new insights into the nature of language.

Notes

1   Michael Polanyi, *Personal Knowledge: Towards a Post-Critical Philosophy* (Chicago: University of Chicago Press, 1962), 4.

2 Gilles Fauconnier, *Mappings in Thought and Language* (Cambridge: Cambridge University Press, 1997), 4.

3 For a recent example, see Fauconnier, *Mappings*.

4 Leonard Talmy, *Toward a Cognitive Semantics*, 2 vols. (Cambridge: MIT Press, 2000), especially chapter 3 of volume 1, "How Language Structures Space."

5 Graham Nerlich, *The Shape of Space*, 2d ed. (Cambridge: Cambridge University Press, 1994), 2, 1.

6 Henri Lefebvre, *The Production of Space*, trans. Donald Nicholson-Smith (Oxford: Blackwell, 1991), 218.

7 Martin Heidegger, "Building, Dwelling, Thinking," in *Poetry, Language, Thought*, trans. Albert Hofstadter (New York: Harper & Row, 1975), 156–57.

8 For an important collection of papers on language and space, see Paul Bloom, Mary Peterson, Lynn Nadel, and Merrill Garrett, eds., *Language and Space* (Cambridge: MIT Press, 1996), which includes work by Ray Jackendoff, Leonard Talmy, Stephen Levinson, Barbara Landau, Melissa Bowerman, and Philip Johnson-Laird. See also Barbara Landau and Ray Jackendoff, "'What' and 'Where' in Spatial Language and Spatial Cognition," *Behavioral and Brain Sciences* 16 (1993): 217–65; Leonard Talmy, "How Language Structures Space," in *Spatial Orientation: Theory, Research, and Application*, ed. H. Pick and L. Acredolo (New York: Plenum, 1983), 225–82; Leonard Talmy, *Toward a Cognitive Semantics*, 2 vols. (Cambridge: MIT Press, 2000); and Ray Jackendoff, "On Beyond Zebra: The Relation of Linguistic and Visual Information," *Cognition* 26 (1987): 89–114.

9 Charles Hampden-Turner, *Maps of the Mind* (New York: Macmillan, 1981), 8.

10 Nerlich, *Shape of Space*, 3.

11 George Lakoff, "The Invariance Hypothesis: Is Abstract Reason Based on Image-Schemas?" *Cognitive Linguistics* 1 (1990): 39–74. See also Mark Turner, "Aspects of the Invariance Hypothesis" in the same issue.

12 Ronald Langacker, *Foundations of Cognitive Grammar* (Stanford: Stanford University Press, 1987–1991), 1:1.

13 Mark Turner, *The Literary Mind* (New York: Oxford University Press, 1996), 7.

14 Philip N. Johnson-Laird, "Space to Think," in *Language and Space*, ed. Paul Bloom, Mary Peterson, Lynn Nadel, and Merrill Garrett (Cambridge: Bradford Books of MIT Press, 1996), 445–46, 448.

15 George Lakoff and Mark Johnson, *Metaphors We Live By* (Chicago: University of Chicago Press, 1980).

16 Turner, *Literary Mind*, 72.

17 For greater detail on these advantages, see Gilles Fauconnier and Mark Turner, *The Way We Think: Conceptual Blending and the Mind's Hidden Complexities* (New York: Basic Books, 2002), 185–87.

18 Sir Francis Bacon, *Of the Interpretation of Nature*, in *The Works of Francis Bacon*, ed. James Spedding, Robert Ellis, and Douglas Heath (London: Longman, 1860), 3:230.

19 Recent books include John A. Lucy, *Language Diversity and Thought: A Reformulation of the Linguistic Relativity Hypothesis* (Cambridge: Cambridge University Press, 1992); John A. Lucy, *Grammatical Categories and Cognition: A Case Study of the Linguistic Relativity Hypothesis* (Cambridge: Cambridge University Press, 1992); Peter Carruthers, *Language, Thought, and Consciousness* (Cambridge: Cambridge University Press, 1996).

20 George Lakoff, *Women, Fire, and Dangerous Things: What Categories Reveal about the Mind* (Chicago: University of Chicago Press, 1987).

21 Dedre Gentner and Phillip Wolff, "Metaphor and Knowledge Change," in *Cognitive Dynamics: Conceptual and Representational Change in Humans and Machines*, ed. Eric Dietrich and Arthur B. Markman (Mahwah, NJ: Lawrence Erlbaum, 2000), 295–342; Eric Dietrich, "Analogy and Conceptual Change, or You Can't Step into the Same Mind Twice," in Dietrich and Markman, *Cognitive Dynamics*, 265–294.

2   Mapping Language

*In the same logic and rhetoric, or arts of argument and grace of
speech, if the great masters of them would but have gone a form
lower, and looked but into the observations of Grammar and syntax; specially enriching the same with the helps of several languages; with their differing properties of words, phrases, and
tropes; they might have found out more and better footsteps of common reason, help of disputation, and advantages of cavillation,
than many of these which they have propounded.*
               —Sir Francis Bacon [1]

*The Yoruba of West Africa regard the line as extremely important,
even associating it with civilization. In Yoruba, the phrase "this
country has become civilized" literally means "this earth has lines
upon its face."*
         —David Woodward and Malcolm Lewis [2]

Strong parallels exist between techniques for mapping the earth and
describing languages. Some of these parallels merely reflect the fact that advances in navigation and language study were informed by the paradigm
changes that characterize the transition from medieval to modern learning.
In both areas, authority and myth gave way to observation, recording, and
analysis. However, I find other salient reasons for approaching language study
from the model of terrestrial navigation. If, as I have already tried
to argue, spatial ideas constantly informed linguistic thought, the technologies of mastering space can also be expected to show up in linguistic thought.
This chapter will suggest that they do. In so suggesting I will use spatial
metaphors self-consciously. That is, I will often bring metaphors of mapping
and navigating to bear on the historical material, rather than rely more passively on the material to provide the metaphors I use to analyze it. My justification for appearing to impose my metaphors rather than eliciting them
from the material goes as follows. Early moderns were not conscious of the
solutions that later generations would offer for known problems of navigation
and cartography. Yet later solutions, in retrospect, helped define the nature of
the problems that early navigators faced. Because, as I will try to demonstrate,

mapping problems so strongly parallel the problems faced in linguistic
inquiry, we are justified, if we are careful not to overreach, in interpreting the
development of linguistic knowledge in terms of them. They help us tease out
pertinent aspects of this history that we might otherwise miss.

The difficulties of mapping and navigation were similar to those of acquiring accurate linguistic knowledge. Both fields depended on representing phenomena in one set of dimensions—whether spheres, solar systems
and stars, or oral discourse and the components of speech—in another
medium—whether maps, charts, vocabulary lists, or grammars. Both
depended on achieving a view of parts within a larger whole. Both depended
on the dynamic relationship between perspectival knowledge, achieved by
viewing things from a vantage point, and objective knowledge, which
seeks to eliminate or, if that is not possible, to conceal our dependence
on situation and vantage point. The chapter will first discuss similar challenges in mapping and linguistic knowledge and, as part of that investigation, present attempts to achieve global perspectives on language in the
Middle Ages. Three senses of "mapping" will emerge: mapping as locating
and relating languages, as deciphering the underlying structure that makes
language what it is, and as projecting that structure onto nature in order
to gain access to those aspects of nature that remained hidden. The chapter
will then argue that the writing of grammars, so crucial to systematic language study, is quintessentially a spatial project and led to a search for
something akin to accurate local maps laid out with the help of rigorous
surveying and, of consequence, employing an overt or implicit metrics.
Grammars convert articulate sounds into written, and therefore spatial,
form and must depict multidimensional grammatical relations within the
parameters of space (two-dimensional surface of sheets of paper) and succession. Universal grammar, with which I will conclude, parallels the production of universal grid systems. It attempts to formalize the knowledge
of many particular grammars and so identify the cognitive or linguistic network in which all human thought can be conceived or expressed. Universal
grammar therefore reflects different strategies for mapping language in a
way that transcended situation and context. Its failure to do so owes to the
fact that its proponents mistook the apparent naturalness of their own
expression for context-free thought.

Islands and Languages

Students of language often explicitly linked land and languages. In a curious treatise written near the end of the sixteenth century, *A Treatise on*

Foreign Languages and Unknown Islands, Peter Albinus, historian to the court of Saxony, links terrestrial discovery and knowledge of languages. He concludes that his century's amazing expansion of knowledge in languages and terrestrial geography must be understood together in a way that goes beyond the obvious fact that unknown lands tend to harbor foreign languages. As Albinus sees them, the exploration of the earth and the increasing study of languages mark the opening of history from its intellectual, spiritual, and geographical confinement. Only by mastering the opportunity that long voyages and travail in languages bring to his day can his contemporaries usher in a new era of learning—more than just an era of learning, actually. Albinus sees in the new understanding of lands and languages a fulfillment of prophecy and sign of a divine era, "the tokens, unmistakable, one may believe, of the last day, and the state of innocence to which we are shortly to return."[3] Increased knowledge of languages—products of the Fall and Tower—will vanquish corruption and give the mind direction in finding its true home again.

To Albinus the growth of linguistic knowledge entailed far more than the gradual increase in vulgar grammars and the accretion of new linguistic information. It entailed also a renewed scholarly focus on studying contemporary languages. This awakening became a sign of God's immanence because, fallen as they were, languages had retained something of the imprint of God's mind and spirit. They were not merely the means by which humans communicated their inner thoughts, not merely the restricted means by which divine revelation had been conveyed and preserved. In their refracted and multiple natures they were kindred media to the same spirit that had recently inspired many great figures to devote themselves to their study. The roll call is striking. Albinus mentions John Picus, Count Mirandola, born in 1463, who learned twenty-two languages by age eighteen; the great linguist Aegidus of Viterbo; Hieronymus of Seripandus, a convert from Judaism who wrote a treatise on the errors of the Talmud, printed in 1602; Hieronymus Aleander, who wrote a Greek and Latin lexicon and a Greek grammar; Frederick Fulgosus, a Greek and Hebrew scholar; Augustine Justinian, Bishop of Nebbio, who made a psalter in eight languages; Sanctes Pagninus of Lucca, a Dominican "celebrated for his knowledge of languages"; Spaniard Aelius Antonius, Cardinal Frances Ximenes, Abbot of Toledo, who in 1517 completed the polyglot Bible in Hebrew, Latin, Greek, and Chaldee, and who "opened at Complut a very rich and spacious refuge for the study of the aforesaid languages"; William Postell, who "wandered over the more celebrated shores of Africa and Asia" and "became master of fifteen languages"; Petrus

Lusitanus, "who besides the Arabic, Indian, and Portuguese tongues, is reported to have been acquainted with the languages of almost all men"; Theodorus Bibliandros, who "fairly boasts in his commentary on the unity of all languages and letters, that, by the grace and gift of God, he had acquired the power of writing and speaking, or at any rate understanding, those languages which are spread far and wide over the whole world"; John Draconites, who undertook a polyglot Bible including German; and finally, "the great Luther" and Melancthon (Albinus, 31–35). Albinus marveled that "never at any period since the Christian era have there been so many in Europe skilled and instructed" in languages (Albinus, 36).

Albinus considered Martin Luther to be a prime mover in the rise of serious language study. Luther examined why the enemy of truth "should have desired so often to prevent the spread of languages." Loss of languages had always for Luther "been followed by darkness in the Church." Emphatically, "errors crept in from inacquaintance with languages" (Albinus, 60). Luther here alludes to the practice of confining a knowledge of Latin and Greek to a special class, the priesthood, and of making the sacred word inaccessible to the common people. By contrast, Luther considered languages "scabbards, in which the sword Spirit, namely the Word of God, is kept sheathed." And if, Luther says, "languages slip away from us through our carelessness as we breathe supinely on our backs . . . we ought to be wholly in fear lest we should lose not only the gospels, but glide on again to the miseries such that we do not know clearly how to speak, and to write correctly, not only Latin, but even the vernacular, which was the case with our ancestors" (Albinus, 61). A scare tactic, but Luther seems to have meant it. At any rate, what is important is the temper of his exhortation. Mastery of languages—and the more, the better—acted as a safeguard against error and decline.

Geographical knowledge played a part in the miracle. It led to safer navigation as unknown areas became charted, it provided a model of venturing into the unknown, and it recovered vital knowledge. As a Pentecostal knowledge of languages had accompanied the Christian gospel in ancient times and had then dwindled through disregard of its importance, so did a more complete understanding of lands and oceans exist in antiquity and then mysteriously disappear. Columbus had reopened the way to the lost world that only select authorities of the past had once understood. From his perspective, Albinus most admired Columbus not for his success, which Albinus deemed assured, given that sooner or later some inquisitive person would have deduced the existence of the Americas or simply risked sailing west. Instead, Albinus admired Columbus for his courage and resolve. Albinus promoted that same resolve in language study.

Albinus brought a bluntly experiential philosophy of knowledge to language. He referred to experience as "the mistress of everything" that must always correct the false assertions of speculative philosophers (Albinus, 57). His linking of ships and tongues is of this order. Ignorance of islands and tongues had bred in Europe the illusion of self-sufficiency, contemplative philosophy squelched the intimations of a world of alterity, and authorities had pronounced on habitable zones and the number of extant worlds before they had been out to see what the world actually contained. Something as mundane as commercial voyages had proved that earthly time was not neatly sliced. When Magellan's crew sailed into Spain they found their calendar one day off because they had "outrun in time six hours a year" (Albinus, 54), an example of how experience introduces complexities of the right kind into learning. "Had the experience of things then overweighed contemplative philosophy?" (Albinus, 55) Albinus asked in reference to recent voyages. Yes. If the world were one and all things coherent, contemplation would eventually yield all truth. But the world was not one and all things were not plain. To fulfill the world's purpose required that one live in it, take it on its own, rather than one's *a priori*, terms, and use its languages, trusting in the higher design to imbue the apparently lower means with all that God saw as necessary and appropriate.

The linking of islands and languages is intriguing. Certainly languages would be found on inhabited islands, and the more separated islands are, the greater the likelihood that their languages would be different from those already encountered. *Islands* did not necessarily mean small lands surrounded by water. The term could simply mean far places. In the first sense, languages resemble islands in that languages can be very distinct. Although languages had their families and genealogies, some languages seemed to stand alone, and thus in Albinus we detect an intuition that languages may be far more varied and distinct than expected.

When we look for particular understanding of what terrestrial exploration or rigorous language study entails, however, we find little beyond the trust in their linkage and greater significance. Albinus had more of a hunch than a full theory that lands and languages accompanied each other in fulfilling human destiny. But it was a hunch with something to it. He seems to have intuited that lands and languages figured each other in telling ways; that both served as correctives to ignorance and error; and that similar attitudes, risks, and rewards accompanied travel and travail in languages. Thus he closes by admonishing the youth to "strive with all your might, with sails and with steeds, and in a direct course, towards the true glory of learning, which is hidden in the study of languages." Language is a destination, a path, a catalyst, a container of wisdom. The direct course will lead home: the "mind will rise aloft from this workshop of toil to that final home of blessing" (Albinus, 62).

Early Modern Navigation and Mapping

The words "foreign" and "unknown" are key ones in Albinus's title. The venture into new lands and new languages required guesswork and risk. It required motion without accurate mapping. It required trust—not trust that the secret order of existence would crystalize in the mind of a recluse—but that going out to meet the constituents of the world, whether geographical or linguistic, would lead to a knowledge that speculation could never reach. The world was a messy place. One had to sail, to guess, to encounter the lands and peoples and languages.

Mapping required a combination of risky venturing into the particular, conjecturing upon means of finding location, and designing conventions for recording information. The rediscovery that the earth was a sphere constituted a giant leap forward, but it did not solve navigation problems. It did, however, accurately identify what the navigation problems were. And so problems of navigation provide, if we take Albinus one step further, an important analog and complement to the problems of linguistic knowledge. A society had to know more than a few acres or a few languages. And one had to know the shape of things to know what the crucial problems would be.

Mapping the world required accurate and comprehensive geographical knowledge as well as new techniques and conventions for depicting the earth's surface graphically. Because the earth is a sphere, even the act of drawing its surface, especially on a large scale, already entails transforming three dimensions into two, no easy feat for the early moderns. When detailed knowledge of heretofore unknown places met a comprehensive system of representation, one that could be used on any scale and in any region of the earth, modern maps resulted. These developments are among the most ingenious of early modern Europe.

In medieval Europe, three types of maps were available, and although they drew on entirely different semiotics, mappers often blended them in individual maps. First, there were local land maps showing distances, relative sizes of regions, and geographical orientations of towns, rivers, and mountains. Second, there were iconographic maps, religious or mythical in purpose and symbolic in design. These used scale not to convey actual distances, but to depict interest or vantage point. Third, there were *mappaemundi* depicting the entire known world. Accurate land maps depicted countries and kingdoms. Iconographic maps related earthly features

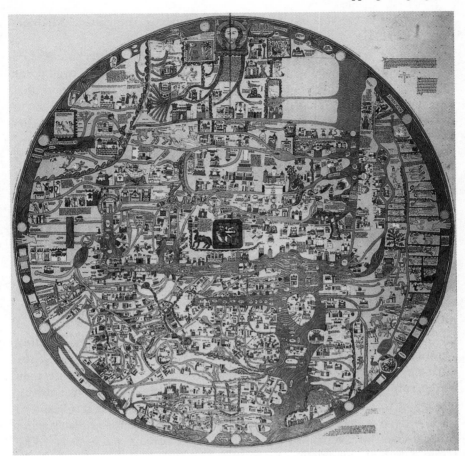

Figure 2.1 The Ebstorf World Map, ca. 1240. This map combines features of the T–O (Jerusalem is at the center) and the iconographic map (note the head, hands, and feet of Jesus Christ at the margins). Reproduction courtesy William L. Clements Library.

to biblical history, dispersions, Christian doctrine, and ancient learning. One of these, for example, divides all the spheres of existence, from the heavenly to the terrestrial, showing at once the dispersion of the sons of Noah, the seasons, the four types of matter (earth, air, fire, and water), and certain important terrestrial features. *Mappaemundi* were designed on the T–O plan, so named because the maps had a circular boundary divided within by a T-like cross. The top portion represented east and Asia, the left bottom portion represented north and Europe, and the bottom right represented south and Africa. These maps provided a holistic grasp of the earth, giving the relative location of the great land masses.

Placing east at the top conveyed the importance of the eastern Mediterranean and Asia.

Advances in mapping required more precise navigational techniques and abstract representational conceptions. Medieval Europeans employed crude technology in mapping land. Roger Kain and Elizabeth Baigent note that "the precise location of a piece of land on a map and the exact measurement of its area were probably beyond the technical competence of medieval surveyors."[4] As technology advanced, two types of land maps complemented each other. Chorographic maps depicted towns from a particular vantage point; geographic maps represented regions and kingdoms. The maps that accompany many editions of Shakespeare are of both types, the chorographic seen in the view of London's buildings (including the Globe Theatre) lining the Thames river, and the geographic seen in the less pictorial, bird's-eye-view plans of London's streets and districts. These two conventions created what Barbara Mundy calls a "standard dual model" for representing space.[5] Chorographic maps became more common as towns grew in size and importance; towns commissioned them to promote their status. Large-scale geographic maps became more common as rulers sought to play up the importance of a whole united kingdom that was more than a league of feudal domains. A "chorographic map overwhelms us with the specifics of an individual city; . . . Its antidote is the geographic map that shows the territory of the whole country" (Mundy, 7). The two types are more than cartographic conventions; they belong to more general cognitive drives, one being the desire to master and represent information as it appears to us in a given context, the other being the desire to transcend context and situatedness. Both, of course, retain elements of context and are shaped by purpose. In both "man defines his relation to the world through his ability to measure it" (Mundy, 4).

Navigation at sea, where no land features could verify a location, created yet more urgent needs for mapping and techniques for determining directions and distances. The compass, thought to have originated in the Orient and mentioned in Arabic texts in the thirteenth century, provided one great advance. It allowed sailors to plot a direction from a known point. The combination of direction and distance, known as dead reckoning, was the chief means of fixing location for centuries. Columbus relied on it. Celestial observation also aided navigation. The *kamal* allowed Arabic sailors to determine the angle between the horizon and the north star, and thus fix their latitude, or north-south location. The *kamal* consisted of a flat board with a rope or string tied to it, the rope having knots at regular intervals. Holding the board close or far from the eye so that it filled the space between the horizon and the pole star, a sailor could count the knots

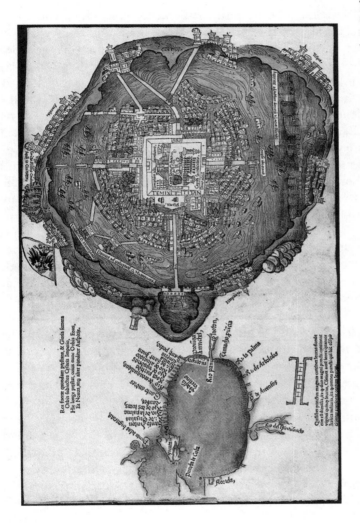

Figure 2.2 Map of Mexico City. This map, published with "The Second Letter of Hernán Cortés" in *Praeclara Ferdinandi Cortesii de Nova Maris Oceani Hispanica Narratio* (Nuremberg, 1524), shows the combination of two cartographic impulses, the perspectival and the objective. Towns around the lake are depicted as if viewed from the surface, while Mexico City and the lake itself are depicted as if from a bird's-eye view.

from his head to the board and convert the number to a distance on a north–south axis. Armillary spheres, concentric bands of metal representing the positions of stars and planets, could predict where the heavenly bodies would be.

Celestial observation differed with location, however. How would one find latitude in the southern hemisphere where there was no north star? King John II of Portugal commissioned a group of scientists in the 1480s to figure out how to find latitude in the south. They found that a calculation of the sun's height at its zenith, corrected for seasons, would fix latitude. Until the southern cross was identified, solar observation had to do. Determining longitude—a position east or west of a known point—was a harder matter. Late seventeenth- and eighteenth-century scientists exhausted their lives and emptied their purses to develop methods for finding longitude using the moon and stars. This method proved too difficult. Not until accurate marine chronometers, the most famous being Harrison's three timepieces in the 1740s and 1750s, did they find a workable and accurate means of determining longitude.

Meanwhile, representational techniques were also developing. Iconographic maps aimed to coordinate terrain with mythic and religious elements of the universe, but they were of no use in navigation. T–O maps of the world gave comprehensiveness but were useless in detail. What mariners and colonizers needed would be mapping conventions that allowed both accurate detail and comprehensiveness. Acquiring accurate detail actually went hand-in-hand with proper schematic conventions. In the fourteenth and fifteenth centuries new schools of cartography revolutionized map making. The first revolution occurred in portolan maps, which combined the advantages of accurate depiction of land mass and coastlines with accurate compass bearings. Portolan charts, from *portolani* or pilot books, used compass roses and rhumb lines to give compass bearings from one landmark, port, or island, and another. Using them a mariner could steer a course using dead reckoning and feel somewhat secure about arriving at his destination. The earliest known portolan chart is the anonymous Carta Pisana of the early 1300s. The Catalan Atlas, produced by Abraham Cresques in 1375, is one of the first portolan charts to depict the known world, using information from sailors as well as from land travelers such as Marco Polo. It also has a north–south orientation.

Since they relied on accurate magnetic compass bearings, portolan charts eventually ran into the problem of incommensurate reference grids. Portolan charts assume that magnetic north aligns with true north, but as the eventual discovery of magnetic declination proved, these two not only differ, they

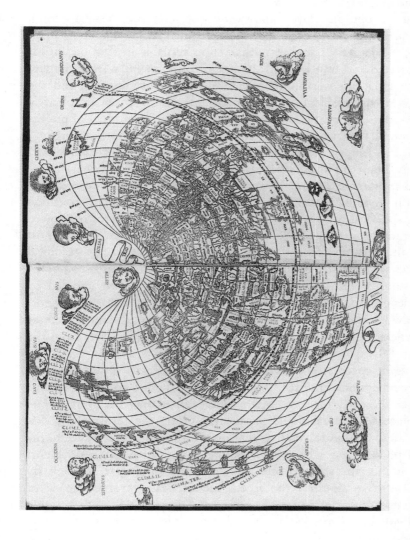

Figure 2.3 Ptolemaic Projection and Grid. World map by Bernardus Sylanus from Ptolemy's *Geography* (Venice, 1511). Courtesy William L. Clements Library.

differ in varying magnitudes according to one's place on earth. Portolan charts of the Mediterranean area, assuming that magnetic rhumb lines corresponded strictly with geography, distort the sea's dimensions in order to make the magnetic bearings work.[6]

A further revolution revived knowledge lost since the classical period. Ptolemy's *Geography* of the second century provided far more accurate maps of Europe, North Africa, and Asia than were available in Europe until it was rediscovered and translated in the late fifteenth century. More important in the long run was another feature, the grid system. Behind the grid system lay the problem of representing a three-dimensional, spherical earth in two dimensions. Ptolemy conceived three different types of projections, but central to all was a grid system, an abstract system introducing regularity into the distances and bearings that portolan charts incorporated. It allowed any point on the earth's surface to be plotted, whether it was visible and prominent or not. It would take another century to reconcile geographical coordinates and straight compass courses in a map projection converting spherical to two-dimensional space. Gerardus Mercator showed it could be done in 1569 in his cylindrical projection maps. Like almost all maps, these entail some distortion, but they are the cartographical masterpieces of the sixteenth century.[7] Because Ptolemy's maps combined ancient authority with a practical orientation meant to be updated by new knowledge and, most important, a universal system that could assimilate that new knowledge, his *Geography* "provided perhaps the most successful of all ancient models for coping with the flood of new facts from the West."[8]

Concepts of space also evolved as navigation became more accurate. Medieval conceptions of space, influenced by Aristotle and Democritus, gave way to the early modern. Michel Foucault defines the shift as one from emplacement to relational proximity.[9] Using the terminology differently, Murad Akhundov defines it as one from finite, filled space to infinite and plural space with both absolute and relative natures.[10] Henri Lefebvre defines the shift as one from absolute to abstract space.[11] By absolute, Lefebvre signifies the filled, hierarchical, governed space of the city-states and kingdoms of medieval Europe. It was thoroughly familiar, divided into orders, classes, and types, filled with no voids or unknowns, and under orderly rule. Foucault treats this earlier conception of space as an

ensemble of places: sacred places and profane places; protected places and open, exposed places; urban places and rural places (all these concern the real life of men). In cosmological theory, there were the supercelestial places, as opposed

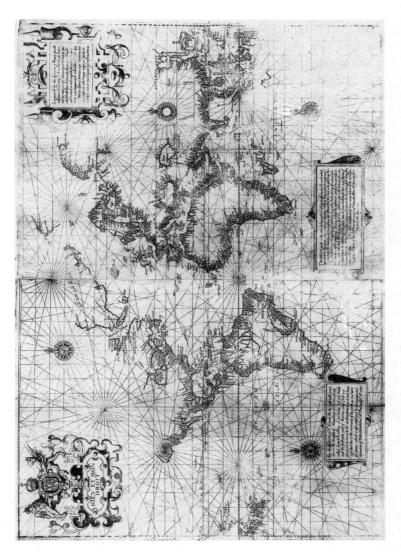

Figure 2.4 World Map, 1599. From Richard Hakluyt, *The Principal Navigations* (London, 1599). Courtesy the Newberry Library.

to the celestial, and the celestial place was in its turn opposed to the terrestrial place. There were places where things had been put because they had been violently displaced, and then on the contrary places where things found their natural ground and stability.[12]

Lefebvre sees this conception of space in decline by the tenth century in response to the rise of private property, towns and cities, the visual logic of art and architecture, and money and accumulation. And, of course, the same technologies used in, and knowledge gained from, voyages also influenced changing ideas of space.

These factors combined to change the conception and social practice from absolute to abstract space—or, as Akhundov would call it, from finite to absolute. For Lefebvre, this type consisted of the comprehensive rationalization of space seen in views and maps of towns. It entailed representations of space from above, perspective, and the appearance of homogeneity produced by consistent scales and conventions such as the facade. Later chapters will develop the shift in greater depth, but here I will note that abstract space combined the sense of local place with an ordered but infinite concept of space that encompasses everything, every place. It also linked place and perspective to conventions for representing space, including perspective and scale as just mentioned.

I propose that the study of languages required a similar shift and similar combinations of orders and conventions. Bearing in mind Albinus's call to venture into unknown lands and languages, let us review what was required to gain accurate knowledge of lands and seas on one hand and languages on the other. Accurate knowledge of terrain required a knowledge of the local area, of the surrounding region, and of the global or big picture. It required schemes and conventions for placing the local into a region and regions into the global picture. It required techniques for specifying a location once it had been placed in accurate relation to its surrounding contexts. These techniques could not be arbitrary or merely imaginative; although variant techniques could be proposed, they had to match the nature of actual cartographic and navigational problems and reflect the spherical nature of the earth. Accurate knowledge of terrain and location also required conventions for representing these elements graphically. In addition, two types of conventions had been developed, the chorographic, or the technique of depicting places from a given perspective, and the geographic which seeks (though not actually attaining) an objective view, usually attained by depicting an area as if from a bird's eye view using symbols.

I would like to suggest that the parallels with language study are strong enough that we can perceive the conceptual needs of expanding language study through those of mapping. Knowing a language is like knowing a locale. Stylistic, rhetorical, and aesthetic treatments of a language, together with travelers' impressions and word lists of new languages, correspond to chorographic maps depicting an area from a given point of view. Having a grammar of a language equates to having a local map, although these can lean toward the perspectival or the objective depending upon the principles informing the grammar. To early grammarians, a Latin-based grammar of an American language approached the objective because Latin grammar was perceived to be a complete description of the elements of language, but as further study revealed the principles and elements of newly discovered languages, two types of more objective grammars evolved, one suited to each particular type of language and one a general grammar suitable to all languages. A knowledge of types of language relates to what I call regional knowledge, whereas the general grammar corresponds to the global knowledge. To attain that global level, something far beyond the general grammar must be reached. This factor would be somewhat akin to the grid lines that made accurate world maps possible (remembering that distortion is always an ingredient in such accuracy). In linguistic knowledge, the corresponding expertise would lie in something that transcends a general language or grammar: it would lie in some awareness of the relations of different types of language and the challenge they pose to general grammar, and growing out of this, an awareness of the nature of language itself.

While aware that the following list will sound a little tendentious, I suggest that something akin to iconographic and T–O maps occurred in the legendary figure of seventy-two languages. Something akin to the hybrid geographies and cosmographies occurred in encounters and collections of random linguistic information from abroad. Something akin to the grid system occurred in reflections on different grammars, and something akin to accurate longitude in typologies and linguistic genealogies. As in the invention of methods for determining longitude, especially the need for accurate clocks—acccuracy in the time dimension, which is not apparently related to space at all—to locate oneself in space, concepts from a dimension outside language itself would be needed to give coherence and order to the world of languages. Initially, this dimension was the rationality of the mind itself and the stability of a nature that was universally the same. These dimensions would fail, to be replaced by the idea that the mind and language interacted differently according to the culture and language of the speaker. What held true universally was that language and mind placed constraints on each other.

Medieval Charts of Language

Cartography and navigation advanced as people rationalized the problems of location that sailors experienced. A similar complementary movement characterized advances in language study. In the history of linguistics G. A. Padley has similarly observed "a regular swing of the pendulum between periods of 'observational adequacy' (to use the term popularized by Chomsky) in which the province of grammarians is the 'practical knowledge of the general usages of speakers and writers,' and periods of 'explanatory adequacy' in which the aim is to demonstrate the underlying 'causes' of a language by applying to it a logical or philosophical metalanguage."[13] The main problems in language were, as Padley suggests, to collect accurate information and to explain and rationalize it.

The medieval world of language was strong in explanation but weak in the observation of details. However, the explanatory element relied on faulty rationalizations and insufficient observation of particulars. As with terrestrial charts of the time, people had local knowledge, in this case of their own and nearby languages, including grammars of Latin, but their techniques for collecting and representing language-specific knowledge reflected little knowledge of anything beyond the horizon. Curiously, even though scholars had little knowledge of distant terrains and languages, they seemed to know the big picture, and their satisfaction with the overall plan left them comfortable with gaps in particular knowledge. That is to say that because they knew exactly how the gaps would be filled in if only they could travel to far places, they felt less of that curiosity and courage that Albinus praised in Columbus and the pioneers of language study. In the absence of the flood of knowledge of languages that would come later, thinkers mapped language onto the world geographically, mystically, and semiotically, seeking in its internal secrets the key to other realms of knowledge.

The relation between this kind of universal knowledge and the particulars that would complete it can be seen in the legend of seventy-two languages, which provided a comprehensive framework for the descent and number of tongues spoken around the globe. This number provided boundaries to diversity and made it comfortable to the human mind. Number does not seem to be a spatial concept, perhaps, but some cognitive linguists have suggested that the idea of number grows out of bodily experiences with space, magnitude, and objects. The legend that seventy-two languages came forth from Babel was accepted by many scholars, perhaps because it combined the learning of several traditions with biblical history and numerology. Arno Borst documents the spread of the idea, tracing its origins probably to Egypt as Greek influence spread there around the second century A.D.

Ireneus already knew about the seventy-two languages in A.D. 183. As the Egyptians assimilated the Greek base-six number system, rather than a decimal system based on multiples of ten as the Egyptians knew it, the number seventy-two took on special meaning as the product of six [(2 x 6) x 6]. Horapollo Nilous, a grammarian from Constantinople, writing on Egyptian antiquities and influenced by Hermetic and gnostic thought, said that the world was made up of seventy-two countries. Eventually, with antiquity backing them up, scholars throughout the Christian world started taking the idea of seventy-two countries and seventy-two languages seriously. The medieval Christian explanation was of course not based on a hexagonal numeric system but on a combination of Christian beliefs and sacred numbers. Between A.D. 612 and 615 a monk named Isidore of Seville published a book in which he attempted to explain the significance of the number seventy-two. He did this by taking the number twenty-four—the number of hours the earth needs to revolve about its axis once—and multiplying it by three, the number of the holy trinity. Wed this figure to the story of the flood and the sons of Noah, and it became generally believed that the confusion of languages at Babel had not only resulted in seventy-two languages but also that these languages were identical with the seventy-two people that originated from Noah's sons Ham, Sem and Japheth. It was generally accepted that the world had been divided up among the thirty-two tribes of Ham in Africa, the thirty-two tribes of Sem in Asia, and the fifteen tribes of Japheth in the cold north.

Medieval scholars who compiled lists of languages according to the "seventy-two tribes of Noah" had to consider all parts of the world without knowing what peoples actually inhabited them. Thus, the number had to correlate with the dispersion and variety of humanity across the earth's terrain. In the twelfth century a popular language list was that of an anonymous Armenian knight or merchant who included languages from Ethiopia, India, and Russia as well as from northwestern Europe, including the Semitic tongues, with some precision. Yet as soon as he ran out of real languages he filled in the missing amount with Armenian city and place names. Another twelfth-century figure, Rhoderich or Roderigo, a historian at the Spanish court, tried to stick closely to the concept that because the fifteen Japheth tribes came to Europe, there must also be fifteen different languages there. In the end he only comes up with thirteen European languages because he argues that German, Dutch and English are one and the same language. His list also does not differentiate between French, Italian, and his own native language Spanish, because he recognizes Latin to be the language from which they all stem. Rhoderich is credited with an early breakthrough in linguistics because he recognized that some languages are too closely related to be considered separate languages and also that several languages may have evolved from one mother language.[14]

Not everyone accepted the legend of seventy-two languages. Thomas Aquinas believed that languages were produced by people and therefore followed no preset pattern; they simply reflected differences in the character, temperament and environment of nations. Dante Alighieri separated linguistic analysis strictly from theology. Believing in the happenings of Babel as well as the confusion of languages by God, he argued that languages were prone to constant change which defied their being pressed into any number or scheme. In Italy alone Alighieri found fourteen languages and one thousand dialects. Origines believed that the earth had been separated from the beginning (even before Babel) into different dominions which were nourished and watched over by specifically assigned angels. According to him the separation of languages had not even taken place.[15]

The legend of seventy-two mapped languages onto the physical world. Working in a different trajectory, some scholars were convinced that language was the compass to everything that could be known. The idea that language mapped onto, and indeed governed, other types of knowledge permeates the work of one of the great medieval encyclopedists, Isidore of Seville. Isidore lived in the seventh century and compiled many books of learning. Chief among them was his *Etymologies*. An encyclopedia of all knowledge fit for a believing Christian of the time, the work contains twenty books covering grammar, rhetoric, mathematics, medicine, law, music, astronomy, theology, human anatomy and physiology, geography, architecture, surveying, mineralogy, agriculture, and warfare. Isidore saw the queen of all these studies, however, in etymology. Why?

Isidore trusted that all these disciplines could be mastered and related not by individual methods but by one, words. His reasoning seems to have run thus: as the world combines many orders of existence and equally many types of knowledge, yet there is only one universal means of representation found among humans, that being language, we should take the hint and see that in language the key to all other knowledge can be found. As one study explains:

His confidence in words really amounted to a belief, strong though perhaps somewhat inarticulate, that words were transcendental entities. All he had to do, he believed, was to clear away the misconceptions about their meaning, and set it forth in its true original sense; then, of their own accord, they would attach themselves to the general scheme of truth. The task of first importance, therefore, in treating any subject, was to seize upon the leading terms and trace them back to the meanings which they had in the beginning, before they had been contaminated by the false usage of the poets and other heathen writers; thus the truth would be found.[16]

Behind this description of Isidore's ideas we find root spatial metaphors. First, going back and clearing away the encrustations of human history to locate an original meaning of each word entails both routes and layers to objects. Second, the notion of an original meaning that will provide a much-needed pattern or reference point to the mind entails setting one object or pattern over another to view the second in terms of the first. Isidore thus provides the linguistic equivalent of space as emplacement, Foucault's term for the fitting of knowledge into the right niches of sacred and profane, earthly and celestial, natural and displaced. While language had been displaced by the Fall from its natural site, it had an important role in the finite, filled world. Since that world in all its disruption still mirrored in subtle and indirect ways the unity of prelapsarian existence, the vestiges of meaning still encoded in original words could guide one through chaos to knowledge.

Or signs themselves could do so. Inspired by the Franciscan dream of converting the world, Raymond Lull (ca. 1235–1316) anticipated achieving this end more readily by mastering the arts of signs. His *Ars Magna* posited that by designing and then combining signs in specified ways, people would be able to produce keys to knowledge that could be communicated among any who knew the method. Umberto Eco says, "The Lullian art was destined to seduce later generations who imagined that they had found in it a mechanism to explore the numberless possible connections between dignities and principles, principles and questions, questions and virtues or vices."[17]

Another mapping of language onto other types of knowledge in the Middle Ages took a yet more mystical turn. Just as the number seventy-two had significant properties, the study of individual words could open the door into all other types of knowledge. One version of this was the branch of numerology that read into words an esoteric knowledge based on the numbers to which individual letters corresponded and the numbers that a word's letters totaled when added up. The cabalists founded their mystical interpretations on the fact that each letter of the Hebrew alphabet also represented a number. Since numbers were felt to have special significance in reflecting the harmony of the universe, especially in relationship to divine revelation and sacred history, words could be studied for their numerical equivalents, which would then yield their meaningful correspondences. Different words whose letter-ciphers added up to certain total figures such as seventy, for example, were felt to have mystical equivalency. A special confidence was placed in such relationships. Indeed, followers of Guillaume Postel, in whom these mystical ideas culminated in the early Renaissance, believed that the infinite combinations of letters in words, when analyzed numerologically, could yield all that could be known in spiritual as well as secular realms.[18]

Many linguistic projects continued the search for core mysteries. Etymologists influenced by Isidore of Seville forged along on the assumption that names revealed essential information about their referents and that etymology uncovered yet more of their original power. Others contemplated the exotic writing systems of distant peoples, often triggered by speculation on Chinese characters that stood not for sounds but concepts. The publication of Horapollo's *Hieroglyphica* in 1505 led, as Donald Lach states it, "to the growth of a popular cult which viewed the enigmatic hieroglyphs as ideographical devices for conveying philosophical insights and moral maxims which could be interpreted by the enlightened everywhere without reference to literary or verbal explanations."[19] Giovanbattista Palatino published a work in 1540 designed to help people learn the letters and scripts of any language whatever, ancient or modern. Blaise de Vigenère produced his *Traicté des chiffres* (1586) on secret methods of writing, or what we would now call cryptology, inspired largely by the conviction that many nations—Chinese, Japanese, and Egyptian among them—had two languages and forms of writing, one ordinary, the other an occult form that preserved their highest learning. Filippo Sassetti reported on a most attractive feature of Chinese writing, that it contained an infinite number of characters for different concepts, and that these allowed speakers of different dialects and languages to communicate ideas without having to pass ideas through the filter of sound-based writing.[20]

The terrestrial discoveries of the sixteenth century helped scholars recognize that a knowledge of signs and numbers would not be sufficient to unlock the secrets of nature. To arrive at a truly fruitful knowledge, scholars saw that they must collect and analyze the fullest possible range of individual languages. They believed that with the right logic of analysis and lucky insight, they would fasten quickly on the core principles of all language and this core would in turn clear the mists of linguistic diversity. These types of reports and studies helped establish foundations for the large-scale collections and analyses of language of the Renaissance. Guillaume de Postel, Konrad Gesner, Theodore Bibliander, Peter Albinus, and Claude Duret were all convinced that a well-constructed collection of linguistic information would propel learning forward on many fronts. Looking back on them, we can see more clearly that they were desperately seeking something to make the collections achieve the proper rationalization of relations between particular specimens of language and a larger frame of knowledge. In her classic study of early anthropology, Margaret Hodgen examines at length the problems of collections. If the collector "was unable to discern the likenesses or uniformities in his materials, if he failed to verbalize their associations with or similarities to one another, if he was unable to convey to others his conceptual organization of alien ways of living, then, in spite of all his labors in getting them together, he had no collection."[21]

Hodgen finds that social and cultural ideas were often more challenging than natural history. "It was primarily in the contemplation of man's religions and his languages that the presence of conformities first challenged the interest of scholars at least in the sixteenth century" (Hodgen, 301). In linguistic matters the collection problems were aggravated because divinity had instituted diversity. Since "neither the plurality of tongues nor their similarities could be imputed to the devil . . . there seemed to be nothing left for the scholar but to count diverse tongues or, when that failed, to try to reach a decision as to which among them was the original" (Hodgen, 304). Although Hodgen is wrong on two counts (missionaries did impute linguistic diversity to the devil, and there were, as this and other chapters show, strategies behind collections), her main point is of use here. Linguistic collections posed an extreme challenge. I refer again to Padley's distinction between periods of observational and explanatory adequacy. Collections being generally as much about general principles as about the detailed particulars, these compendia make evident the leap Bacon so often criticized, that of going from a few instances to the loftiest generalities. As we review some of these collections, what I want to notice is the growth toward more and more generous inclusion of details until it is clear that the lofty generalities fail to account for them. Collections were overwhelmed by what they contained.

Guillaume Postel (1510–1581), a linguist, visionary, and believer in the esoteric, foresaw an imminent concord of the world under a universal Christian monarchy. Greater understanding of languages and their underlying unity would help bring about this goal. Postel's writings were undertaken to this end in spite of his being ejected from the Jesuit order in 1545, prohibited from teaching in 1553, and arrested for heresy in 1555. He helped produce the polyglot Bible of 1571 in Hebrew, Chaldaic, Greek, and Latin. His *Linguarum Duodecim Differentium Alphabetum Indroductio* (1538) combed through the characters of twelve languages to uncover the original writing style that primitive Hebrew had used. Owing to the changes that all languages had undergone, Hebrew included, these primitive characters had largely vanished, but Postel believed that comparisons among current writing forms could reveal them.

Konrad Gesner's *Mithridates* (1555), a comprehensive survey of languages with little analysis, professed to offer information on all the known languages and printed the Lord's Prayer in many of them. Theodore Bibliander's *De Ratione Communi Omnium Linguarum* (1548) made an important argument for missionary linguists and armchair philologists alike, that all languages could be described grammatically, just as Greek and Latin could. The assertion appeared in the middle of the sixteenth-century's flow of linguistic information and meant that those drawn to search out the secrets of language could apply their familiar tools and methods, confident that knowledge of all languages could, at the least, be collected and disseminated without staggering anomalies. Yet travelers would continue to report populations who communicated with gestures and inarticulate sounds, as Thomas Herbert reported of the Troglodites of East Africa in 1634. Their speech, he said, "sounded rather like that of Apes, than men."[22] Bibliander's assertion helped reorient students of language to the underlying rationality and order of all tongues.

Claude Duret's *Thresor de l'histoire des langues de cest univers*,[23] published in Cologne in 1613, resembles Albinus's work in seeing the divine plan reflected in the multiplicity of languages, but it pretends to know how to read God's secrets more than the earlier text. Duret catalogs a seemingly vast array of languages in the hopes that these languages would yield important principles and insights. What the catalog illustrates is the growing difficulty of framing existing linguistic data in comprehensive frameworks held over from an earlier age.

Duret aimed at producing the first language compendium and the first history of all the languages known to humanity. This purpose itself is noteworthy. Duret filled more than a thousand quarto pages of small print with information drawn from classical, sacred, and contemporary sources. In the late 1500s and early 1600s a number of general histories of the new world had been written. Also, the first collections of voyages had been published. Duret used many of these contemporary collections as well as dozens of classical works to produce this curious encyclopedia. He had already written a treatise on the causes of the advance and decline of nations, a discourse on the causes and effects of the movements of the ocean, and a history of marvelous and miraculous plants.[24] His treasury of the history of languages now afforded him the opportunity to survey the extent of known linguistic variety, to connect that variety to the history of humanity, and to postulate the causes of flourishing and decay in language.

We might say that in the *Thresor* Duret combined two treatises in one. The first treated Hebrew, in whose original form Duret perceived language as instituted by God at the beginning of the world. As a divine creation, language stood beside any other of God's handiworks as having a special type of meaning, and as such, it rewarded detailed contemplation. The fall in Eden affected this tongue in that from then on Adam and his descendants lacked the insight to bestow names on creatures commensurate with their nature. Consequently, from that time the search for names had been "very difficult, if not impossible" (Duret, 39). Almost a third of Duret's treatise plods through topics related to the Hebrew language. His second track surveys languages born during or after the fall of Babel. These follow the "fatal course of nature" (Duret, 1014) of growth, perfection, and degeneration. These were subject to environmental forces such as "situation and region," as well as to the vicissitudes and disruptions caused by conquest, alliance, and the proximity of other languages. Duret exhausted little effort on trying to understand the processes by which humans received and developed the language gift (Duret, 5). Rather, he reflected on why God gave humans reason and language and on how writing gave "the means of comprehending in a few small things the multitude and sounds and voices."

On the issue of how diverse tongues related to some broader pattern, Duret advocated the idea of infinite resemblance in all creation, following in particular Postel's cabalistic view of Hebrew.[25] Even the act of writing could have special resonance. On this topic Duret followed one of his sources, José de Acosta, a historian of the Americas, but note what Duret added. Acosta observed that the Latins and Greeks wrote from left to right, the Hebrews from right to left, the Chinese from top to bottom, and the Mexicans from bottom to top or, in the case of their inscribed wheels or calendars, from the middle of space with the figure of the sun, then circling outward. Acosta observed that in these four main types of writing one could see "the diversity of human ingenuity."[26] In a passage clearly modeled on Acosta's, Duret did something quite different. Rather than seeing mere diversity of genius, Duret stated that taken together the modes of writing manifested, in Michel Foucault's words, "the secrets and mysteries of the world's frame and the form of the cross, the unity of the heaven's rotundity and that of the earth."[27] What matters here is not so much any one particular language or a knowledge thereof. Instead, Duret assumed that to see meaningfully one must know more than each part; one must contemplate the parts in relation to each other, and from that, the parts in relation to the whole. Even the decayed and decaying languages that sprang from Babel could teach the truth of all things when contemplated together. Foucault made the following point:

> The relation of languages to the world is one of analogy rather than of signification; or rather, their value as signs and their duplicating function

are superimposed; they speak the heaven and the earth of which they are the image; they reproduce in their most material architecture the cross whose coming they announce—that coming which establishes its existence in its own turn through the scriptures and the Word. Language possesses a symbolic function; but since the disaster at Babel we must no longer seek for it—with rare exceptions—in the words themselves but rather in the very existence of language, in its total relation to the totality of the world, in the intersecting of its space with the loci and forms of the cosmos.[28]

Duret rhapsodized on the different manners of writing, but by implication his comments apply to language in general. He had grand intuitions of language's relations to the world, but notice that he instantiated them only in the rudimentary spatial paradigm of directions in which people write. He did not offer clues as to how language in general reflected the infinite web of creation. Such a view entailed a mystical comprehension of several related types of knowledge, including how lexicons and grammars differed and how those played out a set of inherent relations in the origins and destiny of human beings and the workings the human mind. Duret explicitly beckoned toward such kinds of knowledge but fell mute after providing the voluminous particulars out of which it would be inferred. In fact, we might say that the particulars he so painstakingly assembled were not of the sort he would need to answer these kinds of questions. His is a map of language with a mystical compass but no meridian, no grid lines, no means of surveying the whole his treasury promises to reveal.

Grammar as Spatial

Don Lorenzo Hervás y Panduro, the accomplished Spanish linguist and author of the *Catálogo de las lenguas de las naciones conocidas* (1800–1805) provides a milepost from which to look back on Duret's *Thresor* and other works like it. Hervás eschews the hidden links and sacred resemblances of languages, but his organizational principle indicates that for him, at least, the strands that connected all languages had not been found. His catalog merely lists and describes languages by their location. Thus what holds the collection together is just the earth: these are the languages to be found in such and such a place.

In another way, Hervás depends on penetration into the nature of each language. He provides grammatical detail as far as it was available; therefore he recognizes the immense debt later students of language owed to those early workers who, with no more training than could be derived from the study of Latin in preparation for ordination or civil appointment, dedicated years to mastering and analyzing foreign languages until they could systematically present the principles governing their sounds, grammar, and word order. One such figure was Ruiz de Montoya, who wrote one of the finest early grammars of Guarani, *Arte y vocabulario de la lengua guaraní* (1640). Hervás y Panduro said of him: "One cannot read these works of the Jesuit Ruiz without admiring the author as a prodigy of talent and effort, reducing to clear rules the grammatical artifices and many varied sounds of the Guarani language, one of the most difficult of America."[29] These achievements are all the more significant when we note that the first grammar of Greek to appear in Europe came in 1495, of Spanish in 1492, and of Portuguese in 1536.

We may not recognize at first the spatial constituents of grammar. In order for a language's grammar to be composed, the language must first be in written form, a condition so obvious that we overlook it. Unwritten languages have grammatical principles, but they do not have a grammar in the other sense, a formal plan that can be preserved and transmitted. Writing is inherently and inescapably a spatial (and highly reductive) act—the translation of spoken sounds, not to mention the visual and bodily sensations of talking and listening, into marks on a surface. As J. M. Y. Simpson succinctly puts it, language is "a patterning of recurring elements. In speech these elements are arranged in a dimension of time, in writing they are arranged in a dimension of space."[30] The forms of writing solve differently the problem of translation from sound in time to a two-dimensional surface. Semasiographic writing conveys ideas without regard to sounds and, in some cases, without regard to the number of words it takes to express an idea conveyed by one sign. Glottographic writing, which includes morphemic and syllabic systems, represents sounds. Syllabic systems, a branch of the glottographic, use symbols, sometimes pictures, to stand for syllables or in some cases for initial sounds of syllables. These stylized pictures are then arranged in lines or clusters. Alphabetic writing systems break sounds down beyond the syllable and combine letters into words.

Great ingenuity appears in creating a writing system. Writing systems ideally conform in some way to the nature of the language they record. Let me explain. A syllabic writing system, that assigns one script unit to a given combination of consonant–vowel–consonant, works well in languages with a restricted number of these combinations. Such is the case in Japanese. English, by contrast, has so many combinations that it would require thousands upon thousands of symbols just to represent its syllables. Alphabetic writing, which assigns script units to individual sounds of which syllables and words are made, works much better for English.

A logographic system, which assigns a script unit to an entire word, can work optimally only with a language that does not vary its word forms with prefixes, suffixes, and inflections. Chinese writing functions extremely well in that each character represents a word without inflections, conjugations, or declinations. The Chinese language utilizes no such features. Rather, time, person, and case are conveyed by separate words or word order. Notably, "among the writing systems of the world there is no logographic script that represents words consisting of more than one morpheme by single symbols."[31] By contrast, agglutinating languages, that combine many ideas into one sound-string word, would make any kind of logographic writing impossible, since each possible word would need its own symbol. Even managing individual sounds in a glottographic writing system can require considerable ingenuity. For example, in English *talk* and *take* have different pronunciations, but nothing intrinsic to sounds or to the writing system says which is which. The base vowel is assumed to be the same, so other markers, in this case the final addition of *e* or the insertion of *l* before the final consonant, signals the difference.

Since grammar has long been intrinsic to language study, we easily overlook how it is conceptually influenced by space. We need also to be reminded that parts of speech are not literal but metaphorical parts—pieces of larger composite, each with its location and function. Grammar requires translating from living language, which is sound in time coming from a body in three-dimensional space, to principles that can be remembered in separation from the flow of speech, related along multiple paths, and presented in writing—that is, in two-dimensional space and time. In this feature it resembles maps which convert the topical features on the surface of a sphere into marks on a plane. Maps require distortion from the sphere to plane; selection of features (not every feature can be represented in a single map; maps are of time and of different phenomena such as population, elevation, and temperature); and development of conventions and symbols and means of relating features to each other. Somewhat as a set of blueprints, each one of which relates to and converges in a single building, grammars must represent a language in successive views that relate to each other in multiple ways. A grammar is a breaking apart of an extremely complex phenomenon so that it can be examined a part at a time and reassembled. It requires the separation of parts, the creation of categories by which parts are nested within other parts, and definition of changes that happen under different conditions, or, to put it spatially, grammar isolates the effect of multiple forces upon a single linguistic unit. Grammar demands extreme ingenuity in allocating linguistic phenomena that occur in different planes to their specific places in an overall plan. Latin grammar so powerfully attracted students of non-European languages because it demonstrated that such a template was even possible.

The conventions governing grammar are in some ways as arbitrary as those that govern any writing system. We all know that careful study of a single language has led to multiple and varying grammars. Most grammars are grounded on a spatial concept: divide language into apparently discrete parts such as sounds, word classes, morphology (how words change form under different conditions), clauses, and sentences; put them in proper sequence; and have some means of identifying how changes in one part or level influence those in another. An example of the overt spatial foundation can be seen in the grammar of the Timucua language formerly spoken in northern Florida. The linguist tackles its verb morphology by conceptualizing the verb as having thirteen potential slots, including slots for subject pronoun, object pronoun, the base verb, transivity, locus (whether proximate or distant in time), and mode (indicative or imperative).[32] At another level spatial concepts also operate. Grammar, especially as practiced in the early modern era, entails rules. The word *rules* derives from *regula*, a straight stick or pattern; its verb form derives from *regere*, to set a line or direct. A regular verb follows the line. The move from Latin-based to structural and transformational grammars reflects not only different conceptions of the intersecting planes of syntax and word formation, but different types of conceptual space. The deep structures and branching trees of transformational grammar match the incremental changes that can be made in a simple NP–VP (noun phrase–verb phrase) structure. To write a grammar is to get close to language and create a schematic pattern whose elements correspond to the parts and relations of living, spoken language.

Grammars were among the most important early linguistic documents. Henrique Henriques sent the first grammar of Tamil along with translations of prayers and syllabary to Portugal for printing in 1551. In 1552 Mariano Vittorio published the first grammar of "Chaldean," actually the Geez language of Ethiopia, called *Chaldeae seu Aethiopicae Linguae Institutiones*. In 1560 Domingo de Santo Tomás published in Valladolid the first grammar of an American language, Quechua. Jesuit missionaries in Japan were composing a grammar and dictionary there as early as 1563. Father João Rodriguez, who assisted in preparing several compilations of Japanese vocabulary and characters, produced the first published grammar of Japanese, *Arte da lingoa de Japam* (1604–1608), "a practical and sophisticated presentation of the nature of the Japanese language and its grammar that remained the best available in Europe until after the reopening of Japan in the nineteenth century."[33] After decades of preparing catechisms and other preliminary work, Spanish missionaries in the Philippines printed the first grammar of Tagalog, *Arte y reglas de la lengua tagala*, by Friar Francisco de S. Joseph, in 1610.

The first published New World grammar, by Domingo de Santo Tomás of the Quechua tongue of the Andean region, began with this comment on the difficulty of discovering the regular aspects of a newly learned language:

> To give or discern the rules and modes of speaking in any language is among the most difficult and variable things one can do in this world of human variety. And if it is so in respect to the most learned and used languages, for which erudite men have already made grammars, how different it will be in this language of Peru, so strange, so new, so unknown, so foreign to us, a language never until now reduced to its rules nor placed under their precepts?[34]

Students of language in the sixteenth century would not incline to think that each language would have its own principles and rules. Indeed, the idea of grammar was probably linked in their minds more to languages of erudition, whose parts of speech and rules would be seen as somewhat universal. No wonder, then, that once they perceived some of the regular features of a new language, they began to esteem it more. The rigors of spatialization involved in writing a grammar led to a deeper aesthetics of language— deeper because it could be displayed and demonstrated in other than samples of speech. Santo Tomás announced what would become a theme for many grammars, praise for the fullness and artfulness of the target language. Indeed, Santo Tomás wrote the grammar partly to show the crown

> how false it is of which many have been persuaded, that the natives of Peru are a barbarous people, unworthy of being treated with the gentleness and liberty that your other subjects enjoy. All this your majesty shall clearly see to be false, if you survey in this grammar this language's grand politeness, its abundance of vocabulary, the correspondence these have with the things they signify, the diverse and curious manners it offers of speaking, the suave and pleasing sounds its pronunciation offers the ear, the ease with which it can be written with our characters and letters. (Santo Tomás, 9–10)[35]

Santo Tomás saw in the beauty and regularity of Quechua a refutation of a prevailing notion of barbarous languages, that they were confused and disordered. Note that his appreciation is figured in terms of lines and enclosures and regularity, the last term signifying lined up right.

> How easy and sweet is the pronunciation of this our language, its declinations ordering and adorning it appropriately, and also its propriety of nouns, modes,

tenses, and verb changes for person. And briefly, in many things so conforming to the Latin and to Spanish in its rules and artifices, that the whole language seems but a prognostication that Spaniards would eventually possess her. It is a language, your Majesty, so polished and abundant, so regulated and enclosed within its rules, that it is hardly that kind referred to by Quintilian and others as barbarous, by which they mean one full of defects and barbarisms, without modes, tenses, cases, rules, order, or concert. On the contrary, one may call this language very delicate and polished. (Santo Tomás, 10)[36]

By his reference to Quechua's affinity to Latin grammar, he addressed whether to use Latin grammar as a template on which to teach languages whose intrinsic features might be incompatible with Latin. In the case of Quechua, of course, he found a surprising congruence that would justify the Latin template. It is tempting to criticize this practice as yet another imposition of European ideas on non-European subjects. This criticism is highly unhistorical. One must remember first of all that the grammars were not written to explain these languages to the indigenous who spoke them. Native speakers had no need of instruction. Grammars were prepared to serve outsiders—European outsiders—who in many cases knew only one grammar, the Latin. Using Latin grammar to teach the workings of a new tongue made great sense, even if new terms had to be invented and exceptions noted as the new language was unfolded to view. We should not be surprised then that Andrés de Olmos used Nebrija's highly influential Latin grammar, *Introductiones Latinae* (1481) in his sketch of Nahuatl. During the fifteenth century, European grammarians were just discovering, through direct study of Roman grammarians, that the respected authorities of antiquity disagreed on principles of Latin grammar. This discovery made their attitude toward grammar more flexible.[37] Indeed, I would say that because they had learned Latin using then-available grammars, missionaries appreciated the variety and beauty of new languages much more than would have been the case had their language learning proceeded with no external grammatical model. Only with distinct categories in mind could one begin to compare the way in which another language expressed similar thoughts. Creators of grammar usually saw quite clearly how the target languages differed from Latin and made competent adjustments.

Like medieval cosmologists trying to harmonize epicycles and other celestial aberrations into a geocentric universe, grammarians worked hard to lay the template of Latin grammar onto other languages and still preserve their unique features. For example, the succession of Nahuatl grammars forms a record of continuing struggle to understand and define its lexicon, syntax, and grammatical parts.[38] Nahuatl presented many challenges to grammarians. These linguists, inclined to apply either Latin or Nebrija's Castilian grammar, were aware of the unique aspects of Nahuatl words and syntax, and at the same time they felt motivated to place in the hands of fellow missionaries the most convenient guide to learning the language for the specific purpose of teaching doctrine and receiving confessions from the Indians. The first notable Nahuatl grammar, that of Andrés de Olmos, assured learners that Nahuatl contained all the parts of speech found in Latin, yet Olmos found reasons to break from the usual order for presenting grammatical discussions and began his with pronouns and possessive pronouns because of the way Nahuatl combines these with verbs. Nahuatl is agglutinative rather than inflectional; it expresses genitive relationships using possessive pronouns in a syntax different from anything the missionaries had seen ("the cat's meow" is expressed as "her meow the cat"); it utilizes glottal stops missed by most transcribers; and it expresses spatial relationships not by prepositions but by location nouns like "aboveness" and "belowness." Alonso de Molina, another early student of Nahuatl, went further than Olmos, noting that "the language and syntax of these natives, especially of the Nahuas and Mexicans, is very different from the Latin, Greek, and Spanish language and syntax."[39] Antonio del Rincón, also a grammarian of Nahuatl, asserted that it was not possible to keep "in all languages to one method and art, being that they are so different and distinct one from another. To impose uniformity in this would cause great disformity and, of consequence, confusion and obstacles for whoever learned them."[40]

Writing a grammar entailed a search for the right spatial concept in which to represent a language. One of the most admired grammars of the sixteenth century, Diego González Holguín's *Arte de la lengua general del Perú, llamada quichua* (1586), opened its discussion by stating that the Quechuan language had the eight parts of speech of Latin; Holguín treated each part clearly, providing examples and explaining the exceptions. A section of annotations provided names for classes of relationships that didn't exist in most European languages, for example, for familial terms which differed depending on the gender of the speaker. Under transitive verbs he drew attention to "certain interpositions in verbs by which the transition from the verb to one person or another are noted" and which affected the conjugation. These varied in four ways, from a single to a single person, from a single person to plural persons, from plural to singular, and from plural to plural.[41] When Holguín described sounds that change the signification of the verb when inserted in it, what would he call them? Particles, a very useful term for describing anomalies to the eight parts of speech.

In the first published grammar of Japanese, *Arte da lingoa de Japam* (1604–1608), Father João Rodriguez followed the Latin, but similarly paid close heed to the particles and honorifics in which Japanese differed from Latin. One kind of particle was used to denote the cases of nouns, and other particles he treated as a separate part of speech. He referred to Japanese experts on these points of grammar. As one historian has written, Rodriguez "at no time missed the principal features of the Japanese language. For example, he explained honorifics minutely in every section. Other Jesuit grammarians called the Japanese adjective *Nome adjectivo*, but Rodriguez called it *Verbo adjectivo*, seeing that it was not the same as that found in European languages, but properly belonged to another class of irregular verbs."[42]

As Victor Hanzeli has said of the French missionaries in North America, grammarians of newly encountered languages took part, though on a smaller scale, in some of the most important intellectual activity of the period.

> The qualitative examination of these printed sources gives us the first glimpses of the basic tension which will characterize the entire linguistic work of the missionaries: the tension between acquired intellectual habits and techniques in dealing with languages and the realities of new patterns of speech which cannot be adequately handled in the framework of these habits. Essentially, this was the same tension that was felt by the Renaissance man on a much larger cosmological scale, when new discoveries and new observations began to expand explosively his traditional view of the universe.[43]

Within this large frame, Latin-based grammars functioned as a kind of linguistic cosmology straining to give way to a new world.

It might be of interest therefore to consider briefly what was happening to the concept of space. Just at the time when linguists were beginning to think that numerous languages might have their own independent grammars, one of the most heterodox and stubborn thinkers of the sixteenth century was proposing an infinite universe with a plurality of worlds. The idea of multiple grammars was the linguistic equivalent of that decentered, pluralistic universe. Although it would be a stretch to assert any direct influence of the cosmology of Giordano Bruno on language study, it is no stretch to argue for a diffuse influence. Bruno's ideas were a strange blend of hermeticism, early modern science, and idiosyncratic imaginings that brought him to trial for heresy in Rome, where he was burned at the stake in 1600. Bruno's travels, his interest in Copernicus, and his willingness to think beyond current opinion led him to ideas that parallel what was occurring in language study as the implications of different grammars were being fathomed.

Bruno was born in Italy, studied in France, lectured and composed some of his most important works in England, sought patronage and protection in Germany, and was eventually extradited back to Italy to defend his ideas. His opinions and changing religious affiliations led him to be excommunicated or otherwise expelled in turn by Catholics, Calvinists, and Lutherans. Bruno taught the Copernican universe when many church authorities and university officials viewed it with suspicion. Copernicus proposed a finite heliocentric universe; Bruno proposed an infinite universe with plurality of worlds and solar systems. The human world, he argued, was but one of many possible worlds, with our solar system not necessarily at its center. While endorsing a divine unity that wasn't perceptible to humans, Bruno also envisioned an atomistic composition of the universe that had ingrained in it the possibility of multiple points of view. Not surprisingly, given both his cosmology and his changing commitments to church doctrines, Bruno supported religious toleration and mutual understanding based on open discussion.

The lessons of pluralism can prove difficult to assimilate. It would be easy to look down our noses at the linguists of the past, but we do so in ignorance. I will make a short digression to illustrate how interpretive templates can enforce ideology. The key to deciphering Maya glyphs had been lost since the demise of the classical Maya people. Various theories, some of them mystical, had been advanced, and even the descendants of the Maya living in Central America today had no clue. In trying to figure out how the Maya wrote, the Russian linguist Yuri Knorosov had recourse to the writings of Diego de Landa, one of the first serious students of Maya. There Knosorov found the key: some parts of the glyphs expressed sounds. In some cases these were not the phonetic sounds of Maya, but the Maya equivalent of the letters of the Spanish alphabet as Landa's informants had provided them for transcription. Knosorov disputed the leading Mayanists' theories to state:

> Signs given by D. de Landa, in spite of a century of attack upon them, have exactly the phonetic meaning that he attributed to them. This does not mean, of course, either that these signs cannot have other meanings, or that they exhaust the phonetic signs of the Maya hieroglyphs.[44]

Walter Mignolo has attempted to expose the degree to which alphabetic literacy and colonization cooperated to produce a linguistic tyranny of Latin over Amerindian traditions.[45] The risk of taking Mignolo's position occurred to me when I read his discussion of Diego de Landa. Mignolo was perhaps too eager to accept the judgment of the linguist Roy Harris, who claimed that Diego de Landa's search for a phonetic element in the Maya glyphs was foolish. Mignolo quotes Harris: "Landa's Maya alphabet stands as a kind of permanent folly in the history of linguistics. What it reveals is the depths of incomprehension which centuries of alphabetic culture can inculcate about the nature of writing."[46] In one of those embarrassing twists of history, Landa turned out to be right. Working with a Maya informant, Landa perceived that Maya glyphs were a form of syllabic writing. A glyph for the sound *ku* represents a fishhook, which word is pronounced *ku*. By combining logographs, or symbols that represent ideas rather than sounds, with syllabic glyphs, Maya writers could write of events, ceremonies, and histories in a detail that surpassed logographic writing.[47] Their accomplishment is all the more astounding in light of the lack of writing among most of their neighbors of the Americas.

Grammarians and other students of language often, though not always, of course, learned that the world was linguistically pluralistic and that distinct languages encompassed not only distinct beauties but points of view. Controversy over the identity and number of the parts of speech continued to simmer into the eighteenth century. In 1798 Horne Tooke, when asked how many parts of speech grammar encompassed, responded that it was an important but not settled question. The answer might be two or twenty, depending on the language and what one thought of as parts of speech.[48] The idea that the parts of speech even within a single language might vary according to the principles of the grammar upon which one defined them, and that these might additionally differ from language to language, came as one of the great benefits of grammar writing in a world of linguistic diversity.

From Grammars to Universal Grammar

Grammars were plans of individual languages. If local plans and town maps and drawings had their cartographic complement in geographic maps of entire regions or even the whole world, grammars also begged to be linked so the coastlines and interiors of the linguistic world could be viewed in its entirety, if not in its detail. Local mapping and a more global conceptualizing of cartography can take place separately, but at some point they depend on each other. For example, if a person from one place wants to read a map made in a distant place, he or she needs conventions and symbols that apply to both. Further, if a person wants to know the location of a place depicted in a map or know to what area the map pertains, he or she must have access to some type of locating procedures. Similarly, knowledge of languages could proceed apart from general concepts of language, but only to a degree, and at some point the two domains must connect explicitly. A sufficient number of particular grammars will begin to suggest something about language itself, and a general linguistics starts to suggest something about how particular grammars should be written. Attempts to link these two domains comprise one of the driving forces in the history of language study. Students of language required, at a local level, many grammars of individual languages and, together with those, some conjectures about the true extent and limits of linguistic diversity. At the more abstract level, linguists required a set of descriptions, laws, and principles that defined language.

The seventeenth century responded to the need for comprehensive linguistic understanding with universal grammar. Such a grammar would in a sense map language itself, and, in so doing, help refine and correct the grammars of individual tongues. A valid universal grammar would also be an aid to thinking and an aid to truth. The trick would be in the word *valid*. A universal grammar would have to pertain to all languages and yet not be identical to any particular language. The problem lay in rightly discerning the principles upon which comprehensive understanding would build upon particulars. Bacon saw that few in his time could resist the urge to leap from a few instances to make sweeping generalizations and skip the intermediate inferences that would link them to the particulars.

Bacon saw another way in which language study could fall prey to the wrong methods. As an example of how the "sweet falling of clauses" grew more in price than the "weight of matter" and "worth of subject," Bacon cited Bishop Jerome Osorio, the "Portuguese Cicero," who chronicled Portuguese discoveries and conquests in a much-admired style. Through Osorio's writings Portuguese national achievement and prestige became bound up in the "round and clean composition of the sentence" (*Adv L*, 3:283).[49] This was a map of the world, but a bad one. It confused style with knowledge, just as Renaissance expedition chronicles, such as Walter Raleigh's *The Discoverie of the Large, Rich and Bewtiful Empyre of Guiana* (1596) often were written to redeem failed expeditions by creating textual versions of success.[50] Aware of the linguistic reports and grammars that traders and missionaries were supplying to Europe, Sir Francis Bacon believed that the proper study of language—and particularly of grammar—would help breach the seemingly endless cycle of sterile learning. Real voyages provided a model of discovery and new information upon which errors could be corrected: "Nor must it go for nothing that by distant voyages and travels which have become frequent in our times, many things in nature have been laid open and discovered which may let in new light upon philosophy" (*New O*, 4:82).

Languages, Bacon hoped, would eventually figure as a thing in nature that had been "laid open and discovered." Indeed, if the masters of logic and rhetoric had taken their eyes off of tropes and style and had

> gone a form lower, and looked but into the observations of Grammar and syntax; specially enriching the same with the help of several languages; with their differing properties of words, phrases, and tropes; they might have found out more and better footsteps of common reason, help of disputation, and advantages of cavillation, than many of these which they have propounded. (*IN*, 3:230)

This task involved diversity and comparison, by whose means scholars could escape the confines of their learned traditions. What Bacon proposed was, finally, a new type of language study, modeled on exploration of the world, that required two stages, firsthand sampling of languages to isolate their best features and then meticulous scrutiny of what he would call "conformities," or those similarities in form that nature—or language—repeats, and by which we can perceive their most basic and underlying elements.

Praising grammar as a guard against the confusion of tongues and "the harbinger of other sciences," Bacon saw the outcome of this type of study as a new kind of grammar and one of the desiderata of the new sciences. This kind, a philosophical grammar, would probe the relations of words, things, and reason as never before:

> But the noblest species of grammar, as I think, would be this: if some one well seen in a number of tongues, learned as well as vulgar, would handle the various properties of *languages*; showing in what points each excelled, in what it failed. For so not only may languages be enriched by mutual exchanges, but the several beauties of each may be combined (as in the Venus of Apelles) into a most beautiful image and excellent model of speech itself, for the right expressing of the meanings of the mind. (*Adv L*, 4:441–42)

Bacon wanted a grammar that would help people determine which types of linguistic encoding enabled them to express their thoughts about the world in the clearest and most appropriate manner. He sought a model— a generalized and abstracted scheme that captured the essential functions and relationships of thinking and reduced complexity to the simplest structure that could correspond to the true nature of things.

Such a grammar would be the equivalent of the longitude. It would require multiple types of knowledge and judgment, types that seemed always on the brink of attainment yet constantly eluded the most dogged inquirer. The most achievable of the required types of knowledge was an ability to speak and write in many languages. This knowledge would have to be supplemented by something unavailable in Bacon's time, however. It would require an ability to relate different kinds of expression to similar grammatical and syntactical functions, the judgment to evaluate better and worse ways of expressing ideas, and an ability to declare the grounds on which to make this judgment. For example, one would have to know whether it would be better to isolate each element of meaning into separate words or to cluster many meanings into one word, or whether it would be better to inflect nouns for nominative, dative, and objective cases, or to mark these cases through prepositions and particles. Should verb tenses and conjugations follow the Latin model, or should other tenses and voices be advantageous? Should syntax be comprised of words in a certain order, or of a root word inflected and marked for case, person, relationship, and time? To answer these questions would further require a firm grasp of the "meanings of the mind" as entities quite apart from the particular expressions of them that different languages yielded. Such a grasp seemed eminently achievable because Bacon's contemporaries could easily find phrases and structures in which different languages communicated similar thoughts. Yet such a grasp was constantly elusive in that it presumed a pristine conception of thoughts as they existed prior to and apart from their expression in any particular language. The fulfillment of these expectations would presume a systematic knowledge of language built on a thorough understanding of diverse tongues but would also transcend these tongues: a sort of meta-grammar derived from all known grammars but not necessarily contained in one. All this was happening at a time when Europe had produced only a few grammars of its own languages.

Given that language was already at one remove from that type of matter which could provide checks on learning, Bacon's call faced an additional challenge. In every field, Bacon held, drawing part of his imagery from navigation, "the proceeding has been to fly at once from the sense and particulars up to the most general propositions, as certain fixed poles for the argument to turn upon, and from these to derive the rest by middle terms: a short way, no doubt, but precipitate; and one which will never lead to nature, though it offers an easy and ready way to disputation" (*GI*, 4:25).

Between Bacon's critique of system and his call for what he termed natural histories of phenomena, one brackets the problem facing the seventeenth century. Bacon's new learning rested on the possibility that gross and inaccurate senses could be refined and made reliable through the use of carefully designed experiments. One searches Bacon in vain for ways to subject language to such experimental control, however. He had isolated four causes of erroneous inferences that plagued rigorous research into nature. If we try to apply these to language, we see in each case an additional set of problems for which no solutions had been conceived. First, sensory impressions could be faulty. What would be the counterpart of the failure of sense impressions in studying language? The sounds that reach the ears have significance only in relation to the meaning they carry and are not easily separated from it. Does one study the sounds or the meaning, or both at once? A second cause of error occurs when indefinite and confused notions are drawn from the sense impressions. In language, we would have to differentiate two levels of notions, first the derivation of plain meaning from sounds, and second, notions about language itself. How could one determine whether a notion about language was indefinite or confused without already having solved part of the problem of understanding the nature of language? Third, "the induction is amiss which infers the principles of sciences by simple enumeration, and does not, as it ought, employ exclusions and solutions (or separations) of nature." That is, collections of similar materials and enumerations of their traits could impede understanding because they failed to differentiate the distinct components and constituents inherent in the objects of study. Rather, collections often proceeded on the belief that larger piles of information would of themselves yield more insight. In language, with its interlocking grammatical, semantic, syntactical, psychological, developmental, and social dimensions, it would be extremely important but difficult to clearly identify these natures and reason upon them separately. Fourth, as stated earlier, many thinkers too quickly leaped from a few particulars to the most general axioms and in turn used the axioms to derive the intermediate knowledge that ordinarily should link the particular instance with the most general principles (*GI*, 4:70). One aspect of this problem in language would be how to approach an individual language, much less language as a collective phenomenon, to derive general principles that would be capable of either validation or disproof. If Bacon could say of the mind, that no mere "excellence of method . . . can supply it with the material of knowledge" (*GI*, 4:28), and if language was itself a great seducer of the understanding, how was one to develop anything approaching a systematic understanding of it?

Bacon never tried to answer his own call for a philosophic grammar, but he anticipated one of the major language projects of the seventeenth century, the creation of a universal grammar. In the mid-1600s a group of Jansenists gathered at the convent at Port Royal, near Paris. Jansenists, named for the Dutch Catholic theologian Cornelis Jansen, wanted to halt the Church's drift away from the doctrinal purity of the early patriarchs. They particularly opposed the Jesuits' liberalizing influence. At Port Royal they educated the young, created model educational materials, and gave intellectual support to their movement. Augustinian in outlook, Jansenists deeply distrusted human nature, which they believed must be disciplined to Christian doctrine and restrained by behavioral edicts. The role of education was to train the mind to that discipline, to learn judgment and logic so as to think clearly, and to learn language so as to express thoughts clearly. In France, language study, under the sway of Vaugelas, a proponent of the beauties of correct French, concentrated on elegant, correct French and Latin. The Jansenists, by contrast, hoped to provide insight into language itself, not style. Their universal grammar was to function in the intellectual realm in a way analogous to the universal grid system in mapping the world. That is, it would be an abstract system by which any variety of linguistic information could be regularized. It would also be a navigational aid to the intellect, helping people learn and use language in adherence to truth and logic.

In 1660 Claude Lancelot and Antoine Arnauld, working in conjunction with other intellectual reformers at Port Royal, published the *Grammaire générale et raisonnée* (A General and Rational Grammar). Its preface states:

> As I have been engaged for some time in drawing up grammars of different languages, rather indeed by chance, than from any choice of my own; this has often occasioned my enquiry into the reasons of several things, which are either common to all, or particular to some languages.[51]

As this passage makes clear, the authors intended to offer a grammar that would identify things "common to all" and those "particular to some languages." It is easy to forget the extent to which general grammar reflected this "dual purpose," which Lia Formigari has described as follows: "On the one hand, it must undertake the logical and semantic analysis of languages and distinguish between what is necessary in them and what is incidental to their specific grammatical rules, and on the other, it must inquire into the individual character, or genius, of each particular language."[52] Pierre Besnier makes this quite explicit in his *A Philosophical Essay for the Reunion of Languages* (1674), which, like Lancelot and Arnauld's grammar, had a strong pedagogical motive. Besnier begins with two propositions: "First, that there is a certain accord between the severall Languages: and that therefore they are attainable by comparison, Secondly, they are unquestionably founded upon reason, and therefore that must be made use of in their mutuall reference."[53] Those items that accord in all languages reveal language as a thinking tool, an instrument of reason.

It might seem far-fetched to claim that spatial models informed universal grammar. However, I make that claim. We recall that making a grammar is itself a spatial act, turning into writing, which is spatial, and further arranging in two-dimensions (in successive spaces on sheets of paper) those elements, principles, and rules that inform utterances made in a given language. Those utterances are composed of sound in time and achieve their effects both serially and simultaneously: serially in that we utter sounds one at a time and simultaneously in that we also grasp the meaning of sentences and longer passages holistically, as single units. Universal grammar adds a new dimension to these spatial aspects of grammar. It correlates entities in two different realms, the surface language, whether written or spoken, and the logic of thought to which the surface gives expression but which may have an entirely different type of organization. Acts of thinking, after all, may proceed in mentally constructed spaces through the convergence or activation of three, four, five, or six dimensions, modules, or inputs, all of which language then converts into a temporal string of sounds. By attempting to correlate mental logic with speech, universal grammar attempts to identify and then relate objects in different planes or spheres of thought. It also, as practiced by the Jansenists, tends to reduce reason to a simple set of procedures in order to make the conformity between logic and grammar as tight as possible. That is ultimately its greatest fault, not what it does to grammar, but what it does to logic.

However, my primary claim is that universal grammar is an exercise in filling in space in one realm—the verbal—by knowing what belongs in the gaps within it and between the verbal and the mental. This filling in requires a procedure for identifying and correlating missing material. One must, then, know and examine the complete mental representations that precede speech. Universal grammar thus parallels developments in the philosophy of space alluded to earlier, in its attention to the unfilled parts of nature that lie between the objects that abstract space gives position. The roots of universal grammar in the Middle Ages and Renaissance illuminate the point that universal grammar helps identify what is actually missing.

The roots of universal grammar reach into the medieval concern for the *essentialia* of language—those traits thought to be found in all spoken tongues. Padley has summed up this study:

> The belief in the existence of an underlying (logical) content entails an accompanying belief that the framework of this content will be applicable to any language, and in this respect the late medieval theorists, though they confine

themselves to Latin, are universal grammarians. Their basic assumption is Aristotle's dictum that though men differ in speech, 'the mental affections themselves, of which words are primarily the signs, are the same for the whole of mankind.' (Padley, 219)

The modistic grammars that flourished in the thirteenth and fourteenth centuries assumed that certain modes of thought common to all people provided what we now might call a deep structure of thought.

Peter Ramus (1515–1572) opposed the identity of logic and grammar, insisting that they are not at all congruent and must go their separate ways. Padley describes a crossroads in the practice of universal grammar during the Renaissance when the search for the "underlying cause" of language was "temporarily in abeyance." From that point, studies of this type "must either continue with the now exhausted method of description . . . ; or launch out into a thoroughgoing formalism in which the content level of language is ignored; or return to the search for some kind of ratio or cause" (Padley, 220). By "formal" Padley means the study of logic without reference to language's semantic content. All three courses were pursued, but the second and third eventually culminated in the universal grammar of the seventeenth and eighteenth centuries.

Spanish grammarian Franciscus Sanctius (Francisco Sanchez de las Brozas) freshly approached grammar from the vantage of its underlying logical level in his *Minerva: Seu de Causis Linguae Latinae* (1587). *Minerva* pursued the notion that all things, language included, bore explanation through access to their causes. Sanctius examined what we might call surface expression, the language people actually use to express their thoughts, and demonstrated that a type of ellipsis was at work there. Sanctius's study made it clear that one could differentiate particular expressions from the thoughts they conveyed. Then he proceeded to show that surface expression actually abbreviated an individual's underlying, complete thoughts. Another Spaniard, Gonzalo Correas, amplified the matter in *Arte grande* (manuscript, 1625) and *Trilingue de tres artes* (1627) by emphasizing that Spanish and Latin rendered similar concepts with different syntactical structures. "Behind this lies the desire to prove that the vulgar tongues can, by recourse to periphrasis, express everything that Latin can" (Padley, 281). And beneath this concept also lies the belief that all languages express similar ideas. To say this, however, is to be able to identify what is missing in a given utterance, to draw a barrier between what words are and what we know them to be saying.

Between the appearance of the first Port Royal Latin grammar in 1644 and that of the *Grammaire générale et raisonnée* (hereafter referred to as *GGR*), Lancelot had read and absorbed Sanctius's *Minerva* (Padley, 284).

Thereafter he and Arnauld, the former with an eye on technical matters and pedagogical efficiency and the latter on the logical substrate of language, tried to resolve grammatical categories by reference to their logical understructure. This project required that the parts of speech and their relations be at once ascertainable in the well-known languages and reflective of the most basic logical relations one makes among objects of thought. Both *GGR* and *La logique, ou L'art de penser*, often called the Port Royal logic and published in 1662 but prepared alongside the grammar, made clear reference to the logic of grammar. The heading to the first chapter of part two proposed "that the knowledge of what passes in the mind, is necessary, to comprehend the foundation of grammar: and on this depends the diversity of words which compose discourse." Later in that chapter we find, "We cannot therefore perfectly understand the different sorts of significations, annexed to words, without first considering what passes in our minds."[54] As Desmarais confidently claimed in his 1706 *Traité de grammaire françoise*, a grammar sponsored but then abandoned by the French Academy, "One must use logic and metaphysics to discuss the principles of each part of speech: it is necessary to enter into the reasons which have rendered all these principles common to all societies of men, and which have established such a great variety in the application which each people has made of them."[55] The spirit of the general grammar was to allow one to receive, through the encoding of signs, the mental operations behind the signs and, as Jean-Claude Pariente expresses it, achieve the paradox of dissolving the signs through which people communicate to get at that which precedes the signs.[56]

The *GGR* made possible a more probing analysis of the parts of speech.[57] That is not to say its proponents believed that every language had only those parts of speech or the same grammar found in the *GGR*, but that in the varying grammatical makeup of different languages there existed common forms of thought, regardless of historical change or place. Nor did the *GGR* view the parts of speech or surface forms of language as conforming in every way to the rational substrate of thought. The relationship between the logical substratum and the surface grammar was what mattered; one needed to attend to both. In fact, one could more readily comprehend the varying surface features after studying rational grammar and its way of reflecting the common forms of thought. Indeed, today's linguists find one of rational grammar's most intriguing aspects in its attention to ellipsis and implicature. Ellipses show that the elements of a complete thought may not all appear in an actual utterance, but that such elements are recoverable and capable of analysis in relation to the already known surface expression, which in turn is more fully exposed and comprehensible in light of its complete elements. Implicature suggests that a great deal of contextual information can be inferred but is not expressed in many sentences. "Green light!" may assume that the listener is driving a car, has not been paying attention, and can now drive forward. Obviously, the mind connects the words with a context and intention that the words themselves do not name.

The *GGR* has been subjected to careful evaluation by modern linguists reacting to Chomsky's claim that it launched a revolutionary shift in language study and lay a ground for concepts of deep structure. A few samples will be given of how the *GGR*, in claiming to reflect the operations of the mind and apply to all languages, itself omitted much. Symbolic of these gaps is the missing chapter. Chapter twenty addresses auxiliary verbs; chapter twenty-two, conjunctions and interjections. There is no chapter twenty-one. I don't want to overplay this point, except to say that a system like this may captivate our attention and incline us to forget what is absent. Part II of the *GGR* opens with this heading: "That the knowledge of what occurs in our minds is necessary for understanding the foundations of grammar."[58] This assertion seems safe enough, yet look at what it requires. We are still nibbling at the edges of knowledge of how the brain thinks. Lancelot and Arnauld knew what happened in the mind because they inspected the language that came out of the mouth. Propositions show us how we link substance and accident, and grammar shows us how we link persons, actions, and manner, how we differentiate relationships such as action (accusative) and ownership or belonging (genitive), and how we think of and express conditions such as place and time. No doubt. Since grammar expresses these distinctions, we can safely assert that we think them. But this route makes the argument circular: we know what is in the mind because of language, and having determined what passes in the mind, we now illuminate grammar. The seamlessness holds up only until languages with different grammars are ushered into the fold of universal grammar, or until we think of all the mental and linguistic activities not encompassed in the *GGR*.

Chapter twenty-three, treating syntax and certain figures, contains propositions that have proven of enormous interest to Chomsky and his followers. Consider, "There is never a nominative which lacks a relationship to some verb either expressed or implied." In a complete, grammatical sentence this may be true, but what about the earlier case of "Green light!" wherein the nominative may only be subordinate to the more pertinent nominative in "You can drive forward." Another proposition reads, "There can be no adjective which is not related to a substantive." Again, in a grammatical French sentence, this may be true. But in terms of actual expression, one can utter adjectives without their related substantives: "Blue!"

The figures of syllepsis, by which, as Tsiapera explains, "our speech agrees more with our thoughts than with the rules of grammar. . . , pleonasm, the use of more words than is necessary,"[59] and ellipsis, which uses fewer than is necessary, all require a precise determination of what thoughts are being expressed and exactly how many words are necessary to do so.

Antoine Court de Gébelin's *Monde primitif,* one of the last comprehensive projects on language that proposed a universal grammar in the late eighteenth century, illustrates by its images of weaving and tapestries how essential conformities and gaps are to universal grammar and how difficult to express without resorting to spatial language. Court de Gébelin said,

> All grammars, in whatever language they are found, agree in their general principles and laws, without which there would be no language, no grammar, no mental images at all. These principles, taken from the nature of ideas, are themselves derived from the universe that they depict to our minds, as long as the mind itself conforms to eternal ideas that can be had from a supreme being.
>
> These necessary principles weave the tapestries of speech, in whatever times and places. Everything carries their imprint. But if the nations haven't been able to escape these laws, if they are driven to follow the laws' impulse, they are also free to follow their own genius in the manner of executing the laws, in arranging the different parts of the tapestry, in emphasizing the forms most congenial to them, and with the greater or lesser force they bring to the drawing.[60]

Although Court de Gébelin emphasized eternal ideas at the expense of structures and relationships, the comfort he delivers helps us perceive the crucial importance of presence or absence in universal grammars. He trusts that every nation has retained, and indeed cannot escape, the ideas and laws that govern them. At the same time, he leaves open the possibility that nations have conformed in different degrees to ideas implanted within us. Only by knowing what should be there could one determine whether the nations had in fact conformed to the laws that govern ideas and language.

Universal grammar constitutes one of the seventeenth century's best attempts to negotiate the tricky boundary between a general explanation that encompasses all known difference and the full recognition of difference itself. The boundary always has pitfalls: stress on the general and universal can swallow up the very differences that motivated people to form general theories in the first place, until one no longer sees real difference but only variations in an underlying similarity. However, because the *GGR* assumed "the existence of perfectly formed thoughts produced by a closed logical system"[61] that existed prior to language, it also implicitly defined what would pass as rational thought common to all humans. Padley has observed, following the cue of Basil Willey, an assumption that governed much of general grammar: that whatever could be clearly conceived was therefore true, or in other words, that the structure of things conformed to the structure of human thought. This assumption would incline linguistic theorists to devote analysis to the operations of the mind and to produce grammars of concepts rather than study the material component of the linguistic sign (Padley, 290–91). But such a focus would always privilege the logic and concepts of those who designed the general grammar and those that were embedded in the grammars of their own languages. Relatedly, the Port Royalists who composed the *GGR* harbored some rather deep, Augustinian suspicions of human nature. These suspicions, not explicit in the *GGR* but discernible in its rigor and brevity, would lead students of language to suspect any population who seemed to think differently or who lacked the intellectual and social discipline so crucial to the formation of Christian souls. Universal grammar could therefore influence its followers to ignore or, if not ignore, derogate those who spoke and thought differently, even when their differences motivated the universal grammar project in the first place. For all its pretense to universality, universal grammar profoundly and deliberately ignored the exotic languages, although these were spoken by far more people than spoke all European tongues combined. In their intense concern for Latin and vernaculars such as French, *GGR*s practitioners attempted to patch the dike against linguistic diversity. Their map of language incorporated a much broader knowledge of languages than did medieval maps of language, but ultimately it provided a mapping of language onto other realms of knowledge.

This chapter began by describing attempts to navigate and map the earth. Such efforts raised new problems that required great ingenuity to solve. At sea especially, the shape of the earth and the movement of heavenly bodies almost conspired to deprive mariners of the reference points by which their position could be known. In mapping, one faced the problem of transferring the topical features of a sphere lacking sure reference points onto a plane surface. Language posed similar difficulties. Successes in exploration and navigation created a desire for parallel success in resolving those difficulties. The apparently sure reference points of one's own language were taken away when one studied another tongue, but the juxtaposition of one language with another created opportunities to define the structures of each. And when reducing those newly understood structures to a grammar, one had, as with maps, to convert phenomena from several dimensions into a coherent order in written space which would point to the relations and intricacies of the language. The history of medieval maps of language and Renaissance collections, and the trajectory from many grammars to a universal grammar, reveal a struggle to align particular knowledge with general principles when particular knowledge kept undoing the theory formulated to contain it. In this feature, language study shares with terrestrial mapping a dual impulse, to portray the local terrain as it appears from a given vantage point and yet to master and represent the entire space that surrounds the local, seeing it as if free from perspective and context.

Notes

1 Sir Francis Bacon, *Of the Interpretation of Nature*, in *The Works of Francis Bacon*, ed. James Spedding, Robert Ellis, and Douglas Heath (London: Longman, 1860), 3:230.

2 David Woodward and G. Malcolm Lewis, introduction to *The History of Cartography*, vol. 2, bk. 3 (Chicago: University of Chicago Press, 1998), 7.

3 Peter Albinus, *A Treatise on Foreign Languages and Unknown Islands*, trans. Edmund Goldsmid (Edinburgh: Biblioteca Curiosa, 1884), 31–35.

4 Roger J. P. Kain and Elizabeth Baigent, *The Cadastral Map in the Service of the State: A History of Property Mapping* (Chicago: University of Chicago Press, 1992), 6.

5 Barbara E. Mundy, *The Mapping of New Spain: Indigenous Cartography and the Maps of the Relaciones Geográficas* (Chicago: University of Chicago Press, 1996), 5.

6 Luís de Albuquerque, "Portuguese Navigation: Its Historical Development," in *Circa 1492: Art in the Age of Exploration*, ed. Jay A. Levenson (Washington, D.C.: National Gallery of Art, 1991), 37.

7 David Woodward, "Maps and the Rationalization of Geographic Space," in Levenson, *Circa 1492*, 87.

8 Anthony Grafton, *New Worlds, Ancient Texts: The Power of Tradition and the Shock of Discovery* (Cambridge: Belknap Press of Harvard University Press, 1992), 54.

9 Michel Foucault, "Of Other Spaces," *Diacritics* 16, no. 1 (1986): 22–27.

10 Murad D. Akhundov, *Conceptions of Space and Time: Sources, Evolution, Directions*, trans. Charles Rougle (Cambridge: MIT Press, 1986).

11 Henri Lefebvre, *The Production of Space*, trans. Donald Nicholson-Smith (Oxford: Blackwell, 1991).

12 Foucault, "Of Other Spaces," 22.

13 This and all subsequent Padley citations are found in G. A. Padley, *Grammatical Theory in Western Europe, 1500–1700: Trends in Vernacular Grammar*, vol. 1 (Cambridge: Cambridge University Press, 1985), 9.

14 The summary of the legend of seventy-two languages follows Arno Borst, *Der Turmbau von Babel: Geschichte der Meinungen über Ursprung und Vielfalt der Sprachen und Völker*, 4 vols. (Stuttgart: Hiersemann, 1957–1963).

15 Borst, *Turmbau von Babel*, 234–35, 810–15, 869–71.

16 Ernest Brehaut, *An Encyclopedist of the Dark Ages: Isidore of Seville* (New York: Columbia University Press, 1912; reprint, New York: Franklin, 1912), 33–34.

17 Umberto Eco, *The Search for the Perfect Language*, trans. James Fentress (Oxford: Blackwell, 1995), 64.

18 William J. Bouwsma, *Concordia Mundi: The Career and Thought of Guillaume Postel (1510–1581)* (Cambridge: Harvard University Press, 1957).

19 Donald Lach, *Asia in the Making of Europe*, vol. 2, *A Century of Wonder* (Chicago: University of Chicago Press, 1977), 519.

20 Filippo Sassetti, *Lettere edite e inedite de Filippo Sassetti*, ed. E. Marcucci (Florence: Monnier, 1855), 408, 497.

21 Margaret T. Hodgen, *Early Anthropology in the Sixteenth and Seventeenth Centuries* (Philadelphia: University of Pennsylvania Press, 1964), 165–66.

22 Thomas Herbert, *A Relation of Some Yeares Travaile into Afrique, Asia, Indies* (London, 1634), 16.

23 Unless otherwise stated, Claude Duret will be quoted from *Thresor de l'histoire des langues de cest univers, contenant les origines, beautez, perfections, decadences, mutations, changements, conversions, & ruines des langues . . .* (Cologne, 1613).

24 Duret, *Discours de la vérité des causes et effets des décadences, mutations, changements, conversions et ruines de monarchies, empires, royaumes, et républiques* (Paris, 1595); *Discours de la vérité des causes et effets des divers course, mouvements . . . et saleure de la Mer Océane* (Paris, 1600); *Histoire admirable des plantes et herbes esmerveillables et miraculeruse en nature* (1605).

25 Bouwsma, *Concordia Mundi*.

26 José de Acosta, *Natural and Moral History of the Indies* [1590], Hakluyt Society Publications, 1st ser., no. 61 (London, 1880), 408.

27 Michel Foucault, *The Order of Things: An Archaeology of the Human Sciences* (New York: Vintage Books, 1970), 37.

28 Foucault, *Order of Things*, 37.

29 Don Lorenzo Hervás y Panduro, *Catálogo de las lenguas de las naciones conocidas y numeración, división y clases de éstas según la diversidad de sus idiomas y dialectos* (Madrid, 1800–1805), 1:29–30.

30 J. M. Y. Simpson, "Writing Systems: Principles and Typology," in *Encyclopedia of Language and Linguistics*, ed. R. E. Asher (Oxford: Pergamon, 1994), 9:5052.

31 Simpson, "Writing Systems," 9:5055. This paragraph summarizes a passage in this source.

32 Julian Granberry, *A Grammar and Dictionary of the Timucua Language*, 3d ed. (Tuscaloosa: University of Alabama Press, 1993), 90–99.

33 Lach, *Making of Europe*, 499.

34 "De aquí es que, entre las cosas más difficultosas y más variables en la variación humana es dar Arte y modo de hablar en qualquier lengua. Y si esto es assí en todas, aun en las muy sabidas, entendidas y usadas, y de que ay Artes hechas, por varones de grande erudictión: quánto mas lo será en esta lengua del Perú, tan estraña, tan nueva, tan incógnita, y tan peregrina a nosotros, y tan nunca hasta agora redduzida a Arte ni puesta debaxo de preceptos dél?" Domingo de Santo Tomás, "Prólogo del Autor, al Christiano Lector," in *Grammatica, o Arte de la lengua general de los indios de los reynos del Perú* [1560], ed. Raúl P. Barrenechea (Lima: Universidad Nacional de San Marcos, 1951), 14. Author's translation.

35 "Quán falso es lo que muchos os han querido persuadir, ser los naturales de los reynos del Perú bárbaros, & indignos de ser tractados con la suavidad y libertad [que] los demás vassallos vuestros lo son. Lo qual claramente conoscerá V. M. ser falso, se viere por este Arte, la gran policia que esta lengua tiene, La abundancia de vocablos, La conveniencia [que] tienen con las cosas [que] significan, Las maneras diversas y curiosas de hablar, El suave y buen sonido al oydo de la pronunciacion della, La facilitad para escrivirse con nuestros caracteres y letras." Santo Tomás, "Prólogo," 9–10. Author's translation.

36 "Quán facil y dulce sea a la pronunciación de nuestra lengua, El estar ordenada y adornada con propriedad de declinación, y demas propriedades del nombre, modos, tiempos, y personas del verbo. Y, brevemente, en muchas cosas y maneras de hablar,

tan conforme a la latina, y española: y, en el arte y artificio della, que no parece sino que fue un pronóstico, que Españoles la avian de posseer. Lengua pues, S. M., tan polida y abundante, regulada y encerrada debaxo de las reglas y preceptos de la latina como es esta (como consta por este arte) no bárbara, que quiere dezir, (según Quintiliano, y los demás latinos) llena de barbarismos y de defectos, sin modos, tiempos, ni casos, ni orden, ni regla, ni concierto, sino muy polida y delicada se puede llamar." Santo Tomás, "Prólogo," 10. Author's translation.

37 W. K. Percival, "Renaissance Linguistics: General Survey," in *Encyclopedia of Language and Linguistics*, ed. R. E. Asher and J. M. Y. Simpson (Oxford: Pergamon, 1994).

38 Grammars were written by Francisco Jiménez, Alonso Rengel, Andrés de Olmos (available 1547), Alonso de Molina (1555 and 1571), Antonio del Rincón (1595), Diego de Galdo Guzmán (1642), Horacio Carochi (1645), Agustín de Vetancourt (1673), Balthazar del Castillo (1683), Antonio Vázquez Gastelu (1689).

39 "El lenguaje y frasis destos naturales, especialmente de los nahuas y mexicanos, es muy diferente del lenguaje y frasis latino, griego, y castellano." Alonso de Molina, "Epistle Nuncupatoria," in *Vocabulario en lengua castellana y mexicana y mexicana y castellana* (Mexico, 1571; reprint, Leipzig: Teubner, 1880).

40 Antonio del Rincón, *Arte mexicana* [1595] (Mexico: Secretaría de fomento, 1885), xxv.

41 Diego González Holguín, *Arte de la lengua general del Perú, llamada quichua* [1586] (Lima, 1607), 15.

42 Tadoa Doi, "Researches in the Japanese Language Made by the Jesuit Missionaries in the Sixteenth and Seventeenth Centuries," *Proceedings of the Imperial Academy of Japan* 13 (1937): 235.

43 Victor Hanzeli, *Missionary Linguistics in New France: A Study of Seventeenth- and Eighteenth-Century Descriptions of American Indian Languages* (The Hague: Mouton, 1969), 63.

44 Quoted in Michael D. Coe, *Breaking the Maya Code* (New York: Thames and Hudson, 1992), 148.

45 Walter Mignolo, "Literacy and Colonization: The New World Experience," in *1492–1992: Re/Discovering Colonial Writing*, ed. René Jara and Nicholas Spadaccini, Hispanic Issues, vol. 4 (Minneapolis: Prisma Institute, 1989), 87.

46 Mignolo, "Literacy and Colonization," 54.

47 I am indebted to John Robertson of Brigham Young University's Linguistics Department for information on the Maya language.

48 John Horne Tooke, *The Diversions of Purley*, 2d ed. (Menston: Scholar, 1968), 1:44–48.

49 Unless otherwise noted, subsequent quotations of Francis Bacon are cited in the text according to the abbreviations listed below: Each citation will include the abbreviated title followed by the volume and page number as given in *The Works of Francis Bacon*, ed. James Spedding, Robert Ellis, and Douglas Heath, 14 vols. (London: Longman, 1860).

Adv L	*Of the Dignity and Advancement of Learning*
GI	*The Great Instauration*
New O	*The New Organon or True Directions Concerning the Interpretation of Nature*
NWS	*The New World of Science or Desiderata*
IN	*Of the Interpretation of Nature*

50 Mary Fuller, *Voyages in Print: English Travel to America, 1576–1624* (New York: Cambridge University Press, 1995).

51 Claude Lancelot and Antoine Arnauld, *A General and Rational Grammar* (Grammaire générale et raisonnée) [1660] (Menston: Scholar, 1968), A3ʳ.

52 Lia Formigari, *Language and Experience in Seventeenth-Century British Philosophy*, Amsterdam Studies in the Theory and History of Linguistic Science, vol. 48 (Amsterdam: John Benjamins, 1988), 46.

53 Pierre Besnier, *A Philosophical Essay for the Reunion of Languages* [1674], trans. Henry Rose (Oxford, 1675), 3.

54 Lancelot, *General and Rational Grammar*, 22.

55 Quoted as translated in Maria Tsiapera and Garon Wheeler, *The Port-Royal Grammar: Sources and Influences* (Münster: Nodus, 1993), 157.

56 Jean-Claude Pariente, *L'analyse du langage à Port-Royal* (Paris: Éditions de Minuit, 1985), 48.

57 Garon Wheeler, "Port Royal Tradition of Grammar," in *Encyclopedia of Language and Linguistics*, 6:3229–33.

58 As translated in Tsiapera and Wheeler, *Port-Royal Grammar*, 128.

59 Ibid., 143.

60 "Toutes les Grammaires, de quelque langue qu'elle soient, s'accordent sur leurs principes généraux, sur ces loix, sans lesquelles il n'y auroit point de langue, point de Grammaire, point de peinture d'idées: principes pris dans la nature des idées, puisées elles-mêmes dans l'Univers qu'elles peignent à notre esprit, tandis qu'il est conforme lui-même aux idées éternelles qu'en eut l'Etre suprême.

"Ces principes nécessaries, dirigent les tableaux de la parole, dans quelque temps & en quelque lieu que ce soit: tous portent leur empreinte; mais si les Nations n'ont jamais pu s'écarter de ces loix, si elles ont été forcées de suivre leur impulsion, elles ont pu se livrer à leur propre génie dans la manière d'exécuter ces loix, dans l'emplacement à donner aux diverses parties d'un tableau, dans les formes dont elles pouvoient être susceptivles, dans le plus ou dans le moins de force avec laquelle on les dessine." Antoine Court de Gébelin, *Monde primitif, analysé et comparé avec le monde moderne* (Paris, 1774–1796), 2:24. Author's translation.

61 Tsiapera and Wheeler, *Port-Royal Grammar*, 160.

3 Language Barriers

Language differences comprised an obstacle and a protective barrier. Living in a dangerous world, early modern Europe most wanted to safely manipulate the boundaries between peoples and between the mind and nature. Their attempts to cross or circumvent language barriers disclosed boundary features they rarely articulated explicitly, but strongly suggested spatial metaphors help disclose these features.

Positioning and boundaries are essential to knowing space; they are also essential to conception and communication. We think of the boundaries as lying at the limits of given spaces, but insofar as language is a condition of our existence, we live within the boundaries in two senses: within the area the boundaries circumscribe, and within the very line that conceptualizes or figures boundaries. Thus, to encounter the language barrier was to encounter, in however a fumbling way, fundamental existential and political principles. Boundaries and separations make individual and group identity, knowledge, and consciousness possible. Yet it is apparently a condition of knowledge to make us desire simultaneously to exist in a position and yet be released from the fact that existence requires position.

Babel: Language as Impediment

The story of Babel ties together language and space in a saga of unity and separation. In the Bible account, unity breeds mischief: when it comes to communication, there can be too much of a good thing. "And the whole earth was of one language, and of one speech." Since difference is necessary to consciousness, a similar people will eventually define and measure themselves against other beings. In the Bible, they turned their envious eyes on God. "And they said, Go let us build us a city and a tower, whose top may reach unto heaven; and let us make us a name, lest we be scattered abroad upon the face of the whole earth" (Genesis 11:1, 4). The tower-builders' fear suggests that scattering and, with it, linguistic change, was already taking place. Tower building is an attempt to make a name, and both tower and name-making are efforts to avoid fragmentation, perhaps in this instance the ungoverned dispersion of people across the land.

The cabal or king who mandated the tower was the first architect of national symbols designed to boost pride and give people a comforting identity around a grand project. God saw the threat as aimed not only at him but at the limits placed on humanity's powers. So his punishment fit the crime: limit unity and communication, and you also limit power. "And the Lord said, Behold, the people is one, and they have all one language; and this they begin to do: and now nothing will be restrained from them, which they have imagined to do. Go to, let us go down, and there confound their language, that they may not understand one another's speech" (Genesis 11:6–7). The punishment accomplished the condition that the tower and name-making were to forestall: scattering.

Linguistic confusion and geographical scattering accompany each other. Languages hold people apart, and distance accelerates language change. In the Bible account God invented language barriers as an impediment to co-operation. Language barriers draw their meaning from impediments to motion across space. However else we have conceived of barriers, they are, at root, separations by distance or obstacle. They restrict freedom, they confine, they hinder movement, they shackle, they retard. They produce stasis, from the Greek root for standing.

Babel was a dual curse. It divided people from people and aggravated the initial linguistic fall at Eden, when the pure Adamic tongue decayed and words lost their power to name the inner nature of the things they named. As Robert Stillman puts it, "On the plains of Shinar, the perfect bonds between words and things were shattered. As man fell from the garden into history, there was born a terrible division between words and things, the signifier and the signified."[1] In the seventeenth century William Whately summarized the dual heritage of Babel: on one side, increased barbarism, hatred, and warfare bred by lack of understanding among peoples, on the other "errour and mistaking in all Arts and Sciences." Except for the expulsion from Eden and the Flood, the confusion was "the heaviest punishment the world hath felt, yea in respect of the succession of men it was worse than the floud, that onely drowned the men who lived in the present time, this hath drowned in ignorance and errour all succeeding times."[2]

Beyond installing a wall between word and thing, the confusion was also believed to have created such disorder within individual tongues that they became crude, unstable means of communicating even human ideas. The English translator of Salust du Bartas's *Les semaines*, or *The Divine Weeks*, published in 1578, in a section on the dispersal of peoples and tongues observed: "It may be saide of every toong since the confusion: that it is nothing but corrupt jangling, weake, uncertaine, and changing ever from time to time."[3] Godfrey Goodman's *The Fall of Man, or The Corruption of*

Nature (1616), one of the most thorough Renaissance studies of post-Edenic conditions, viewed all post-Babel languages as permanent punishments. He reasoned that nature and language, reason and grammar should share some alliance, but he detected "no likelihood or affinity among them."[4]

Further, the confusion left humanity with a double mystery. In placing the means and mechanisms of change within the realm of miracle and therefore beyond human comprehension, the Genesis history of Babel threw up a screen between us and the workings of language. It also left the continuing mystery of how humans with similar minds could persist in using radically different tongues. John Calvin saw this point: "And truly the diversity of tongues is to be regarded as a prodigy. For since language is the impress of the mind, how does it come to pass, that men, who are partakers of the same reason, and who are born for social life, do not communicate with each other in the same language?"[5] Whatever the nature of that "impress," for Calvin it obviously entailed, after Babel, distance and indirection, making possible multiple ways of perceiving, naming, and expressing what should be the same thing in nature. This approach to language masked from view another explanation, however, that the nature of language makes possible that very manifold impress of mind on thought and communication, since language entails multiple ways of naming a single idea.

Demonic Meddling

Seeing the confusion as an evil, missionaries often took the next short step to believe that Satan aggravated the language barrier to increase confusion, make languages inherently idolatrous, and prevent the spread of Christianity. In the first extensive history of the Americas, Gonzalo Fernandez de Oviedo marveled over the linguistic variety of the Americas. He explained it not simply as a result of Babel but of demonic intervention in the already degraded linguistic state: "One thinks that this heathen people, of whom the devil has been lord for so many centuries, have been taught these diversities of language by him who takes such joy in their souls and who has deceived them and left them defenseless until our times."[6] In his lengthy speculations on the origins of the Indians published in 1607, Gregorio García accounts for the number and heterogeneity of Indian languages in the same way. He quotes Psalm 19:7, "La lei del Señor es lucida, y con su luz alumbra los ojos del Alma," which can be rendered, "The law of the Lord is bright and clear, illuminating with its light the eyes of the soul," and then leaps to conclude, "and so the Lord's light had no part in the diversity of languages." He continues:

The Devil shrewdly conjectured that the gospel would be preached in these kingdoms. Knowing that if the Indians understood it, and as a result converted, and envying the happiness that would accrue, he arranged that God's ministers would encounter great difficulty in preaching it. By inducing the Indians to invent new languages and abetting them with his subtle ability, he made sure that the great number and diversity of languages would hold the miserable Indians in perpetual slavery to him.[7]

Many thus viewed language as an impediment to communication, with that communication going primarily in one direction—from Christian Europe to everyone else.

The more interesting story is that in the minds of many missionaries, languages themselves posed dangers. Crossing this barrier was far more difficult than scaling a wall or crossing a river. It so turned out that the linguistic wall could imprison souls; the linguistic river carry away or drown them. Religious officials viewed the vocabulary and structures of indigenous languages as being intertwined with the idolatrous practices of the people who spoke them. A *cédula* of 1538 expressed concern over a catechism in the Tarascan language: "And take particular heed that examiners determine whether these terms present any difficulties for the teaching and practice of the Christian religion, because of the meaning the Indians give them in their language."[8] Diego de Landa (1524–1579), who arrived in the Yucatán in 1549 and became bishop of the area, offers a case of linguistic immersion and distrust. He learned Maya quickly (he reportedly preached his first sermon in Maya after a few days' study) and eventually became an authority on the area's languages and customs. His *Relación de las cosas de Yucatán*, one of the most thorough ethnographic works of the sixteenth century, makes note of dialects and language boundaries, phonetics, prospects for a grammar of Maya, and forms of indigenous writing. These facets of language naturally had an instrumental appeal to Landa: by creating grammars, attending to dialect variations in the area, and deciphering the native writing, priests could more easily preach and could use native customs and beliefs to persuade. Coming to understand the Maya language, writing, and customs created many puzzles which absorbed Landa's attention. The language and writing systems intrigued him, but his admiration never advanced to deep cultural sympathy. His suspicions still centered on the content of Indian writings. "We found a large number of books [written] in these characters and, as they contained nothing in which there were not to be seen superstition and lies of the devil, we burned them all, which they regretted to an amazing degree, and which caused them much affliction."[9]

In about 1617, Hernando Ruiz de Alarcón expressed wonder that native paganism still continued after a century of Christianity, especially given the apparent ignorance of the Indians: "The ignorance or naivete of almost all the Indians . . . is so great that, according to general opinion, all are very easily persuaded of whatever one might want to lead them to believe."[10] Priests like Ruiz de Alarcón traced Indian credulousness to the amazing ability of their languages to absorb the new and yet retain the old, an ability linked to their figuration. "The more figures and tropes the language has, the more difficult it is to understand," he observed, "and the language I report is nothing but a continuous use of metaphors, not only in the verbs but also even in the nouns and adjectives and at times passes into being a sustained allegory." Etymologically, a *figure* is a shape; a *trope*, a turn. A language full of unusual shapes turns ideas on a different axis. The frustration of attempting to convert the indigenous languages to his own use led Ruiz de Alarcón finally to damn Indian tongues. Only the devil could be this clever, he thought, inventing languages to influence "his veneration and esteem by means of the difficulty of the language" (Ruiz, 40).

The problem was to take the unusual shapes and turns out of the language and leave it standing. Ruiz de Alarcón was ordered by his superiors to discover all the superstitious terminology and idolatrous practices he could and compile them "in order to erase them, and even to scrape them, from the memory of men" (Ruiz, 39). The irony has been remarked before: in order to erase seductive tropes and allegories, early missionaries had first to record and circulate them. As Richard Andrews and Ross Hassig have summarized, "There was a danger—long recognized by the Spanish clergy—that any record of the native ways could permit their continued practice."[11] A preacher had to become intimate with the language in order to detect those metaphors and double-meaning words that would ultimately taint the purity of any Christian concepts expressed through them. At the same time, he had to retain the distance that his own language and belief system provided. Missionaries less expert in the language faced an additional burden. They would have to rely on the authority of a Ruiz de Alarcón to learn all the pagan connotations latent in the language they were using, while having to implement linguistic change among those whose language they understood only superficially. Ruiz de Alarcón advised that his work would serve only those clerics who had already worked among the Indians and knew their language.

In their curious way, these missionaries were the first, I think, to perceive the strong bond between language and cultural norms that we now refer to as ideology. They often conceived this connection in terms of overlapping fabrics bonded that one couldn't separate them without ruining them and intertwined so tightly that one could not pull the strands apart. How could they use indigenous languages to teach concepts of Christianity that were wedded to the language in which Europeans expressed themselves? Only by trusting the mental powers that superseded language. And they faced the same challenge that cultural and linguistic relativists still face, that of having sufficient knowledge of a language to perceive its implicit values, norms, and cognition-shaping factors as an insider might experience them, and at the same time, having an outside framework sufficient to identify foreign elements as distinct and different from those in their own language and culture, and at the same time a still larger framework that allowed them to relate the insider and outsider knowledge to a more comprehensive system of connections between language and thinking. Ruiz de Alarcón and others like him were constantly traversing the boundaries between insider and outsider knowledge. They had to reach a state in which they could converse and teach a people freely in their own tongue, recognize the often subtle ways in which expressions could reinforce desirable or undesirable opinions and attitudes, and negotiate the various ways of expressing ideas so that only correct opinions were reinforced. It seems that they often found themselves trying to fix the point at which sufficient knowledge of a language brought the advantages of understanding without increasing the dangers of seduction.

In Asia, Jesuit priests and friars of the mendicant orders faced off over similar disagreements over the degree of contamination inherent in target languages. The Jesuits, whose policy in China favored accommodating Chinese religion as much as possible to Christianity, wanted to attract converts from the literati of China; they therefore painted Confucianism as largely compatible with Christianity. The other missionary orders, who interpreted Confucianism as essentially atheistic, had written to Rome in the 1650s to denounce those Chinese ceremonies they viewed as incompatible with conversion. The Jesuits and the friars then debated accommodation before the ecclesiastical rulers in Rome, but in the end the Jesuits failed to win approval. As interesting as the outcome was the possibility of disagreement. Both parties saw different valences in the complex fabric of Chinese intellectual and spiritual life, and perhaps in Christianity as well. Both assumed, though in very different ways, that past traditions and present contexts shaped meaning. Some differences involved only competing chronologies, but others hinged on something as crucial as whether the Chinese words used to express Christian teachings had theistic or atheistic bearings. For example, the Chinese referred to the "sovereign Lord of the Universe" as *Chang ti* or *Tien*. But these words had ambiguous references. *Tien* could mean either "the material heavens" solely or a being who created heavens and earth.[12]

Domingo de Navarrete, who spent many years in China and the Philippines during this period, wrote "Eight Doubts concerning the Sacraments," one of which was "Whether the Form of Baptism in the Chinese Language Be Valid." Navarrete gave the Chinese wording as "*Ngo is ul*, or *Ni in fu, kie zu, kie xing xin ming che*" and added: "Many deny it, and urge, that the Chineses do not know either a true Spirit, or true Sanctity; nor do the words *xing xin* in their first Institution dignify the Holy Ghost: Nor is the Unity of Essence, Power, or Virtue expressed."[13] Book VII of Navarrete's *Account of the Empire of China* documents many doctrinal disputes and problems arising from the encounter of two cultures with highly developed spiritual and literary traditions. Although many missionaries to China were pleased to work among a literate and intelligent people because they assumed that literacy made translation of Christian doctrines and terminology more feasible, many others assumed that tradition kept language static and prevented words from taking on the new meanings and valences that would aptly convey new doctrines.[14]

Many linguists classified as good those languages whose terminologies easily lent themselves to Christian doctrine and European thought. Garcilaso de la Vega praised the Inca language, and Gabriel Sagard dismissed Huron on that basis, and all around the world similar judgments were made. If language was simply the assignment of names to things and ideas, the problem was sizable. But if language was saturated with perceptions, attitudes, and beliefs, as Ruiz de Alarcón, Sahagún, and others seemed to indicate, then the problem was enormous. How did one teach a people concepts alien to their own frame of mind? One could adapt the terminology of an indigenous language, but its vocabulary could bring with it networks of incompatible associations. One could teach a new language, assuming that no adaptation of their own vocabulary would quite capture the doctrines as Christians knew them, but aside from the sheer logistics of teaching a people a new language, there were more intrinsic problems. Robert Ricard has defined two strategies adopted by the missionaries. One group imported whatever words they needed to teach doctrine without the contaminating residue of indigenous vocabulary. Another translated the closest available native words so they wouldn't have to dwell endlessly on the strange meaning of new terms. Either method brought trouble.

The first method was a better protection against heterodoxy, for under it all misunderstanding and confusion in the minds of the neophytes could be averted. It would have been vain to try to Christianize a word which had thus far been used only by the pagans, for it would have run the risk of retaining a part of its meaning and of being associated with ideas that were not at all Christian. . . . The procedure presented a much graver and almost fundamental difficulty, to wit, that Christian ideas, presented in foreign dress, ran the risk of remaining perpetually foreign to the native mind. . . . Not only will the ideas be badly assimilated, or not at all, but Christianity will appear as the religion of foreigners, the Universal Church as an institution peculiar to one nation or race, and the convert as a traitor to his country. The history of missions proves beyond question that there is no more fatal mistake.

   With the second method this danger is averted; but another appears, for the instrument is a very ticklish one to handle and requires a thorough knowledge of native language and civilization. In his *La religion de Tupinambas*, Métraux gives a typical example of the errors that missionaries are exposed to. When they tried to find in the Tupinamba language a word to convey the idea of God, they chose, *faute de mieux*, the word *Tupan*, which means thunder. But this Tupan, in the mythology of the Tupinambas, was only a secondary spirit. Fortunately, the Indians were aware of the confusion and realized very well the difference between Tupan and the Christian God. Similar confusions occurred in Mexico.[15]

These problems continued to plague missionary efforts. Barriers are relative, and no language is simply a barrier. As Wilhelm von Humboldt would eventually see, language is a world of its own, and to recognize that fact means living inside the barrier.

Managing the Barrier

Seen as a curse, linguistic separation brought with it a need for caution and, rightly managed, brought certain advantages in a world where nations sought to dominate and gain from each other. Sir Francis Bacon, one of the great advocates of new knowledge and of contact with other nations, surveying the state of learning in the early 1600s and wanting to influence its advancement, imagined the ideal institution for sifting, ordering, and expanding knowledge. This institution, located on the imaginary Pacific island of New Atlantis, was called Solomon's House. Because it collected and disseminated the light of knowledge it was revered as the "eye" and "lantern" of the New Atlantis. Bacon intended it as a model college "instituted for the interpreting of nature and the producing of great and marvelous works for the benefit of men" (*New A*, 3:127).[16] For all its appetite for learning, however, New Atlantis assured its prosperity and intellectual vigor not by free exchange with the outside world, but by rigorous control over the flow of information. Language was a key to that regulated flow, that flood control project of ideas.

The kingdom's position at the forefront of learning depended partly on its geographical position—far from the main paths of communication, isolated from and unknown to the rest of the world. Citizens of Bensalem (the republic's name) could not travel to other parts of the world, and strict interdictions governed the arrival and departure of strangers. Recognizing, however, that total ignorance of the outside world could turn New Atlantis into a China, the epitome of the "curious, ignorant, fearful, foolish nation" (*New A*, 3:144), yet still wary of unfruitful systems of learning that could stagnate its fresh pools of knowledge, the founder of Solomon's House instituted a network of informants resembling a modern spy ring. Periodically, fellows of Solomon's House traveled to other countries, where they learned languages and mastered the knowledge of nations without divulging their own identity or secrets. Thus, they also depended on language as part of the key to managed superiority. The informants who traveled the world and passed as members of other societies collected information on "the sciences, arts, manufactures, and inventions of the world" and brought back "books, instruments, and patterns of every kind" (*New A*, 3:146). Their goal was to know, yet not be known. In the words of Bacon's informant, the kingdom undertook these measures for "preserving the good which cometh by communicating with strangers, and avoiding the hurt" (*New A*, 3:145).

J. H. Elliott has shown that the influences of New-World discoveries spread quite slowly in Europe.[17] Bacon's *New Atlantis* helps us understand why they did so and why, when the influences did spread, representations of the exotic often took forms most appealing to European minds. Even intellectual commonwealths find covert and overt means to regulate the flow of new knowledge into their domains. Communication with strangers, or in other words, new knowledge, promises to result in both trouble and profit, and because it is difficult to anticipate the form its good or evil will take before it becomes familiar, societies must absorb the new knowledge slowly or have mechanisms to test and filter the newness and difference that strangers bring. Bacon gives us the rudimentary economy of communication: good and hurt. Contact with strangers may bring comfort or peril on any level, from the physical or economic to the intellectual and moral.

In every realm there were reasons to remain figuratively at a distance from new tongues and the implications of their existence. Languages were difficult to learn, and if a few informants or translators allowed venturers to achieve their aims without having to learn languages, then for the rest, new languages were superfluous. Also, those on the front lines of exploration and conquest most often viewed indigenous languages as inferior, just as they judged indigenous technologies and military prowess to be inefficient or backward. On the religious level, new languages always raised the possibility of new gods. On the political level, these other languages promised to confirm, or, more threatening, to disconfirm, Europe's cultural superiority and its right to dispossess and rule other peoples. On the level of culture and ideology, the same alien points of view that became intriguing objects of study made it possible to critique Europe's societies as if from the outside. There was, however, a fine line between that study which gave Europeans a new vantage on their own beliefs and customs and that study which finally threatened European beliefs. Complicating matters, the process of self-critique as if from the outside was itself open to abuse and critique because it depended on a carefully managed process of selection and partiality. Europe proved very adept at strategically exploiting the mix of insider and outsider knowledge to manage the flow of information and power.

Ignoring the Barrier

The language barrier therefore raised great ethical questions. The questions were: What rights do invading and proselyting nations have in the new lands where they arrive? What rights to genuine communication do indigenous peoples have when they must choose whether to learn new languages or to adopt new masters and religions? Weighed in the cool atmosphere of the study or classroom, these questions today have fairly obvious answers. This section claims that in the council rooms where colonial policy was mapped and on the ground where policy was carried out, the greatest harm came from ignoring the language barrier altogether, pretending that communication differences were nonexistent, or, if existent, not crucial factors in the relations between the indigenous and the colonizers. Often the languages of colonized peoples disappeared from consideration except as nuisances to be replaced as soon as possible with that of the conqueror. When that happened, the rights of the people as human beings also tended to disappear.

European nations that conquered and colonized viewed their own languages as unique gifts to be bestowed on the people they subjected. In *Musophilus* (1599), the English poet Samuel Daniel pondered the future of the English language:

And who, in time knowes whither we may vent
The treasure of our tongue, to what strange shores
This gaine of our best glory shall be sent,
T'inrich unknowing Nations with our stores?

What worlds in th' yet unformed Occident
May come refin'd with th' accents that are ours?[18]

Peter Martyr, first chronicler of the age of discovery, wrote of the "large landes and many regyons whiche shal herafter receave owre nations, tounges, and manners."[19] Probably the best known of these statements came from the Spanish grammarian Antonio de Nebrija, whose volume of Spanish grammar was presented to Queen Isabella in the same year that Columbus first sailed to the west, with Nebrija's comment that "language is the instrument of empire" (Pagden, 57–58).[20] As Stephen Greenblatt has observed, such Europeans viewed peoples across the world as intellectually void, their minds so many *tabulae rasae* to be filled as Europe reversed the flow of riches from west to east with cargoes of language flowing from east to west. He says of Daniel, "he hasn't the slightest sense that the natives might be reluctant to abandon their own tongue."[21]

Poets, chroniclers, and grammarians were not, of course, policy makers; however, they expressed a general wish to see their languages spread; thereby they hoped for evidence that national power and cultural excellence formed obverse sides of the same coin. Their linguistic ambitions legitimized their disciplines. Nebrija and Daniel wanted others to see that those devoted to learning were performing a service as valuable as that of traders and settlers. By contrast, those who carried out the work of empire also knew how much that work hinged on language and even on attitudes to language. Julian Garcés, Bishop of Tlaxcala, complained in a letter to Pope Paul III that ecclesiastics who belittled the Indians "sweated little" and showed no zeal for native languages. In his opinion, "this is a voice that comes from the avaricious throats of Christians, whose greed is such that in order to slake their thirst for wealth they insist that rational creatures made in the image of God are beasts and asses."[22] The Viceroy of New Spain, Antonio de Mendoza, advised his replacement to believe neither those who praised the Indians as humble and charitable nor those who accused them of avarice and laziness without taking the informants' ulterior motives into account. He commented: "There are few persons in these parts who are not motivated by some interest, whether by temporal or spiritual gains or by passions or ambitions, whether virtuous or vicious."[23]

Bernardo de Aldrete's *Del origen y principio de la lengua castellana* (1606), the first history of a European vulgar tongue, reveals in another way the political gratification accompanying the spread of a colonizing nation's language. Aldrete wrote after a century of conquest and rule and following decades of wrangling by religious orders and the Spanish crown over the extent to which indigenous languages should be tolerated and how much of the purity of Christian doctrine relied on its being taught in Spanish. Aldrete's is the first history of the Spanish language to incorporate the spread of Spanish to vast areas outside Spain. Tracing its development into a vehicle of communication fit to accompany the banner throughout the world, Aldrete sees in Spanish an artfulness corresponding to its prestige as the language of an unprecedented world empire. It had in a sense become the new Latin. Aldrete raised many issues familiar to modern students of language—innovations and loans, the relationship of dialects and the standard language, the question of a linguistic area, and the problem of diffusion.[24] Related issues, such as the fitness of Latin grammar to describe exotic languages and the uniformities of grammars, eventually surfaced more explicitly in linguistic thought. But these are secondary matters compared to the grand narrative, Spain's destiny as its language spread across the Americas, displacing and replacing all less artful languages in its path.

Aldrete helps us see in retrospect that, insofar as a linguistic agenda existed in Spain, one of its purposes was to supplant indigenous languages. Aldrete sees in Castilian's power to displace other tongues the confirmation of its superiority and deserved prestige. This was largely accomplished, of course, by the force of arms, followed by coercion and suppression. "The conquered receive the language of the conquerors, delivering theirs up with their arms and persons."[25] If anything, Aldrete views force as justified: the Spanish honor the humanity of the native populations by giving them the Spanish tongue, Christianity, and the opportunity to join an unrivaled world empire. Even enormous declines in population are converted by Aldrete into signs of the glory of Castilian. In one notable passage, he observes:

> It is certain that when our people first arrived on the island Hispaniola there were a million and a half Indians, of whom not one remains today; in Cuba there remain only a few; and the same holds true on the other islands. On all these everyone speaks Castilian, and the remaining Indians have so totally lost their own former tongue that today it is not known what it was. This is very surprising, since these are such large islands.[26]

Observe the rough analogy: death or extermination of the native peoples appears alongside the triumph of the language of the colonizer.

When we move from the learned and the on-site agents of expansion to the level of national or imperial policy, we find in some cases a striking absence of attention to language. In its policy discussions the Spanish crown and its body for governing New Spain, the Council of the Indies, more often ignored language than its vital role in empire might lead us to expect. However, ruling bodies had powerful incentives to ignore many aspects of language when they deliberated on the nation's presence in the New World. Language matters could have massive and direct consequences on Spain's legal justifications for its presence in the Americas.

We must therefore view divided opinions on native languages in the context of a more encompassing disagreement over Spain's right to conquer and subject the Indians to Spain's rule. In his study of Spanish imperialism, Anthony Pagden has examined Spain's persistent qualms over the legitimacy of its overseas empire and its right as a Christian state to rule kingdoms subdued and retained by force.[27] This became an issue as early as 1512, was commonly disputed at universities by the 1530s, and continued to be debated through the sixteenth and seventeenth centuries and well into the eighteenth century. At one point Charles V was even rumored to be pulling Spain out of America to calm his troubled conscience (Pagden, 32). From the very beginning of the discoveries, "the crown remained . . . overwhelmingly concerned with the need to defend its claims to sovereignty (imperium) and property rights (dominium) in America before an increasingly hostile world" (Pagden, 13–14). Pagden notes that

the extent and the intensity of the struggles over the rights of Spaniards in America are, perhaps, unequaled in the history of European colonization. These debates belonged, however, to a tradition of ritual legitimation that the Castilian crown had, since the later middle ages, regularly enacted when confronted by uncertain moral issues. (Pagden, 5)

"With the accession of King Ferdinand and Queen Isabella," when Spain "effectively secured the consensus of its own political nation" and, consequently, became more aware of "its self-appointed role as the guardian of universal Christendom" (Pagden, 5–6), it became imperative that the crown act in "accordance with Christian ethico-political principles" (Pagden, 6). In a fascinating chapter on legal theory and political realities Pagden reviews in some detail the grounds on which this right was defended or attacked. Pagden doesn't foreground issues of language, but his book offers many insights into why language, which could have played a vital part in Spain's ethical and political discussions, is so often missing from the debates, and why, when it does appear, it generally does so only as a tool for carrying the cultural conquest to completion after a military conquest has already been made.

One of the main issues here was property rights. Notice that a discussion framed this way seldom accommodated attention to language. Language would have to be seen as a space between the conquerors and conquered that would have to be crossed by communication. Communication with people in their own language meant reversion to persuasion and permission. To acknowledge language was to acknowledge a degree of humanity which debates over property circumvented:

> What the crown wished to be told by its advisors was not whether it might *rule* the Indians ... but whether it might legitimately benefit from the fruits of their labour and from the profits to be had from their land, and, more crucially, from what lay beneath their land. (Pagden, 15)

The Spaniards believed that the societies they had conquered were, according to Roman law, not civil and therefore not legitimate. The Roman jurists believed that civil society was based on property, and "property relations were what constituted the basis for all exchanges between truly civil men." Since the inhabitants of America were not civil, their lands were not their own, "but merely open spaces which they, quite fortuitously, happened to inhabit" (Pagden, 15). With Spain's first contacts in the Antilles, such determinations, absurd as they may appear today, were considered relevant. However, with the incursions into Mexico in 1519 and Peru in 1531, Spain's denial that America's indigenous peoples lacked civil society became more tenuous. The question became, how could Spanish rights to possess the lands and goods of indigenous peoples be maintained even with regards to more technologically advanced, complexly organized societies?

The "dense" term *dominium* that lay at the heart of the debate changed meaning considerably over time. This term is in part a spatial one, but it was carefully configured to signify rule over less tangible things such as time, labor, and freedom. In the mid-sixteenth century it alluded generally to "certain natural and hence inalienable rights," of which property and its use were foundational. In the seventeenth century the term expanded to include people's rights "over not only their private property, their goods (*bona*), but also over their actions, their liberty, and even—with certain important qualifications—their own bodies" (Pagden, 16). Two questions were: Did the American peoples have *dominium*? And, if not, what right could Spain exert over their property, lives, and even bodies? Such determinations involved the state of society. By basing the determination on particular grounds—say the existence of property and exchange—and excluding other factors we would call cultural, some crown advisors nicely avoided the issue of language, even though language was manifestly considered a reflection of the degree of civilization in other contexts. It was

as if the interlocking realm of culture, language, the arts, social organization, and religion were reduced to a specific legal issue—whether people
had deeds, taxes, and coinage.

Yet as some advisors seemed to recognize, a serious look at languages
could affect the determination that the Indians were or were not a civil
people. In Gines de Sepúlveda's *Democrates Secundas*, Democrates states that
since the Indians "had no rulers and no laws in their pre-conquest state,
they might legitimately be appropriated by the first civil man to reach their
shores" (Pagden, 28). Pagden points out that "Sepúlveda was committed to
a far starker reading of Aristotle's theory of natural slavery than any previous author had been. The Indians, he claimed, were evidently not civil
beings since they consistently violated the law of nature." According to
Sepúlveda, "the Castilian crown's claim to sovereignty in America . . . rests
on the dictate of the natural law which grants dominium to all those who
are civil beings over all those who are not" (Pagden, 28, 29).

Among the advocates of Spain's rights to possess America and its peoples,
those who gave any notice to language usually wanted Spain to impose its
own language and obliterate the others. Giovanni Botero, author of *The
Reason of State*, states that "the victors will do well to introduce their own
tongue into the countries they have conquered, as the Romans did extremely
successfully."[28] In 1492 when Antonio de Nebrija offered his Spanish grammar to Isabella, "she is said to have asked what use she, who spoke Spanish
already, could have for such a work. To which he is said to have replied,
'Madam, language is the instrument of empire'" (Pagden, 57–58). Many
believed that the "acquisition of another language, other speech habits, and
another cultural vocabulary, led ineluctably . . . to the acquisition of the cultural habits, the customs and mores that give meaning to that language"
(Pagden, 58). Hence, to some minds it was expedient to impose Spanish on
conquered peoples.

The eccentric Tommaso Campanella argued that empires are founded
upon language, wealth, and the sword; and that language, by far, was the most
important: "Those who conquer by the sword alone, as had the Assyrians
and the Turks, 'swiftly gain and swiftly lose.' The true science of politics is primarily concerned with the exercise of power over the minds (*animi*) not
the bodies of men" (Pagden, 56). He advocated the "Hispanization" of the
American inhabitants—the prime instrument of which would naturally be
language (Pagden, 56–57). According to Campanella, "power, or 'the sword,'
is exclusively the domain of the secular ruler. But 'language' is the domain of
religion and also of the religious" (Pagden, 58). Because "the priesthood . . .
has control of 'language,'" Campanella points out that "no secure political
power has been possible without its support" (Pagden, 59).

The reason Spain overlooked the phenomenon of language should be clear from this material: to admit language and its problems of understanding, communication, and translation would already be to place the Indian peoples more on a level with Spain. It would place Spanish administrators in the position of evaluating cultures and languages they hadn't, with few exceptions, bothered to study in sufficient detail, and that effort could radically reframe the premises of the Spanish presence.

Among the defenders of Indian rights we find some, however, who at least implied the role of language in Spain's rights, even though they approached the question in the abstract and without much direct knowledge of American peoples. In the absence of such knowledge, what became important was their governing conception that language was a space between peoples that must be crossed on terms of mutual respect. In 1539 Francisco de Vitoria made a meticulous examination of the different grounds on which *dominium* might be asserted, only to conclude that the rights that Spain could enforce upon the Indians fell short of the right of possession, but not short of rule. The Spaniards could assert several rights which derived from *ius gentium*, or the law of nations. Among these were the rights of society and communication, or in other words, the right of access to other lands and to trade; and *ius predicandi*, the "right to preach their religion . . . without interference—although it did not compel anyone to accept it" (Pagden, 21). The right to preach without compulsion is a conception that already makes language a medium and individual determination a condition of communication.

Several disciples of Vitoria refuted even the limited rights Vitoria had upheld. The Dominican Melchior Cano in 1546 reasoned that Spain had no defensible right to travel and access, since any prince may restrict the travel of foreigners in his domains. Cano insisted only on *ius predicandi* and the right to defend the innocent. Another disciple, Juan de la Peña, insisted that as humans with rational capacities, the Indians had *dominium rerum* and could not be deprived of it. Having been deprived, they were now in the position of "persons from whom a judge has taken far more than the law allows and, like all such persons, they were entitled to restitution" (Padgen, 31). Peña defended only one right of the Spanish—again, *ius predicandi*—only the right to preach and be heard. Notice what this finding does, not only to property rights in the New World, but to the status of language in all of Spain's foreign "possessions." To reduce themselves to achieving their goals through communication, persuasion, or invitation, the Spaniards would risk the chance of losing what they had conquered. If Cano and Peña prevailed, the most likely conclusion would be that the Spaniards must give the Indians back all that they had taken.

In light of these deliberations and the absence of a concern for indigenous languages in them, the ludicrously sad *Requerimiento* document becomes more predictable. Crown policy in 1513 required expeditions to read this document—in Spanish—to newly encountered peoples in order to give prior notice and therefore legal weight to the thin fiction of Spanish jurisdiction. As with the protocols for claiming territory, the *Requerimiento* had as its real audience the states of Europe. The document informed baffled native listeners, at the peril of their lives, of the authority of the Spanish crown and its viceroys to occupy their territories and spread the Christian faith. The fact that the native inhabitants didn't understand the document's claims, its justification, and its threat of enforcement didn't bother those who pronounced it, as long as the steps were properly followed and recorded by notaries. Bartolomé de Las Casas, an informed and sympathetic witness of conquest depravities, stated that he didn't know whether "to laugh or cry" at the *Requerimiento*.[29] Stephen Greenblatt says, "A strange blend of ritual, cynicism, legal fiction, and perverse idealism, the *Requerimiento* contains at its core the conviction that there is no serious language barrier between the Indians and the Europeans."[30] I argue rather that the *Requerimiento* assumes an absolute language barrier that could be exploited fruitfully only if language was left out of the discussion. The act of reading the *Requerimiento* can be explained only in the context of Europeans' awareness that they were treading on others' territory and that communication about their presence was necessary, yet the content of the document and the procedures followed in presenting it denied any of the consequences of that recognition. In this extreme case, venturers simply denied that a full cycle of communication was needed—no need for the native inhabitants to understand what officers read to them, and certainly no need for a return communication.

The debate between Sepúlveda and Bartolomé de Las Casas in 1550, before the Council of the Indies, on the question of whether the church should wage war on the Indians in order to subject and convert them, succeeded at least in bringing the language question into the open. Sepúlveda argued that war was indeed right and necessary in order to convert the Indians. Las Casas, clearly a disciple of Vitoria, responded that war was not only unnecessary but wrong. Las Casas pointed out that the Indians did, in fact, have intellectual capacity, as evidenced by their intellectual gifts. He argued that the issue hinged on ignorance of language, and he noted that in order for the Indians to be converted, the Spaniards would have to take the time to make their message adequately understood. His view was controversial because it meant a thorough overhaul of Spain's policies and practices.

Las Casas, a former conquistador and reformed *encomiendero* who entered the priesthood and eventually rose to Bishop of Chiapas, had intimate acquaintance with several Indian groups. Although he apparently never learned any Indian languages himself, Las Casas saw the Indians' language learning capacity as evidence of their intellectual gifts:

> In the liberal arts that they have been taught up to now, such as grammar and logic, they are remarkably adept. With every kind of music they charm the ears of their audience with wonderful sweetness. They write skillfully and quite elegantly, so that most often we are at a loss to know whether the characters are handwritten or printed.[31]

Las Casas implicitly grasped the crucial role language played in Spain's perceptions of the inhabitants of conquered territories. He distinguished types of barbarians, most of which are merely construed as such by Europeans. One of these types "includes those who do not have a written language that corresponds to the spoken one, as the Latin language does with ours, and therefore they do not know how to express in it what they mean." The lack of a written language corresponding to Latin didn't prove a people barbarous. Many such peoples had been known to be "wise, courageous, prudent, and lead a settled life." The issue hinged not on writing, but on ignorance of another's tongue: "In this sense he is called a barbarian who, because of the difference in his language, does not understand another speaking to him" (Las Casas, 30–31).

But Las Casas's most radical tack in refuting Sepúlveda involved his respect for the integrity of Indian intentions, even in such practices as human sacrifice, and his attaching great importance to their right to understand the Christian message through the medium of language. Men like Sepúlveda had reasoned that since human sacrifice could not be tolerated, the Spaniards had the duty and right to stop it by any means. Las Casas countered in a strange way, reasoning that some might view the practice of human sacrifice as a way to please God. This being so, what could be done to stop the Indians from practicing it? He observes, "It is not possible, quickly and in a few words, to make clear to unbelievers, especially ours, that sacrificing men to God is unnatural." Las Casas then makes the case that, since "they do not understand the preacher," the obligation lies on the Christian, with the help of the Holy Spirit, to overcome what may appear to be invincible ignorance (Las Casas, 241). He cites church fathers who stress that it is not sufficient simply to forbid certain beliefs and practices. Ministers must attract the ignorant and unbelieving by teaching and by gentle behavior in accordance with the gospel itself (Las Casas, 250–52).

The proper path involves a strong emphasis on language as open communication between parties and on the language of the Indians. Las Casas frequently returns to this kind of scenario:

Let us put the case that the Spaniards discover that the Indians or other pagans sacrifice human victims or eat them. Let us say, further, that the Spaniards are so upright and good-living that nothing motivates them except the rescue of the innocent and the correction of the guilty. Will it be just for them to invade and punish them without any warning? You will say "No, rather they shall send messengers to warn them to stop these crimes." Now I ask you, dear reader, what language will the messengers speak so as to be understood by the Indians? Latin, Greek, Spanish, Arabic? The Indians know none of these languages. Perhaps we imagine that the soldiers are so holy that Christ will grant them the gift of tongues so that they will be understood by the Indians? Then what deadline will they be given to come to their senses and give up their crimes? They will need a long time to understand what is said to them, and also the authority and the reasons why they should stop sacrificing human beings, so that it will be clear that evils of this type are contrary to natural law.

Las Casas gives language the status of a barrier that must be crossed appropriately.

Further, within the deadline set for them, no matter what its length, they will certainly not be bound by the warning given them, nor should they be punished for stubbornness, since a warning does not bind until the deadline has run out. Likewise, no law, constitution, or precept is binding on anyone unless the words of the language in which it is proposed are clearly understood, as the learned jurists say. . . .

Now, I ask, what will the soldiers do during the time allowed the Indians to come to their senses? Perhaps, like the forty monks Saint Gregory sent to convert the English, they will spend their time in fasting and prayer, so that the Lord will be pleased to open the eyes of the Indians to receive the truth and give up such crimes. Or, rather, will not the soldiers hope with all their hearts that the Indians will become so blind that they will neither see nor hear? And then the soldiers will have the excuse they want for robbing them and taking them captive. Anyone who would foolishly and very unrealistically expect soldiers to follow the first course knows nothing about the military mind. . . .

Further, let us suppose that such a thing does not happen to the Indians and, after more or less time, they may come to understand the warnings of the Spaniards. What if they say they do not kill the innocent for sacrifice or cannibalism but only those condemned to death for their crimes, or those captured in a just war, or those who have died a natural death? Therefore they do no harm to innocent people but only to themselves in eating the flesh of humans like wild beasts. In this case, will not the reason for freeing innocent people from an unjust death cease to be valid? (Las Casas, 217–19)

Lewis Hanke believes that Las Casas risked heresy in expressing these views, in that he accorded the Indians not only the intelligence to govern themselves, but the unconstrained freedom to choose or reject Christianity after having the opportunity to hear and understand it.[32] Whatever the degree of his heresy, we can see why the Council of the Indies, together with soldiers and colonial administrators in New Spain, would resist by any measure the position Las Casas advanced. To concede that Indians had the right to be taught Christian doctrine in a language they could understand, before the Spanish could even debate their own right to employ force against them, would be to overthrow in a moment the foundations of Spain's political, economic, and spiritual empire.

Language and the Conditions of Knowledge

So far, this chapter has concentrated on the language barrier as one between peoples. We turn now to language as a barrier between the mind and the world it seeks to understand. In exploring this barrier, linguists and philosophers were also exploring the conditions of knowledge and existence.

Unity and diversity are both necessary for thought to take place. Without unity and identity, reality is a kaleidoscope of difference, fragmented and incoherent. Without difference, reality is one continuum with no distinct objects for the senses to perceive and the faculties to grasp. The most rudimentary division perhaps is that between *Self* and *Other*, whereby we recognize that we are the same type of beings but different instances or embodiments and that we exist in that play of sameness and difference. As contemporary phenomenologists have noted, in our desire for understanding we have a tendency to reduce the *Other* to the *Same*, or in plainer words, to assume that others are like us or are in some manner simply extensions of ourselves. Yet our existence depends on the fact that others are different, that they constrain our freedom and make demands upon our attention, time, and resources. The quest for unity is a quest to collapse the distance between us and also between us and our objects of knowledge, when our existence as knowers and as individual beings depends on the distance we want to collapse. The desire to move boundaries is thus a desire to test the nature of, and perhaps alter, existence. The many attempts throughout history to fathom linguistic diversity, create unified or perfect languages, and close the gaps among words, things, and ideas are reconfigurations of and experiments with the conditions of knowledge and being.

Medieval and Renaissance students of language predominantly believed that the fall at Eden had split language from nature and that the confusion at Babel had obliterated whatever remnants of the divine language had remained beyond Eden. So far were language and nature sundered that little could be gained from studying languages—little, that is, beyond the immediate benefits of better communication of fallen knowledge—and if the mind found the variety enticing, the danger was only the greater. For Anglican bishop Lancelot Andrewes, the gulf between word and thing was introduced by humanity itself. Adam disobeyed and lied, thereby severing language from the world. He allowed signifier and signified to part.[33] Andrewes's contemporary Godfrey Goodman said, "Neither do tongues follow the order and course of nature, for in many things which nature hath rankt in one kinde, and given them the same properties, yet in grammar you shall find them infinitly to differ in their genders, their numbers, declension" (Goodman, 301). One might expect "some kind of affinity between Logick and Grammar, the one directing his understanding, the other framing his speech, and both of them should ranke things *in serie praedicamental*," but one does not find this affinity. He added, "Though speech be proper and naturall to man, yet this, or that language, follows the frank and free imposition of man, and hath no ground work in nature" (Goodman, 303). Indeed, "their [*sic*] seems to be a kind of opposition, between the studie of nature, and the knowledge of tongues" (Goodman, 300). Notice the types of separations here involving the order and courses of nature and languages, the ranks and hierarchies of nature and those found in grammar, and the frames of logic and grammar.

Languages, in this view, offered no privileged view of the world, although many people in the sixteenth and seventeenth century banked their careers on demonstrating some type of linkage. The great language projects of the seventeenth century all reflected the assumption that the breach between language and nature must be healed. The problem was to find the secret upon which they could be brought back together. Lancelot Andrewes thought the mending could be accomplished only spiritually and morally. When truth and righteousness were severed from mercy and peace, only an act of reconciliation could bring them back together. Christ's birth restored truth; righteousness was possible in the hands of those who followed him. Mystics like Jacob Boehme depended on a visionary insight into the power of language. For many others, the healing was a more intellectual matter. Various etymologists searched for vestiges of the Adamic tongue, whose syllables still harmonized with the objects and ideas in the world and would assist the mind in thinking rightly about them. Framers of philosophical language and real characters depended on designing systems of sounds that, although established by convention and not by divine decree, would designate an idea's nature and its exact location in the tables of knowledge.

The great question was, did language correspond to reality in some hidden and nonarbitrary way? If so, then to the degree that one could tease out the inner structure of language, one could learn thereby the secrets of the world. One early modern insisted that the answer was no. He was Francis Bacon. Robert Stillman observes that

> long before *The Advancement of Learning* (1605), increased historical awareness and philological sophistication of Renaissance humanism led the way to greater consciousness of linguistic abuse, mutations in language over time, and inadequacies in the vernaculars and scholastic Latin. In spite of which, the humanists as a group expressed no great awareness of an epistemologically fatal division between words and things. Bacon was not alone in opening a breach between words and things, but he was uniquely effective in exploiting that breach in order to advance the claims of a new, culturally superior form of knowledge.[34]

One of the keys to Bacon, I think, is in fact his insistence that language and nature belonged to two completely different orders of things, so much so that little or nothing about nature was to be learned by studying words.

Bacon wanted to police the language barrier, first by standing as sentinel against the wrong kind of language study and second by fostering the proper study of nature, which meant a study carried out as free as possible from linguistic seductions. Others, even accepting the Babel legend, believed the semiotic system held the key. Their presumption went as follows: whatever knowledge we have comes to us by language; therefore, we will understand the structure of the knowledge we have better by understanding the sign system. The claim, incidentally, is still central to semiotics. Bacon said no, the structure of nature and the structure of language are two different things, and we will advance by learning the differences, respecting them, and focusing our attention where knowledge can truly grow: on matter. He warned that "the first distemper of learning" occurs "when men study words and not matter" (*Adv L*, 3:284). In other words, the road to useful knowledge did not lie in the study of language but in the study of the phenomena that language names and communicates. Language was a barrier, after all, but a far different kind than his predecessors had perceived. In the context of the above discussion of language similarity and difference, we see that part of his project was to negotiate the boundaries between language and reality, and those between languages, in a proper way. He gave emphasis to both kinds of boundaries and had a place in his new learning for both of them.

The spatial metaphor here is not casual. Bacon used many figures rhetorically to convey his points. Among these are images of light, genealogy, prison, affections, and the breath of life. Spatial figures function both rhetorically and conceptually for Bacon. "The world is not to be narrowed till it will go into the understanding (which has been done hitherto)," he remarked, "but the understanding is to be expanded and opened till it can take in the image of the world."[35] The metaphor at work here is more than just an expression. Just as the exploration of the New World depended on the discovery of the mariner's needle, or compass, the student of nature needed something to guide the mind. And reaching a proper destination hinges on the way of setting out. The two main ways of proceeding, one speculative, logical, and respectful of authority and the other inductive and experimental, are two paths. "The one, arduous and difficult in the beginning, leads out at last into the open country; while the other, seeming at first sight easy and free from obstruction, leads to pathless and precipitous places" (*GI*, 4:8). Another passage, with its marital imagery, is also implicitly about closeness and separateness: "By these means I suppose that I have established forever a true and lawful marriage between the empirical and rational faculty, the unkind and ill-starred divorce and separation of which has thrown into confusion all the affairs of the human family" (*GI*, 4:19). What is curious about this passage is the way it depicts unity and separation. The so-called divorce of reason and observation had occurred because philosophers had conceived of them as closely allied. The divorce was one of results. Bacon marries them by recognizing how different they are and laying rules for their compatibility. Thus, the true marriage is one that recognizes distance.

These and many other spatial concepts were fundamental to Bacon because he was concerned about proper distances and affinities among mind, language, logic, the senses, and nature. Each of these had a structure. The problem was that in so many centuries, working along the same lines, assuming the same conformities of logic and mind and the external world, scholars had produced so little verifiable understanding. Nature was presumed to have a structure, but Bacon arrived at the conclusion that it had far different characteristics than generally conceived. Nature was more subtle than logic could ever pretend to be. "The universe to the eye of human understanding is framed like a labyrinth; presenting as it does on every side so many ambiguities of way, such deceitful resemblances of objects and signs, natures so irregular in their lines, and so knotted and entangled." Meanwhile, "those who offer themselves for guides are also puzzled, and increase the number of errors and wanderers. . . . In circumstances so difficult neither the natural force of man's judgment nor even any accidental felicity offers any chance of success" (*GI*, 4:18).

As his words indicate—"such deceitful resemblances of objects and signs"—Bacon was particularly (though not solely) concerned with the disconformities of language and logic. The study of words had infected knowledge like a plague in many forms. In rhetoric, for which Bacon had a great respect if properly pursued, the fascination for argument and style had obscured attention to substance. The admirable style pleased the mind and induced a closure to ideas before they had been sufficiently examined. In logic, fascination for syllogism obscured the fact that syllogisms are no match for the subtlety of nature. Syllogisms depend on words that are at best rough approximations of facts, and at worst name downright false or nonexistent things:

> I on the contrary reject demonstration by syllogism, as acting too confusedly, and letting nature slip out of its hands. For although no one can doubt that things which agree in a middle term agree with one another (which is a proposition of mathematical certainty), yet it leaves an opening for deception; which is this. The syllogism consists of propositions; propositions of words; and words are the tokens and signs of notions. Now if the very notions of the mind . . . be improperly and over-hastily abstracted from facts, vague, not sufficiently definite, faulty in short in many ways, the whole edifice tumbles. (*GI*, 4:24)

Thus Bacon pulls apart the certainty to which strict logic was thought to lead. Conclusions from syllogistic reasoning may well be demonstrable given the terms used therein; however, the demonstrability may have no bearings on the matter to which it pretends to relate. The strong urge to spring from a few facts to higher generalities leaps over the intermediate facts and generalities that only patient observation, not propositions, can arrive at. The understanding that works by words trusts in its own powers, when in fact, Bacon observed, the understanding is a thing quite unequal to contend with the obscurity of things (*New O*, 4:50). "The subtlety of nature is greater many times over than the subtlety of argument" (*New O*, 4:51).

Bacon called Idols those false beliefs and practices that constantly retarded understanding. They are different versions of barriers, different paths into the confusion of thing, idea, and word. Idols of the Tribe are the flaws in the senses and mind which, like false mirrors, introduce their distortions into whatever they are held up to (*New O*, 4:54). Idols of the Cave introduce individual quirks and bias. Idols of the Theater reflect our tendency to believe in tidy systems when reality is messy and complicated. We don't stretch Bacon far when we apply this sentence to prevailing views of language: "The human understanding is of its own nature prone to suppose the existence of more order and regularity in the world than it finds. And though there be many things in nature which are singular and unmatched, yet it devises for them parallels and conjugates and relatives which do not exist" (*New O*, 4:55). Idols of the Marketplace relate directly to language. They derive from our dependence on words. Bacon wanted his peers to see that, yes, language can govern thought, but it often does so detrimentally. Words have a faulty alliance with things and thus give a faulty sense of rhetorical control over ideas. Some words name things that do not actually exist. "Prime mover" and the "element of fire" are examples. More troublesome are unskillful abstractions that denote a jumbled variety of things with no constant meaning (*New O*, 4:61). Many of these defects occur because words are not precise even in their beginnings. Most words are framed in vulgar use, without concern for clear ideas. For that reason Bacon opposed the study of etymology to which so many curious minds were drawn on the mistaken assumption that words "were not arbitrarily fixed at first, but derived and deduced by reason and according to significance." Once words pass into circulation, they bring with them such indefiniteness that makes etymological study "a subject elegant indeed," but only "sparingly true and bearing no fruit" (*Adv L*, 4:441). Although words are most germane to Idols of the Marketplace, they affect the other idols as well, because "vicious demonstrations are as the strongholds and defences of the Idols; and those we have in logic do little else than make the world the bond-slave of human thought, and human thought the bond-slave of words" (*New O*, 4:70).

Bacon's project involved the proper separation of mind, language, logic, senses, and external nature. Only by properly appreciating the differences in these interdependent orders of being could a science of results and practical improvements and true comprehension begin. Just as *comprehend* has an etymology that includes not only understanding but surrounding and taking within, so Bacon's project to separate logic and language from their ruling place in the interpretation of nature included not only words and reasoning but the nature of our existence and the condition of knowledge. For much of the Middle Ages and early Renaissance, scholars pushed forward in their work with the firm conviction that words, the human mind, and the universe, though fallen, shared an intrinsic harmony—often secret and unperceived—that would, when teased out by logic and one or another form of semiotics, reveal itself as the ultimate reality. Bacon saw the compelling allure of this equation. It held that there was more to existence than met the eye. Knowledge was a matter of deciphering, and codes have always invited decryption. Bacon saw this philosophy as the great barrier to knowledge.

To dismantle the barrier meant thinking of human nature and knowledge differently and relocating the barriers among them. Bacon promised that new barriers would yield surprising results. Using almost the language of a hermitic philosopher, he promised:

> There is therefore much ground for hoping that there are still laid up in the womb of nature many secrets of excellent use, having no affinity or parallelism with any thing that is now known, but lying entirely out of the beat of the imagination, which have not yet been found out. They too no doubt will some time or other, in the course and revolution of many ages, come to light of themselves, just as the others did; only by the method of which we are now treating they can be speedily and suddenly and simultaneously presented and anticipated. (*New O*, 4:100)

Proper fences make good knowledge. They hinder and separate, but they also protect and demarcate. In a way, they are essential to identity and meaning. Language barriers are essential to the idea of peoples. The search for unity of languages, for primitive words that would heal the breach, was driven by this fundamental irony: the condition of meaning is particularity, or embodiment by mediation in a particular form that can be differentiated from something else. Words exist because they are not the ideas they name, and ideas are different because they have been separated out from the bland continuum of consciousness. To seek wholeness is also to seek meaninglessness, to pursue lack of consciousness, to lose that very separation from others and God by which we exist.

Notes

1 Robert E. Stillman, *The New Philosophy and Universal Languages in Seventeenth-Century England: Bacon, Hobbes, and Wilkins* (Lewisburg, PA: Bucknell University Press, 1995), 30.
2 William Whately, *Prototypes* (1640), 88, 89–90.
3 Salust, Guillaume de [Seigneur du Bartas], *Babilon, a Part of the Seconde Weeke*, in *The Divine Weeks* (Les semaines) [1578], trans. William L'Ilse (London, 1596), 29.
4 Godfrey Goodman, *The Fall of Man, or The Corruption of Nature, Proved by the Light of our Naturall Reason* (London, 1616), 292, 300.

5 John Calvin, *Commentaries on the First Book of Moses, Called Genesis*, trans. John King (Grand Rapids, MI: Eerdmans, 1948), 1:325–26.

6 "de pensar es questa gente infiel, y en quien el demonio ha seydo señor por tantos siglos, les haya enseñado con el tiempo, goçando de tanta ánimas, essas diversidades de lenguajes, hallando aparejo tan manifiesto é abierto para los engañar, é estando estas gentes tan faltas de defensas hasta nuestro tiempo." Gonzalo Fernandez de Oviedo, *Historia general y natural de las Indias* [1535] (Madrid: Real Academia de la Historia, 1851), 1:236. Author's translation.

7 Gregorio García, *Origen de los Indios de el Nuevo Mundo, e Indias Occidentales* [1607], 2d ed. (Madrid: Abad, 1729), 52–53.

8 "Noticia de una Obra en Tarasco," in *Annales del Meseo Michoacano*, ed. Joaquín García Icazbalceta (Morales, 1888), 62–64.

9 Diego de Landa, *Relación de las cosas de Yucatán*, ed. Alfred M. Tozzer, Papers of the Peabody Museum, vol. 18 (Cambridge, MA, 1941), 169.

10 Hernando Ruiz de Alarcón, *Treatise on the Heathen Superstitions and Customs That Today Live among the Indians Native to This New Spain, 1629*, trans. and ed. J. Richard Andrews and Ross Hassig (Norman: University of Oklahoma Press, 1984), 43.

11 J. Richard Andrews and Ross Hassig, introduction to *Treatise on the Heathen Superstitions*, by Hernando Ruiz de Alarcón, 7.

12 I am following P. J. Marshall and Glyndwr Williams, *The Great Map of Mankind: British Perceptions of the World in the Age of the Enlightenment* (London: Dent, 1982), 109.

13 Domingo de Navarrete, *An Account of the Empire of China: Historical, Political, Moral and Religious*, in *A Collection of Voyages and Travels*, comp. Awnsham Churchill (London, 1704), 1:406.

14 Robert Wardy gives an update of the issues behind this controversy, brought into the twentieth century's conflicting images of China and developed in terms of a Chinese translation of Aristotle, in "Chinese Whispers: The Jesuit Policy of Accommodation and Western Philosophy in China," *Proceedings of the Cambridge Philosophical Society* 38 (1992): 149–70. A more general study of the Jesuits in China and their contribution to Sinology can be found in D. E. Mungello, *Curious Land: Jesuit Accommodation and the Origins of Sinology* (Honolulu: University of Hawaii Press, 1989).

15 Robert Ricard, *The Spiritual Conquest of Mexico: An Essay on the Apostolate and the Evangelizing Methods of the Mendicant Orders in New Spain, 1523–1572*, trans. Lesley Byrd Simpson (Berkeley: University of California Press, 1966), 55–56.

16 Unless otherwise noted, subsequent quotations of Francis Bacon are cited in the text according to the abbreviations listed below: Each citation will include the abbreviated title followed by the volume and page number as given in *The Works of Francis Bacon*, ed. James Spedding, Robert Ellis, and Douglas Heath, 14 vols. (London: Longman, 1860).

Adv L	*Of the Dignity and Advancement of Learning*
GI	*The Great Instauration*
New A	*New Atlantis*
New O	*The New Organon or True Directions Concerning the Interpretation of Nature*
NWS	*The New World of Science or Desiderata*
IN	*Of the Interpretation of Nature*

17 J. H. Elliott, *The Old World and the New, 1492–1650* (Cambridge: Cambridge University Press, 1970).

18 Samuel Daniel, *Musophilus: Containing a General Defense of All Learning* [1599], ed. Raymond Himelick (West Lafayette, IN: Purdue Research Foundation, 1965), lines 957–62, p. 86.

19 Peter Martyr, *The Decades of the Newe World* (De Orbe Novo), in *The First Three English Books on America*, trans. Richard Eden and ed. Edward Arber (Birmingham, 1885), 177.

20 Anthony Pagden, *Spanish Imperialism and the Political Imagination* (New Haven: Yale University Press, 1990), 57–58.

21 Stephen Greenblatt, "Learning to Curse: Aspects of Linguistic Colonialism in the Sixteenth Century," in *First Images of America: The Impact of the New World on the Old*, ed. Fredi Chiapelli (Berkeley: University of California Press, 1976), 2:561–62.

22 Alberto María Carreño, *Fray Domingo de Betanzos: Fundador en la Nueva España de la Venerable Orden Dominicana* (Mexico: Victoria, 1924–1934), 318–19.

23 Antonio de Mendoza, "Relación, apuntamientos y avisos que por mandado de S. M. Dió D. Antonio de Mendoza á D. Luis de Velasco, nombrado sucerderle in este cargo," in *Colección de documentos inéditos relativos al descubrimiento, conquista y organización de las antiguas posesiones españolas de América y Oceania* (Madrid: Quirós, 1864–1884), 6:499.

24 Guillermo L. Guitarte, "La dimensión imperial del español en la obra de Aldrete: Sobre la aparición del español de América en la lingüística hispánica," in *The History of Linguistics in Spain*, ed. Antonio Quilis and Hans-J. Niederehe, Amsterdam Studies in the Theory and History of Linguistic Science, 3d ser. (Amsterdam: John Benjamins, 1986), 182.

25 Bernardo de Aldrete, *Del origen y principio de la lengua castellana* [1606], ed. L. N. Jiménez (Madrid: Consejo Superior de Investigaciones Científicas, 1972), 1:138.

26 Aldrete, *Principio de la lengua castellana*, 1: 146.

27 See note 20.

28 Giovanni Botero, *The Reason of State*, trans. P. J. and D. P. Waley (New Haven: Yale University Press, 1956), 98.

29 Bartolomé de Las Casas, *History of the Indies*, trans. and ed. Andrée Collard (New York: Harper & Row, 1971), 196.

30 Stephen Greenblatt, *Marvelous Possessions: The Wonder of the New World* (Chicago: University of Chicago Press, 1991), 98.

31 Unless otherwise stated, all parenthetical citations of Bartolomé de Las Casas are found in his work, *In Defense of the Indians: The Defense of the Most Reverend Lord, Don Fray Bartolomé de Las Casas, of the Order of Preachers, Late Bishop of Chiapas, Against the Persecutors and Slanderers of the Peoples of the New World Discovered Across the Seas*, trans. and ed. Stafford Poole (DeKalb: Northern Illinois University Press, 1974), 44.

32 Lewis Hanke, *All Mankind Is One: A Study of the Disputation between Bartolomé de Las Casas and Juan Ginés de Sepúlveda in 1550 on the Intellectual and Religious Capacity of the American Indians* (DeKalb: Northern Illinois University Press, 1974), 94.

33 Lancelot Andrewes, "A Sermon" [Christmas Day, 1616], in *Lancelot Andrewes: Selected Writings* (Manchester: Carcanet, 1995), 28, 43.

34 Stillman, *New Philosophy and Universal Languages*, 31.

35 From *The Parasceve*, quoted in Loren Eisely, *The Man Who Saw through Time* (New York: Charles Scribner's Sons, 1973), iii.

4 Containing Language: What Language Contains

I . . . presently apply'd my self to the study of that dreadful and stu-pendious [Chinese] Language; there are few but find great dis-couragement in it, I labour'd all I could. . . . I was commanded by my Superiors to study the Characters, and thought it a difficult Task; I began with infinite reluctancy, but in a few months was so fond of it, that I could not put down my Books for a moment.
—Friar Domingo de Navarrete[1]

Travelers and colonizers studied indigenous languages in order to succeed in their enterprises. This motive I will refer to as one of containing language because it bounded and incorporated languages and neutralized, as far as possible, the challenges they posed. This pragmatic motive sufficed for many, but others found that the pragmatic motive gave way to curiosity, aesthetic appreciation, and the love of the different mind-sets that accompany languages. I refer to the latter move as discovering what language contains and even being contained by it. This chapter will present examples of language study that made possible the transition from one state to another. The signs of that transition go beyond sheer appreciation and love of language; they include the finding of new vantage points from which to see one's culture as if from a distance, and a reverse move, which is initially spatial but transcends it: the tendency in those who studied language to see the human face of indigenous people. Who could contain languages? Depending on how containing is conceived—no one, or every-one. What do languages contain? Pioneers found that they contained points of view. People. Worlds.

In saying that languages contain points of view and even worlds, I may seem to reinforce the linguistic relativism of Edward Sapir and Benjamin Whorf, the principle that languages cause differences in thinking as well as in perception.[2] However, my metaphor, containing, implies something else about language and indeed about most cognition. A given language may indeed condition the thought of those who speak it, but it also offers alternate metaphors, points of view, and organizations of reality. Learning new languages merely accelerates the perception of alternate points of view that any language offers. One might venture to give a definition of language based on this principle. Language—meaning both language generally and any specific language—is the possibility of alternate organizations and perceptions of reality.

These points are present already in the dynamics of containing. We like to hold things—water, fuel, thumb tacks, or potato chips—in containers so they are more easily stored, managed, and utilized. We also contain things— unruly mobs, fires, poisonous gasses—to limit and constrain them. When it comes to less tangible entities such as ideas, attitudes, and cultural forces, both aspects of the container metaphor may operate simultaneously, so that our ability to hold and use an idea is linked to our ability to limit and con- strain it. As the linguistic relativity debate illustrates, when it comes to think- ing about language, we have difficulty separating how we can contain lan- guage (define it, limit it, manage it) without recognizing that in some ways it contains our thinking. The early modern experience with newly encountered languages is the story of discovering these multiple aspects of containment.

Failure and the Incentive to Language

Most colonizers left Europe with clear, self-interested agendas; as a result they were slow to feel the pull of languages. For many of them, however, the pull came when their projects appeared doomed to fail. They had planned their enterprises, much in the frame of mind of Sepúlveda in his debate with Las Casas before the Council of the Indies, as if language didn't require special consideration in their conquest and settlement. But the language barrier proved a barrier to their own success. As failure drove explorers and even some conquerors to study languages, language learning sometimes influenced them to redefine success and failure. That is, as they gained abil- ity to communicate with the indigenous peoples over whom they ruled, some military and colonial officers began to measure success not only in military, economic, and managerial terms, but in the moral and spiritual. Among missionaries, a similar pattern held true. Those who studied languages envisioned conversion in new ways, not as mere imposition or adoption of Christian views but as a process of comprehension, transformation, and mutual exchange. And once these moves began to take place among colo- nizers, the practical necessity of language study itself underwent a transfor- mation. Language changed from a means to an end and also to a means by which ends could be assessed.

Explorers, soldiers, missionaries, and colonial administrators rarely concerned themselves with new languages out of a concern for their beauty or the deep implications of linguistic diversity. Pizarro had no interest in evangelizing and cared little about the behavior of his troops or the prospects for intimate contact with the Andeans. When Friar Bernardino de Minaya tried to counsel Pizarro not to rob and despoil the Indians but to "make God known to them" and "explain to the Indians the reason for our coming," Pizarro replied that he "had not come for any such reasons; he had come from Mexico to take away from them their gold."[3] However, to the degree that their enterprises were more than grab-and-run schemes, colonizers found that they needed understanding of new languages as much as they needed ships and weapons.

Initially, Europeans required only enough language to find out where the gold was, barter for goods, and maintain order. Later, they wanted to administer, convert, trade, and perhaps even explain their presence. As long as they held language learning in strict subordination to their goals, they accomplished those goals all the more efficiently. Diversity could even work to their benefit: Gonzalo Fernandez de Oviedo attributed the dramatic military success of the Spaniards in the Americas to the lack of common languages among the natives. A common language would have made it easier for the natives to work together to fight off invaders.[4] Cortés achieved success beyond his dreams in conquering Tenochtitlan and, with it, all of central Mexico, because his interpreter, Doña Marina, a bi-lingual Aztec woman, gave him the ability to cross the language barrier without having to encounter it himself.

In terms of language learning, no more important development occurred in the long history of discovery and conquest than the venturers' recognition that they couldn't assume they were effectively communicating simply because they knew what they wanted, believed themselves divinely sponsored, or had faith in the excellence of their languages. Fernandez de Oviedo observed, in a manner that could be echoed almost everywhere in the New World, that the language barrier was real, that there was a dire need for interpreters, and that in their absence, all the good intended by benevolent Spaniards was at risk because of the vices and greed of the conquerors. Only clear understanding between colonizer and colonized could eliminate the pervasive threat of failure.[5] Of course, we are looking at failure here from the European perspective. Language, which figures in most post-colonial studies as mainly a tool of violence, appeared to Fernandez de Oviedo as just the opposite. A knowledge of the natives' languages would not make the conquerors vanish; on the contrary, it would facilitate their remaining. But it would actually lessen the violence that flourished when two peoples could barely communicate and the conquerors imposed their will solely by coercion.

Language study in turn prompted some conquerors and missionaries to modify their attitudes toward indigenous peoples and eventually to modify their objectives. And, to complete the cycle, closer understanding of peoples and specific languages promoted a new understanding of language itself and created new possibilities for cultural tolerance. This pattern—failure leading to further language study which then modified the relations between conqueror and conquered—did not always occur. But it happened often enough to deserve notice.

It can, of course, be argued that on the spectrum of types of success I have defined, with military and economic and managerial at one end leading to the moral and spiritual at the other, the military really made possible the other types, that no one could talk about moral and spiritual success until military, economic, and managerial successes were being achieved. Thus viewed, effective brutality and warfare bestowed the luxury of moral and spiritual considerations on tender missionary minds. Of course there is truth in this view. But this view is not complete in itself. Those who concerned themselves with the moral and spiritual didn't always accept the methods of the soldier, nor did they want only to make the people obey regardless of their hearts and minds. They also wanted to understand and convert people in the inner sense. As they investigated native customs, thinking, and idioms, they challenged their own people's use of weapons to subdue others without just cause. The two were connected. Such an awareness had already been expressed in Europe, where linguistic divisions had helped create and aggravate political rivalries. In 1450 Aeneas Silvius Piccolomini advised the king of Hungary and Bohemia that "love, no less than the sword, guards kingdoms" and that "intercourse of languages is a promoter of love."[6]

To start the process, adventurers and chroniclers had to decide, usually without consciously thinking about it, what status to grant the sounds and gestures made by newly discovered peoples. To us it may seem arrogant that they had this power, but it was part of the whole complex of attitudes that Europeans brought with them. We must remember that it was somewhat reciprocal, too. The indigenous had their views of the invaders, but their views were less documented. To us it may also seem obvious that other populations communicated among themselves in language, even though no one had constructed grammars of those languages. Upon first contact this was not so obvious. Europeans confronted many issues at once, unaware of the manifold implications of their attitudes. Should unfamiliar languages be considered languages at all, or only inferior forms of barely articulate communication? Did the putatively superior knowledge and languages of European intruders give them, as some seemed to suppose, ready insight into the ideas of the natives? Should new languages be learned, replaced, or conveniently circumvented through the use of informants and interpreters? Were words in the native languages roughly equivalent to the words and corresponding concepts in European languages, including Christian doctrines? Could languages be recorded using European characters? Would their structures lend themselves to description in Latin-based grammatical terms, or indeed in any?

Columbus set the course in responding to many of these questions, not because he had brilliant insights, but because a first discoverer could hardly help reveal the patterns that his fellow explorers would follow. Columbus took with him a man who spoke many languages, but Columbus's sense of linguistic sufficiency stretched oddly between two poles. He wrote that his own words failed to express the wonder of the Indies, but he had implicit confidence in his ability to discern the content of native utterances. He often treated these utterances as transparent media, a set of signs he already knew how to interpret. The natives seemed to say what he wanted them to. He showed not the slightest uncertainty at first: "I made signs to them asking what they [their old wounds] were; and they showed me how people from other islands nearby came there and tried to take them, and how they defended themselves." Or: "We understood that they were asking us if we had come from the heavens. And one man . . . called to all the men and women: Come see the men who came from the heavens."[7] He listened for sounds that had special meaning. *Cybao* must be *Cipango*, or Japan (Columbus, 285). *Cami* must mean *Kahn* (Columbus, 125). In other matters where he had no expectations, he viewed the natives as empty linguistic vessels the Spanish could fill: "They should be good and intelligent servants, for I see that they say very quickly everything that is said to them" (Columbus, 69). Their docility would become a commonplace.

Initially, he transformed even his ignorance into a deficiency in the natives: "I do not give much credit to what they say, from not understanding them well and also from recognizing that they are so poor in gold" (Columbus, 103). Notice that the act of not crediting an utterance implies that one already understands it. That which Columbus didn't understand merely fueled his suspicions, and his suspicions were confirmed by the natives' lack of gold, which here meant two things. It meant that since the Indians had no gold, their directions as to where to find it must be doubted; it also meant that they lacked authority generally. Only after repeated disappointments in his quest for gold did Columbus acknowledge ignorance and seek for remedies. Needing results desperately, Columbus wished for priests who could learn the language. This was imperative: "nothing is lacking except to know the language and to give them orders" (Columbus, 259).

Alternatively, Columbus wanted to capture some of the natives and convey them to Spain, "so that they might learn our language and in order to know what there is in that land, and so that, returning, they might be interpreters for the Christians, and so that they would take on our customs and faith" (Columbus, 143). This tumbling passage prefigured much of the linguistic activity of the conquest: circumvent the language barrier by training informants and supplant native languages by teaching Spanish, all in order to gain information and to convert. Someone, though, would have to speak two languages.

Learning two languages opened a floodgate of other motives. Some wanted only to be correct in their statements about the inhabitants. Translators and grammarians wanted to preserve exotic languages in their true forms. Those who attempted to trace the origins of the Indians used word comparisons to ascertain from which parts of the world Indian ancestors traveled to the Americas. The consequences for the European masters were not dire, but in matters of greater scope, both the dominated indigenous peoples and the dominating Europeans recognized the high cost of misunderstanding. Those who suspected native languages of being devilishly contaminated found themselves in the interesting position of having to learn Indian languages and mores so they could eradicate, not ignorantly preserve, heathen practices. Diego de Durán, who is said to have penetrated the Aztec mind better than any other historian of the sixteenth century, wanted above all to destroy the ancient folk religion of Mexico; he found that doing so required an understanding achievable only through language.[8]

Others were far more sympathetic to the natives. Even though they wanted ultimately to replace non-Christian practices with Christian, they perceived that the Christianity they promoted required a certain type of disposition toward the people and a respect for native customs and viewpoints. In the *Historia eclesiástica indiana*, Geronimo de Mendieta described the encounter between Juan de Tecto, one of the first Christian priests in Central Mexico, and the larger group that arrived after Cortés' victory:

> When the twelve missionaries arrived in 1524 and saw that the temples and idols still stood and that the Indians still used their idols and sacrifices, they asked Friar Juan de Tecto and his companions what they were doing and in what light they understood it. To which Friar Juan de Tecto replied, "We learn that theology which Saint Augustine completely ignored," calling *theology* the language of the Indians, and giving them to understand the great benefits to be derived from knowing it.[9]

Many indigenous temples would be destroyed, and often Christian churches would be built where the temples had stood. Some missionaries wanted to achieve the linguistic equivalent of this destruction, yet those of de Tecto's persuasion recognized a higher way, a much more subtle and respectful process requiring them to learn languages intimately and use them not only as a tool of administration but a source of deep understanding.

José de Acosta's *Natural and Moral History of the Indies* (1590) grieved the damage done by those who lacked concern for the discourse of the native peoples: "We ... enter by the sword, without hearing or understanding; persuading ourselves that the Indians' affairs deserve no other respect, but as of venison that is taken in the forest, and brought for our use and delight." Acosta devoted chapters to "confute that false opinion many do hold of them, that they are a gross and brutish people."[10] He and many others recognized that lack of understanding inhibited clear and effective teaching of Christian doctrine and that to explain one's thoughts to others, one must know something of their thoughts as well. Acosta believed that "having knowledge of the Indians' customs, we may help them more easily to follow and persevere in the high vocation of the gospel." He continued, "The ignorance of laws and customs hath bred many errors of great importance. ... And besides the wrong which is done unto them against reason, it is prejudicial and hurtful unto ourselves, for thereby they take occasion to abhor us, as men both in good and evil always contrary to them."[11] His is a pointed appeal: ignorance creates enemies of those who would otherwise be friends. The kind of understanding Acosta encouraged required not only a grasp of words and syntactical structures, but of the subtle contexts that conditioned their use and interpretation.

Something as simple as place names posed a problem. Colonizers recognized that the territories they traversed were not culturally empty spaces but already had names that they should learn. As Garcilaso de le Vega amusingly noted, many explorers got the names wrong. Soldiers in the Andes captured a man to inquire where they were:

> Having petted him to help him overcome his fear at the sight of their beards and unaccustomed clothes, the Spaniards asked him by signs and words what land it was and what it was called. The Indian understood that they were asking him something from the gestures and grimaces they were making ... but he did not understand what they were asking, so he told them what he thought they wanted to know. Thus fearing they might do him harm, he quickly replied by giving his own name, saying, "*Berú*," and adding another, "*pelú*." He meant: "If you're asking my name, I'm called *Berú*, and if you're asking where I was, I was in a river." The word *pelú* is a noun in the language of that province and means "a river" in general. ... The Christians understood what they wanted to understand ... and from that time, which was 1515 or 1516, they called that rich

and great empire *Peru*, corrupting both words, as the Spaniards corrupt almost all the words they take from the Indian language of that land.[12]

Garcilaso adds another case taken from Gómara's *Historia general de las Indias*. Soldiers in one location asked a native for the place name. He replied, in his own language, "'*Tectetán*,' meaning, 'I don't understand you.' The Spaniards thought that it was the name of the place, and corrupting the word, always called it *Yucatán*, a name that will never cease to be used."[13]

The name Yucatán, from *Tectetán*, or "I don't understand you," is an appropriate place name to be used by soldiers who assumed that the men who answered their question were providing them with a place name. Those in similar situations always risked closure before understanding had actually been reached. Reaching that understanding implies a grasp not only of words but of the contexts in which words have meaning. It implies communicators' freedom to compare and disrupt each other's views until they can sort out what they share and what is truly foreign in each other. Real understanding presumes the freedom to inquire and respond among equals, a condition that rarely held when military or religious soldiers confronted the people they had invaded. Even in the condition of superiors and sub-alterns, however, the study of language made it possible for colonizers to move toward understanding.

The transition I am describing is, again, one that takes the colonizer from containing the indigenous language to discovering what language contains. Among those who best perceived this dichotomy were native inhabitants schooled by Europeans, who then reflected on the European perceptions of their people. Garcilaso de la Vega is a good example. Born in 1528 to a Peruvian mother and Spanish soldier father, Garcilaso wrote his *Royal Commentaries of the Incas* to amplify and correct the perceptions of Inca history and customs he found in the books being published in Spain.

Garcilaso explained that an early interpreter even butchered the concept of the trinity by translating it into the Inca language not as three in one, but as "God three and one make four." In another passage he detailed the many meanings possible for Inca words depending on pronunciation and context and then explained the distortions in Spanish versions. Garcilaso also explained grammatical features that many Spaniards hadn't grasped and that led to poor translation or, at the very least, laughable expression. The Incas differentiated familial terms not only by relationship (brother, sister, etc.) but by the gender of the speaker, so that a boy used a different word for "sister" than did a girl. Garcilaso cited Spanish teachers of the Inca language who mistook words because they could not differentiate between sounds that did not exist in their own language. The Spanish missed many opportunities to communicate their own beliefs effectively. They scorned what they supposed to be devil-inspired Inca beliefs that paralleled Christian truths but which were not in fact valid Inca beliefs. And they failed to comprehend the many features of Inca language and customs they could have deployed to convert the Andeans to Christianity. Here we see that the effective use of language required truer comprehension of the contexts that influenced meaning. Not surprisingly, Garcilaso gave eloquent but practical justification for maintaining the general language and not supplanting it with Spanish.[14]

A thorough understanding of the languages of the indigenous, upon which admiration for their own traditions of learning and communication grew up, often required the type of serious language study that only grammars and extensive lexicons made possible. For example, Donald Lach records that the first generation of Augustinian missionaries in the Philippines achieved little expertise in the Bisayan language, with the exception of Friar Martin de Rada who quickly learned both Bisayan and Chinese. "Systematic study of the native tongues did not begin until the Franciscans decided to prepare a Tagalog catechism, grammar, and dictionary in 1580. Friar Juan de Plasencia, who was taught Tagalog by a Spanish boy born in the islands, was delegated to undertake this task."[15] In response to a question he must have often heard asked, Why intersperse so much grammar in his "arte" or rules for speaking? Ludovico Bertonio, in *Arte y gramática . . . de la lengua aymara*, answered:

> We have seen many of those who thought they had achieved skill in the language, merely from knowing how to decline nouns and mastering quickly some verb conjugations, and learning every day a few vocabulary words, yet they really mastered so little because they failed to interest themselves in the precepts and principles. They didn't know how to explain their ideas, nor say what they wanted to say. They left much in doubt, whereof the damage would be but little if it were only a matter of knowing or not knowing the language, but there followed from that fact great damage to the souls over whom they had a charge to convey the doctrines.[16]

From Bertonio's concern, it is only a short step to respecting indigenous political rights. Domingo de Santo Tomás, author of the first grammar of an American language and admirer of the unique beauties of Quechua, also argued, more directly and insistently than it would be possible for the indigenous chronicler Guaman Pomo de Ayala to do, that the Spanish masters should restore the rights of the Andean lords to govern their own people, believing that they would rule more effectively and profitably than the Spaniards could. Santo Tomás proposed that the Council of the Indies prohibit all encomiendas (plantations and other enterprises based on indigenous bond or slave labor) and Spanish settlements. After publishing his grammar, Santo Tomás returned to Peru with authorization from the Council to convene the native lords to consult over the future of their lands and nations.[17] The grammar writer stood up for the rights of the indigenous people. Publishing his grammar in Spain gave him the opportunity to do so.

Somewhere between the extremes of forceful constraint and true mutual communication are countless instances in which communication was at once necessary and resisted. In these cases a pattern of great interest to the development of language thought emerged. The process of bringing new kinds of failure into consciousness was central to the development of language attitudes and language knowledge. The causes of this liberalizing shift—and I want stress that the shift didn't always take place and, when it did, wasn't always thorough or transforming—are matters for profound speculation. The causes seem to lie both within every language's seemingly infinite ability to foster thought and communication and in living languages' role as metonymic of living humans, who always impose an ethical demand, no matter how that demand is answered, denied, or ignored. Not always did grammar contain an ethics, but there is a worn path from the one to the other.

Sahagún and the Insufficiency of Motive

Missionary linguistic studies were often characterized by a balance of sympathetic penetration and a desire to be thorough and accurate. They were also characterized by goal displacement. That is, their grammars and dictionaries led missionaries more clearly to perceive, then to admire and love, the character and customs of the people they served. Their studies then took on a self-justifying quality that transcended practical motives. Fray Bernardino de Sahagún is one of the best instances of this change. He set out to produce books that would contain the language and beliefs of the people of Central Mexico and wound up consumed by the virtues of both the language and the people.

When Tenochtitlan (now Mexico City) fell to Cortés on August 13, 1521, an entire civilization came under Cortés's control. Eventually Spanish rule included the area from the Yucatán to what is now the southwestern United States. Missionaries faced a daunting linguistic challenge. Initially, the few priests who accompanied Cortés used a combination of pictures, interpreters, and memorized sermons to preach. With these rudimentary means they converted large numbers of the Mexica and soon begged for more missionaries to carry on the work. The first group of twelve Franciscan missionaries, often referred to as the twelve apostles, arrived in Mexico in 1524. They and their followers established missions northwest of present-day Mexico City and eventually became the most productive linguists of the three orders, partly because the peoples in their area spoke no less than ten languages. The Dominicans arrived in 1526 and occupied an area south of Mexico City. They had only four languages to contend with, but even this number created a challenge. The Augustinians arrived in 1533 and established an area between the Franciscans and Dominicans, east of Mexico City, where ten languages were spoken.[18] Although later clerical authorities would emphasize teaching Spanish as well as mastering the native languages, or would even consider restricting gospel instruction to Spanish, there was no question in the minds of the original twelve and following groups that they must preach in the languages of the natives. The vast area contained seven or eight culturally distinct regions and several hundred languages.

Robert Ricard lists a few of the languages the Franciscans encountered in the area they evangelized. Besides Nahuatl,

> other languages were still very much alive: Huastec and Totonac on the shores of the Gulf of Mexico; in the west, Tarascan; the languages of independent territories were even more flourishing. The charms of Tarascan are frequently boasted of. These were the principal languages, but there were many others, spoken by small numbers of people, such as Pirinda or Matlaltzinca, in the Valley of Toluca and at Charo (Michoacán); Popolloca, spoken by some natives of the present states of Puebla, Guerrero, and Oaxaca. . . . But the obstacle was very great, because it was necessary to know at least five or six languages, not, of course, for every missionary, but for the Order in general, and because all these languages were extremely difficult. (Ricard, 25)

Other languages of Mexico included Zapotec, Mixtec, Chontal, Otomí, Chichimec, Tlalpanec, and Ocuiltec (Ricard, 47). The Franciscans, Augustinians, and Dominicans threw themselves into the task. Ricard counts 109 grammars, vocabularies, and doctrines written between 1524 and 1572, considering this only a preliminary figure (Ricard, 48). It is worth noting that grammars of some of these native languages were written before any had appeared for English and Dutch.[19]

Well into the sixteenth century, crown policy favored the teaching of Spanish in the belief that Indian languages were either too numerous or were inadequate for the expression of Christian doctrine, but in actuality the policy had little effect: instead missionaries took the most expedient route to communicate their teachings. The existence of a general language offered an alternative. Nahuatl was spoken in most areas. In 1550, Charles V declared that Spanish must be taught throughout New Spain. In response, Fray Rodrigo de la Cruz wrote: "It seems to me that Your Majesty should order that all the Indians learn the Mexican language, for in every village today there are many Indians who know it and learn it easily, and a very great number who confess in that language. It is an extremely elegant language, as elegant as any in the world."[20] A general language such as Nahuatl could reduce the need to learn many languages and also assist in uniting the various indigenous groups into something approaching one people speaking one language. This tack of course had far-reaching consequences on the cultural integrity of the various tribes and clans who were made to learn Nahuatl, but such considerations fell low among the priorities of missionaries who saw their first task as conversion.

Because the linguistic efforts of sixteenth-century missionaries could occupy a book, I will dwell on one figure, Fray Bernardino de Sahagún, a Franciscan who arrived in New Spain in 1529, just five years after the first twelve, and who spent over sixty years there, until his death in 1590. Much of his life he devoted to the study of Nahuatl so that other friars could more expertly teach the indigenous people. Sahagún, not a minor figure to students of the conquest, figures prominently in Todorov's *The Conquest of America*, Ricard's *The Spiritual Conquest of Mexico*, and several biographies and full-length studies. With the benefit of these materials I will show that Sahagún's legendary mastery and meticulous documentation of Nahuatl language and customs were motivated partly by his fear that the language shielded enormous amounts of idolatry from view—unless one knew it intimately. Only by knowing the language in the context of its actual use in indigenous history, myth, and theology, he came to believe, could missionaries recognize and then eradicate the non-Christian practices that converts still observed.

Sahagún approached his linguistic task guided by concepts of cover, penetration, and attachment. The Nahuatl tongue covered up Aztec idolatry, which was subtly attached to the spoken words. To reveal the language required discovering and penetrating and, eventually, detaching the language from the idolatrous ingredients that could be identified. However, Sahagún's laborious gathering, recording, revising, and promoting of his work went beyond what his stated purposes required. They had to, given the interplay of language and his purposes. Initially, two goals seem to have guided Sahagún's efforts. First and most important, Sahagún wanted to bring to light, and thereby to enable the priests to suppress, all the vestiges of the "evil and imponderable" religion of the Aztecs (*FC*, 45). "To preach against these matters, and even to know if they exist, it is needful to know how they practiced them in the times of their idolatry, for, through [our] lack of knowledge of this, they perform many idolatrous things in our presence without our understanding it" (*FC*, 58). As ancient pagans hid their places of worship in cave, forest, and thicket, the Mexicans hid theirs in songs, psalms, and other apparently innocent practices. Sagahún seemed especially concerned that apparently Christian observances had become shields for ancient religion. Only priests who knew the language and were aware of how religion and language were interwoven could educate the people as to this type of mixing and thus excise the pagan from the Christian (*FC*, 91–92).

Even his material that focused on Aztec gods and rituals—the material most germane to his missionary purpose—would fail to prepare other friars to perceive latent idolatry unless they were as intimately acquainted with Nahuatl as Sahagún was. Ultimately then, Sahagun's fierce commitment to a knowledge of Nahuatl transcended utility. For him the cure for the Aztecs' spiritual problems was not simple translation, not fluency, not even a priestly knack for sniffing out vestigial paganism. It was a familiarity with their way of thinking so intimate and contextual that it exceeded the utilitarian service it was to perform. It was a cure that, as some of his fellow friars recognized, was meant to treat the causes of spiritual illness but risked becoming part of the disease.

Yet Sahagún had a second motive, one that made him a reverse missionary. He believed that the language and culture of the Aztecs comprised a monumental human achievement. This never fully distracted him from his objectives as a Christianizing missionary, but his deep respect for the Aztecs' devotion and civic discipline certainly complicated those objectives. Sahagún was deeply concerned that the conquest had destroyed the Aztecs' noblest traits and that conversion had failed to reclaim, much less increase, their discipline. He insisted that his work would help others "learn the degree of perfection of the Mexican people, which has not yet been known." Resorting to a biblical parallel, Sahagún explained that the Aztecs fulfilled again the prophecy of Jeremiah. Likening the Mexicans to the Judeans and the Spaniards to their enemies, he recited Jeremiah:

I will bring against you a people from afar, a very vigorous and brave people, a very ancient people skillful in battle, a people whose language ye will not understand, nor hast thou ever heard their manner of speech, all powerful and courageous people, lusting to kill. This people will destroy you and your women and children and everything ye possess, and will destroy your villages and your buildings. (*FC*, 47)

Sahagún added, "This has literally happened to these Indians by way of the Spaniards. . . . Thus they are considered as barbarians, as a people at the lowest level of perfection, when in reality (excluding some injustices their mode of governance contained) in matters of good conduct they surpass many other nations which have great confidence in their administrations." Note that if the Aztecs take the place of ancient Israel here, we are required to see Spain as another Babylon or Egypt. In another place Sahagún concluded that whatever their errors of the past, the natives showed themselves able in all crafts, quick to learn the liberal arts, and brave in warfare. "How strong they are in enduring the hardships of hunger, thirst, cold and sleeplessness! How willing and ready they are to undertake all kinds of dangerous missions! They are no less capable of our Christianity" (*FC*, 50).

Learning the indigenous languages therefore entailed far more than making dictionaries and grammars. Some of Sahagún's peers heard of his work and expected a dictionary. Certainly a dictionary would be beneficial, he exclaimed, but before a dictionary must come the groundwork that would inform words with "their meanings, their equivocals and metaphors" (*FC* Intro, 50).[21] Only by starting with what their language contained, recording the beliefs of the people in their own words and signs, could the friars hope to acquire sufficient mastery of the language to solve the problem of adaptation and assimilation. Only this preparation would allow the missionaries to express Christian principles in the people's own language so they would be properly understood, a process at once necessary and dangerous. As noted earlier, if Spanish or Latin terminology were introduced to give names to new teachings, the teachings would often remain sterile concepts learned by rote because the learners lacked any prior understanding of the practices, myths, and values that gave the concepts impact in daily life. Yet any effort to use native words and their connotations to vivify new teachings faced a complementary risk: that doctrines could be so strongly associated with Indian rituals, religious customs, and myths that they lost purity and became assimilated only as variations of former beliefs. Missionaries especially feared that Indians would outwardly follow Christianity yet covertly hold to idolatrous beliefs and customs. They similarly feared that Indians would adopt Christianity in a form so confused and syncretized that their faith would contain more heresy than truth.

Ricard notes that the missionaries usually "respected native languages" and "respected all the usages of current life which struck them as having no bearing on religion" (Ricard, 36). Yet they recognized the dangers of adaptation and compromise, especially when shallow understanding of the target language could "breed confusions and erroneous notions in the spirits of the natives" (Ricard, 34). As a result of these concerns, linguistic policy often shifted. New Spain's Royal Audience, a judicial body, gave a charge to Friar Andrés de Olmos in 1533. He was to "retrieve into a book the ancient ways of these native Indians, particularly of Mexico, Texcoco, and Tlaxcalla, that some memory might remain thereof, that the evil and imponderable might be refuted more easily, and if anything good were found, that it might be noted, just as are noted and held in memory many good things of other gentiles."[22] Olmos was to contain the language and contain the possible damage of contamination.

During the time Sahagún worked, the first Mexican synod, concerned that sermons and doctrines already translated into local tongues might inaccurately convey gospel teachings to the natives, asked that all such works be pulled out of circulation until their accuracy could be verified or until they could be replaced by more accurate renderings. It was in this atmosphere of desire for knowledge and the suspicion of its contamination that Sahagún accomplished his extraordinary work. Inspired by the work of two brothers of his order who came with the original twelve and encouraged by his provincial (the chief friar of his order), Francisco de Toral, to gain expertise in the indigenous language and manners, Sahagún helped establish the College of Santa Cruz at Tlatelolco in 1536. There he assembled a group of informants to help perfect the teaching of Christianity in Nahuatl. So that they could perfect the sermons, Gospels, and catechisms being composed in Nahuatl, students at the College were taught Latin, over the objections of some colleagues who feared that this dangerous enterprise would "place them in danger of becoming heretics" by giving them direct access to scripture and theology, from which they might derive erroneous views of Christian doctrine and practice. Some worried that they might learn that Jehovah had sanctioned polygamy, for example. Sahagún's response reminds us that in many ways he and his brother friars were venturing into the unknown: by teaching the natives Latin, he answered, the missionaries would know "how far their capabilities might be expanded" and from there know "what would seem to be just, as nearly as possible" (*FC*, 83).

In the late 1540s Sahagún, back in Tlatelolco after fulfilling assignments elsewhere, began to interest himself in the Indian "no longer just as a catechumen, but also for the culture and historic past of his people."[23] Working first with questions and answers on specific topics, he expanded his project to a treatise and eventually to a twelve-book compendium of Aztec knowledge and customs in three parallel columns, one in Aztec glyphs, one in Nahuatl alphabetized with Roman characters, and one in

Spanish. His interest would become an obsession and would position him curiously and often precariously in relation to his fellow friars, leaders of his order, and the crown itself. His passion made him part zealot—a zealot in constructing a knowledge of idolatry when Motolinía and other experienced brothers considered the preoccupation with paganism and superstition more harmful than were their traces among the population—and part heretic in pursuing his studies in direct disobedience to his superiors.

The Franciscans, among the more progressive and sympathetic to indigenous cultures, saw immediately that native conversion hinged on missionaries' thorough acquisition of native languages. Sahagún's initial charge to record as much as he could of the Mexican languages and customs came from his provincial, Toral. In 1558 the newly elected provincial again encouraged Sahagún to write what seemed to be useful in the Mexican language. Yet such official support depended to a large extent on the current leadership of the order in Mexico and the tides of opinion among the friars. By 1569 the last of the twelve original friars had died, and the chapter cooled toward Sahagún. When Sahagún tried to circumvent the chapter and appeal to the Pope, his superiors interpreted this as rebellion and scattered his books around the province. The Commissary General, Navarro, arrived in New Spain and favored Sahagún's type of work and encouraged its continuation. Ironically, the scattering had allowed others of the religious orders to become acquainted with his cause. Sahagún's works were again gathered. The decade of the 1570s marks the most turbulent in the changes of official policy toward the study of indigenous cultures. To understand the currents of support and opposition we must remember that debates on such matters occurred among the religious as well as the secular leadership in both Spain and New Spain and that parallel lines of communication were often employed simultaneously to influence policy. At the urging of Juan de Ovando, president of the Council of the Indies, King Philip II issued a *cédula* in which he asked for "moral histories" of the natives, including "the different languages they had; the kind of government and operation of temporal government matters; their religion and worship, the people who taught it and their method, and everything concerning their religion."[24] In 1575 a new Commissary General, de Sequera, who had grown up in Granada and had seen the result of animosity toward the Moors, wanted extracts of important work such as that of Sahagún made so that church and crown leaders in Spain could see and reward the works. This was the year Ovando died; soon after, the Office of the Holy Inquisition was installed in New Spain, and the measures of the Council of Trent, meeting since 1545, were applied there also. Among other measures, the Council of Trent imposed a severe limit on the translation of scripture into vulgar tongues. In 1576 the Holy

Office in New Spain prohibited the recording of any ecclesiastical manual or scripture in any indigenous language. The next year Philip II ordered all originals and copies of books on indigenous customs and religion to be collected at once and sent under guard to the Council of the Indies. The fact that Sahagún's work survived at all is partly owing to Sequera's insistence on carrying a copy with him back to Spain in 1580, even after the crown had reissued orders to confiscate all such work.[25]

Enthusiasm for Nahuatl and antipagan zeal drove Sahagún to explore indigenous culture even more fully. Sahagún felt compelled to survey the culture as widely as possible to catch every fruit that Satan's work yielded in every facet of the otherwise extraordinarily virtuous lives of the Aztecs. Yet in his accounts of Aztec gods and ceremonies, one strains to find the subtle contamination to which Sahagún kept referring. In fact, while the straightforward ethnographic material comes across as authoritative, Sahagún is much less convincing when he gives examples of old idolatries hiding among Christian rituals. In the prologue to the *General History of the Things of New Spain* Book XI, *Earthly Things*, Sahagún described places and rituals he feared might still have pagan significance to the local people. The Franciscans built a Church of Santa Ana near a place where the Aztecs revered one of their gods, *Toci*, which means *Our Grandmother*. Having been told that Santa Ana was the grandmother of Jesus and therefore "our grandmother," the natives would travel some distance to attend feasts there "on the pretext of Saint Ann." "But since," he complained, "the word is ambiguous, and they respect the olden ways, it is believable that they come more for the ancient than for the modern" (*FC*, 90–91). What are we to make of this? If the missionaries chose to build churches on sites formerly sacred to the people (a common practice), and if they themselves chose analogs between old and new religions to reinforce the new faith, the indigenous would always be chargeable with paganism, but the fault lay more with the missionaries who unwisely exploited parallels in the two spiritual frameworks from the start.

Perhaps related to this complex of motives, we can see an additional contradiction in Sahagún's career study, one that still has ramifications for students of language. It involves the mutual impregnation of language and all we refer to as culture. Sahagún only partly accepted the idea of language as culture. He didn't use this term, of course, but he did raise the issue. He accepted the link between language and culture insofar as he believed that missionaries must, to know the language, know all that a simple dictionary could not convey: the associations, connotations, histories, figures, and contextual meanings. To know the natives' language was to fathom their knowledge, their rituals, their past, their greatness. And Sahagún saw the network of language and all these other factors as partial cause of their greatness, discipline, and civic virtue. Yet in wanting to control the language for the use of Christianizing, Sahagún wanted to sever it from the full range of the contextual belief system, including the Aztec religion. His ultimate goal, excision and detachment, implies the manipulation of language to exclude the context that gives it meaning. In this he perceived a clear breach between language and culture. His later despair over the prospects for fully converting the Aztecs, for restoring their greatness and nobility but on Christian terms, might be read as an indication that once the cultural substructure had crumbled, something vital to the language had disappeared, too. The difficulties reached as far as conversion of the soul. To bring the people to believe truly, the priest had to take them as they were, to link their desire to believe to things they believed in, such as their desires to please the gods and live properly. In reinforcing Christian with indigenous beliefs, missionaries planted the seeds of contamination and thus made it hard to distinguish pure from impure conversion. No wonder his colleagues had qualms about his work.

Sahagún began his project with great confidence in the thorough conversion of the Mexicans. The fact that his confidence waned as the project expanded gives an additional azimuth by which to triangulate his motives. How does one explain the fact that the document in which he voiced his doubts most fully also celebrated the material on which he was working, and the fact that he promised still greater results if the church would only provide the support? Part of the answer I offer is that, once the process of containing language begins, it becomes itself contained and entangled in layer after layer and network upon network of word, idea, and context. While writing the *Colloquios y doctrina* in the mid 1560s, Sahagún applauded the great fervor and success of the first few years of his order in New Spain.[26] Yet in 1576, in the last drafts of the *General History*, Sahagún expressed deep misgivings about the endurance of the work of conversion. For fifty years the Spanish had preached Christianity to the Indian people. In the interim Sahagún had witnessed lassitude and backsliding which deepened his disappointment. He had begun with high hopes for an indigenous priesthood. Later he said, "From experience, we learned that, at the time, they were not capable of such perfection" (*FC*, 78). The mixing of heathen and Christian custom produced a "labyrinth of great difficulty" that became "almost hopeless to correct" (*FC*, 79).

Profound conversion was initially impeded by the missionaries' limited language skills. "Hardly ever did we gain the insight as we now have learned it" (*FC*, 79). Yet what benefits accrued from greater linguistic facility? Sahagún concluded sourly: "If they were now left alone, if the Spanish nation were not to intercede, I am certain that in less than fifty years there would be no trace of the preaching which has been done for them" (*FC*, 98). As in many parts of the Middle East where Christianity once prevailed and was now lost, New Spain was now a "sterile land and very laborious to cultivate, . . . and from little cause that which is planted and cultivated withers. It seems to be the Catholic Faith can endure little time in these parts" (*FC*, 93–94). One hope still sustained him: that at least Peru and New Spain might provide a staging ground where the gospel could "pass through and still be on the way in order to communicate with those peoples in the regions of China" (*FC*, 96). In his despair Sahagún didn't seem to realize that the dynamics of containment would play themselves out on new shores.

Sahagún's materials were so comprehensive and his methods so thorough that he has won high praise from today's scholars. His biographer wrote, "He is indeed foremost among the group of Franciscans who are partisans of a scientific and sympathetic study of the indigenous civilization. As he deepens his knowledge of the Indian people, Sahagún comes to be ever more sincerely influenced by them." And elsewhere:

> The Mexican language for Fray Bernardino was not just an indispensable vehicle for preaching, or a rampart against the Indian's contagion by the Spaniards. It was above all the object of a disinterested scientific and artistic study. The greatest token of admiration for a people is to learn their language, not with the utilitarian end of understanding and being understood, but rather with the design of working for its purity and preservation. This sincere homage was rendered by Sahagún to the Mexican people.[27]

I agree with the praise but disagree with its nature. Disinterested scientific study would be an alien concept to Sahagún. Rather, the conflicts among accurate and, to that extent, disinterested study, sympathetic absorption, an instrumental approach to language, and deep anxiety about what he was learning as a result of his study characterize his monumental project.

Sahagún also illustrates a further step in the trajectory I laid out at the beginning of this chapter. I said there that the prospect of failure drove colonizers and missionaries, each in different ways, to plunge into language study. Successful immersion for Sahagún was a return to failure in the larger mission of conversion. Yet in that immersion he achieved something quite remarkable—a love, a fascination, an admiration, a wonder, a desire, and an archival impulse for the sounds, the naming, the ambiguities that don't translate neatly from one sign system to another. Sahagún began creating his twelve-volume cultural labyrinth to achieve an identifiable purpose;

along the way it became its own fulfillment. He set out with a dream of containing and finished with a project that contained, changed, and limited his dream.

Linguistic Wonders of the World

Sahagún was but one of thousands to discover unexpected linguistic and moral virtues among other peoples. As European colonizers collected, catalogued, and penetrated diverse languages, they created a linguistic map that, like the *mappaemundi* and early travel literature, enchanted through its sheer weight of wonders. Perhaps the simplest form of admiration was the borrowing of new words. Sebastián de Covarrubias's *Tesoro de la lengua castellana o española* (1611), the first dictionary of Spanish, included twenty-three words of American origin, including *canoa*, or canoe, and *hamaca*, or hammock, *coca*, and *huracán*.[28] Lach calls this process of bringing exotic words into Europe a "rebabelization," but it reflected an awareness of differences in cultural products and practices as much as sheer novelty in words. By far the most new words came first into Portuguese and from there into French and Spanish. Italian incorporated words from its trader partners, but these lost circulation with Italy's gradual loss of trading interests in the East. Germany brought in non-European words from Spanish, Portuguese, and Italian. The English imported exotic words mostly from translated travel literature. Borrowed words fell mainly into the following classes: place names, geographical features, flora and fauna, and caste or social categories (Lach, 532–39). This passage from Lach captures the richness of Asian imports:

> Practices that were foreign to Europe, such as running "amock," were known only by their native names. For the caste names of India no European equivalents existed and so the native names ("Pariah," "Nāyar," "Chetty") were simply adopted. Words for conveyances that were unknown in Europe, or different in certain ways from their European analogues, were often known by their Asian names: "andor" (litter), "sampan," "jangada" (raft), "junk," "Lantea" (Chinese rowing vessel), "palanquin," "pangara" (small boat of India), and "dhoney." Names for secular administrators ("mandarin," "nabob," "naique," "rajah," "shabandar," "zamorin") as well as religious personages ("bonze" [Buddhist priest], "brahmin," "yogi") were adopted in many European languages. The names of Asian deities ("Shaka" [Buddha], Ganesha, Confucius) and religious buildings ("pagoda" and "varela" [Buddhist temple]) were all used after a time in European writings without explanation. Uniquely Asian products were

commonly referred to by their original names: "achar" (pickles), "areca" (palm seed,) "baju" (short jacket), "bamboo," "bhang" (Indian hemp), "coir," "calambec" (aloes-wood), "calico," "cha" (tea), "curry," "charao" (lacquerware), "saia" (root for red dye), "copra," "datura" (thorn-apple), "gingham," "hing" (asafetida), "jaggery" (palm sugar), "lac" (varnish), "litchi" (dried fruit), "mango," "ola" (palm leaf), "patola" (silk cloth), "kimono," "rota" (rattan), "sago" (palm starch), "zerumbit" (aromatic root). Commercial terms which became permanent additions to the European vocabulary were words such as "banian" (trader of Gujarat), "caixo" (cash), "chop" (seal), "chatinar" (to trade), "chit," "coolie," "fanani" (small coin of south India), "godown" (warehouse), "mangelim" (weight equal to a carat), "tanga" (a small coin of south India). Words which reflect the daily life and the intellectual and artistic advancement of the East are notable for their scarcity. But still there are a few that crept into the European languages at this period: "biombo" (Japanese folding screen), "boy" (servant), "catana" (large Japanese broadsword), "catel" (cot), "lacai" (lacquerware), "pundit," "tank" (place of ceremonial bathing in India). (Lach, 532–33)

Linguistic admiration usually extended beyond words to the structures and artifices. The English Jesuit Thomas Stevens arrived at Goa in 1579 and became ecstatic over the Marāthī language of India, whose "phrases and constructions are of a wonderful kind." He wrote a grammar of Konkani and composed poetry in that dialect. "Like a jewel among pebbles, like a sapphire among jewels, is the excellence of the Marāthī tongue. Like the jasmine among blossoms . . . is Marāthī among languages," he wrote.[29] Pedro Chirino's *Relación de las Islas Filipinas i de lo que in ellas añ trabajado* (1604) includes a chapter titled, "De las lenguas de las Filipinas" in which he most admires the Bisayan language. It has qualities of "the four best languages of the world, Hebrew, Greek, Latin, and Spanish" as follows, "From Hebrew, the mysteries and the fecundity. From Greek, the articles and distinctions, and not only in appellative nouns but also in the proper. From Latin, copiousness and elegance. And from Spanish, good breeding, restraint, and courtesy."[30] He gave the Ave Maria in Spanish and Bisayan to demonstrate their qualities and then, for contrast, curiously presents the same prayer in the "Haraya" tongue, as if a reader could tell from the transcription that it and the other tongues are cruder and harsher (Chirino, 36). He intended not to offend but to show the "idiomatic expressions of these languages,"[31] even though "each one, for its natives, has its beauty, its elegance, which may not shine through for strangers" (Chirino, 34, 36).[32]

The Japanese language gained many ardent admirers. Lourenço Mexia, a Jesuit who worked in both Japan and China, esteemed Japanese as superior to Greek and Latin in its solemnity and expressive fullness and added:

"Then there is another thing which I do not think is to be found in any other language—that a person learns rhetoric and good breeding along with the language, for nobody can know Japanese without knowing how he must address the great and lowly, the nobles and commoners, and the decorum to be observed with them all, for they have special verbs, nouns, and ways of speaking for the one class and the other."[33] Luis de Guzman also believed Japanese surpassed Greek and Latin in its copious vocabulary and forms of courtesy.[34] Allesandro Valignano, another Jesuit, reported the following from Japan:

> They have but one language and it is the best, the most elegant and the most copious tongue in the world; it is more abundant than Latin and expresses concepts better. As well as possessing a great variety of synonyms, it also has a kind of natural elegance and dignity: and so you may not use the same nouns and verbs when talking with different people about diverse topics, but you must employ polite or common words, honorific or depreciative phrases according to the rank of the person and the subject of conversation. The written and spoken languages are very different, and men and women also differ in their way of speaking.[35]

Father João Rodriguez spoke similarly and at much greater length in his *Arte da lingoa de Japam.*

Gabriel Magalhães waxed enthusiastic over Chinese, which from three hundred and twenty root monosyllables could nearly "form a perfect Language." The syllable *po*, for example, "taken after eleven several manners, makes eleven several words," including noun, pronoun, adjective, adverb, participle, and verb forms. He also found Chinese easier to learn than Greek, Latin, or any other European language.[36] Some of the bases for admiring Chinese and Japanese have proven fallacious. For example, Semedo, Magalhães, and other early students of Chinese thought it an extremely simple language because its words were not inflected and could serve as nouns, verbs, and adjectives. However, they failed to notice or to tell their readers that particles, word order, and the combining of single-syllable words into more complex units made Chinese as complex as other languages.[37] Certain characters given by Semedo as examples of Chinese writing were printed incorrectly and then copied in book after book on China.[38] Regardless of these mistakes or the correctness of their assessments, all these early workers in the cultural contact zone were lending their authority to the idea that vastly different structures for organizing and expressing thought could lead to levels of excellence as high as one's ability to perceive and describe.

The study of other languages began with attention to sounds, then vocabulary lists, then grammars, then ethnographic surveys of individual populations. From there it proceeded to universal grammars and philosophical inquiries into the relations between cognition and language. Spatial concepts link these studies. Vocabularies, standard in cosmographies of the sixteenth and seventeenth centuries, quite naturally listed words as features of lands, along with geographical and biological information. Other types of collections were of course strongly linked with geography. In about 1430 Johann Schiltberger, who spent thirty-two years as a slave in Turkey, printed the Lord's Prayer in the languages of Turkey, Armenia, and Tartary and perhaps inadvertently established the tradition of using that text as a device for linguistic comparisons. In the early nineteenth century the last and most extensive of these collections appeared in J. C. Adelung's *Mithridates* (1806), with the Lord's Prayer in five hundred tongues (Lach, 503). Bernard von Breydenbach's *Journey* (1486) gave Europe its first glimpse in print at the alphabet of Ethiopia. John Mandeville's highly fanciful *Travels* contained a number of Asian alphabets, not all of them imaginary.[39] The German priest Johannes Potken published a psaltery in the Geez and Latin languages in 1513 (Lach, 510). A member of Vasco de Gama's first voyage, 1497–1499, compiled a list of 138 words in the Malayālam language of India. Vocabulary appeared in the 1516 publication, by Nebrija, of Peter Martyr's *De Orbe Novo*, an expanded version of the first chronicle of New World exploration, and became standard features of voyages. Antonio Pigafetta, who accompanied Magellan, included Malay, Bisayan, Tagalog, Brazilian, and Patagonian word lists in his *Voyage et navigation* of 1525. These lists found their way into the travel publications of Ramusio (1550), Eden (1555), and Purchas (1625) (Lach, 493). Don Alonso de Ercilla's epic poem of Peru, *La Araucana*, published in parts from 1569 to 1590, introduced many new words to its readers. Cosmographies or surveys like Thevet's *Cosmographie universelle* (1575) or Joannes de Laet's *History of the New World, or Description of the West Indies*, first published in 1625 in Dutch, routinely included vocabularies or sprinkled geographical, botanical, and demographic information with words from indigenous languages.

Polyglot dictionaries implicitly spoke of need for shortcuts to understanding diverse languages. Ambrogio Calepino's *Dictionum Latinarum e Graecarum* (1502) was successively enlarged from two languages to five, six, seven, eight, and eventually eleven by 1590. The century's expanding linguistic horizons are also seen in Megiser's *Thesaurus Polyglottus* of 1603, with an astounding four hundred languages represented by at least a few words. Donald Lach summarizes: Megiser "sought to assemble all the information available on ancient and contemporary languages according to their cognate and derivative affinities. In addition to six principal European groupings based on linguistic interrelationships, he postulates Asiatic, African, and American classifications" (Lach, 517). Catechisms, more challenging if narrower in scope than vocabularies, often followed word lists. It is interesting to note that within three years of the publication of the first grammar of Portuguese, that of Fernão de Oliveira in 1536, João de Barros composed a brief catechism and Portuguese primer that were translated into Tamil in 1542 and Japanese in 1549.

The worldwide work was an immense undertaking. In Spanish America, Alonso de la Molina, in *Vocabulario en lengua castellana y mexicana y mexicana y castellana* (1571), provided the first published treatment of Nahuatl. Ruiz de Montoya's *Tesoro de la lengua guarani* (1639) illustrated the importance of vocabulary to his grammar, which he published the next year in combination with the vocabulary. Robert Ricard counts a "minimum list" of 109 works in native languages published in Mexico alone between 1524 and 1572 (Ricard, 48). Angel Rubio lists 212 works dealing with New World languages in the sixteenth century and 250 in the seventeenth.[40]

The world of language yielded wonders as great in magnitude as the physical and demographic world.

From Sympathy to Self-Critique

We consider a language or discourse competent when it can represent another discourse in its own terms without severe distortion or reduction. Post-colonial studies have sensitized us to the degree to which European discourses swallowed up and silenced indigenous traditions all over the globe. By contrast, Europeans in the cultural contact zones often felt themselves swallowed up by indigenous languages and traditions. These people then adopted the indigenous discourse, showing its flexibility, its eloquence, its related social and political values, and ultimately its superiority. They showed that European discourse, together with its social and political values, could be contained within the foreign in such a way as to reveal the deep fractures and inhumanities in European culture. Their initial curiosity and love of a new language sprouted into cultural self-critique, or the loss of infatuation with their own society, ideas, manners, and values. This change happened because the act of getting close to another language, sometimes described as getting inside a culture or mind-set, figuratively puts distance between a person and his or her own culture, thus providing on the far side of that space a location from which to view one's customs with new perspective.

Sometimes curiosity began as a mere recording of the silences, cadences, tones, gestures, protocols, sighs, and groans of a territory's inhabitants. Those who took from this experience a motivation to study and understand their hosts' language were more likely to discover their own personal and cultural failures. Although there was no guarantee that those who sympathized with an alien host and came to criticize their fellow Europeans would always perceive either the host or their own customs correctly, they felt an impulse to complete the journey outward with journeys both inward and toward home. We see the pattern in the French Calvinist Jean de Léry, who spent part of 1557 and 1558 among the Tupinamba of Brazil in the vicinity of present-day Rio de Janeiro. He records an incident in which the sounds of language compelled him to sneak into a hut to observe a celebration from which, as an outsider, he had been excluded.

Léry's response to Tupi ceremonies offers the linguistic equivalent of the visual splendor of the New World. One morning he happened to be present when *caraïbes*, or sorcerers, were visiting the village:

> While we were having our breakfast . . . we began to hear in the men's house (not thirty feet from where we stood) a very low murmur, like the muttering of someone reciting his hours. Upon hearing this the women all stood up; and clustered together, listening intently. The men little by little raised their voices and were distinctly heard singing all together and repeating this syllable of exhortation, *He, he, he, he*; the women, to our amazement, answered them from their side, and with a trembling voice; reiterating that same interjection *He, he, he, he*, let out such cries, for more than a quarter of an hour, that as we watched them we were utterly disconcerted.[41]

Compelled by his curiosity, Léry sneaked into the men's hut and watched as they continued:

> When I was in the women's house, I had been somewhat afraid; now I received in recompense such joy, hearing the measured harmonies of such a multitude, and especially in the cadence and refrain of the song, when at every verse all of them would let their voices trail, saying *Heu, heuaure, herua, heuraure, heura, heura, oueh*—I stood there transported with delight. Whenever I remember it, my heart trembles, and it seems their voices are still in my ears. (Léry, 144)

Sheer sounds seemed to trigger this rapture. Though he was unaware of the meaning of the chanting, he felt a strong current of emotions and sensations. But in fact his rapture had many constituents. One was his desire for entry and participation in the ritual unity of the host society. Nominally barred from participation, he entered by stealth and so was both there and not there, just as linguistically he was present to the sounds but absent from their signification. The spiritual dimension and his keen desire to know whether the Tupinamba actually had a concept of God increased his interest.

Léry's *History of a Voyage to the Land of Brazil* is a milestone in the textual creation of a sympathy grounded in the attraction of another language even when that language is barely understood. His (for that time) unusual motive for visiting Brazil also prepared him to be open to linguistic pleasure. He came to Brazil not to conquer or convert, but to find a place where fellow French Huguenots might settle and escape the fierce religious persecutions that tore France in the late 1500s. To a degree not usual in soldiers and missionaries, he became attentive to the native people and passionately involved in their customs. Also, in observing the natives and their customs, he often saw critical implications for his own society, and this increased his sympathy for his hosts. Their forthrightness, bravery, and hospitality contrasted starkly with the deceit and cruelty he would, by the time he wrote his memoir, witness in France. Léry did not publish his journal for nearly twenty years, until after he witnessed the horrors of the St. Bartholomew's Day massacres, when Catholic forces laid siege to several French cities and butchered the Protestants who sought refuge there. Compared with these nightmares, Tupi cannibalism appeared humane. In many ways his experience served him in interpreting the continuing polemic between the Catholics and the Protestants. As a Protestant, Léry might even be said to have supplanted the Catholic fixation on ritual and priesthood hierarchy by a focus on the inner state. Léry gives to the indigenous language a deep response that is aesthetic yet social, religious yet detached from motives of dominion.

This detachment enabled him to view the Tupinamba as a reference point by which to criticize his own culture and the presence of Europeans in Brazil. He related an amusing episode in which the French witnessed a boat with thirty natives overturn in the ocean. The French sailors rushed out to sea in another vessel, only to find the natives "all swimming and laughing on the water" and asking, "and where are you going in such haste, you *Mairs* [Frenchmen]?" "We are coming to save you and pull you from the water," responded the French crew, whereupon the natives laughed again and said, "Do you think that just because we fell into the sea we are in danger of drowning? Without putting foot to ground, or touching land, we could remain a week on the surface, just as you see now" (Léry, 97). An interesting anecdote on its own, the story has added bite as a fable of European self-assurance and condescension among people who do not ask for, much less need, their assistance.

In a similar vein, Léry cited a passage in Gómara about a certain nation in Peru who, fearing that the bearded Spaniards roaming their country and looking "so swaggering and so foppish" would "corrupt and alter their ancient customs," referred to the outsiders as "seafoam, fatherless people, men without repose, who cannot stay in one place" (Léry, 103).[42] One Tupi man, upon hearing how hard the French would work to acquire wealth for their children, remarked,

> I see now that you *Mairs* (that is, Frenchmen) are great fools; must you labor so hard to cross the sea, on which (as you told us) you endured so many hardships, just to amass riches for your children or for those who will survive you? Will not the earth that nourishes you suffice to nourish them? (Léry, 102)

Léry reminds us that although the written record has favored Eurocentric views, the indigenous people of other parts of the world always had their discourses, their ways of representing, their humor, their enclosure of the outsiders. The enduring legacy of that recognition exists in the switch of perspective that contact with alien others has always produced.

One question of special interest to students of language arose from such contacts. To what extent did language also bestow the possibility of fraudulence and deception? If words did not relate in some intrinsic, non-arbitrary fashion to the things they named, they could still reveal the truth of fact and intention rather than mislead and conceal. The relations between language and falsehood being so complex, with ramifications at so many levels of discourse, the clearest way through the problem was not to think about it directly, but rather to embed the concern in narratives of encounter with non-Europeans, whether these narratives were based in fact or fantasy. Contact with other peoples and languages unleashed nostalgia and self-criticism—nostalgia for honest and complete communication, and self-criticism of the communicative practices that made deceit, manipulation, and all shades of misrepresentation so common in Europe, where society had developed elaborate strategies, categories, and protocols for lying.

Michel de Montaigne, who helped cut the channel in which the noble savage was to sail through Europe, portrays a culture of language that makes deceit difficult or unnecessary. Writing in the late sixteenth century when new lands and peoples were still being discovered and conquered, and when Spain was still sorting out the moral and political implications of possessing large tracts of America, Montaigne wanted Europeans to question their own standards of civilized behavior as they contemplated the cannibals: "We may well call these people barbarians, in respect to the rules of reason, but not in respect to ourselves, who surpass them in every kind of barbarity."[43] Montaigne depicted their dwellings, eating habits, warfare, religious practices, leisure activities, and treatment of prisoners to illustrate aspects of the cannibals' moral superiority. Language entered into the assessment:

> It seems to me that what we actually see in these nations surpasses not only all the pictures in which poets have idealized the golden age and all their inventions in imagining a happy state of man, but also the conceptions and the very desire of philosophy. . . . This is a nation . . . in which there is no sort of traffic, no knowledge of letters, no science of numbers, no name for magistrate, no riches or poverty, no contracts, no successions, no partitions, no occupations but leisure ones, no care for any but common kinship, no clothes, no agriculture, no metal, no use of wine or wheat. The very words that signify lying, treachery, dissimulation, avarice, envy, belittling, pardon—unheard of. (Montaigne, 153)

Notice that the near-paradise Montaigne found—or imagined—was partly a linguistic one. In pointing out that the Brazilians had no words for lying, treachery, dissimulation, and pardon, Montaigne linked language to moral cognition.

Part of the shock Montaigne must have generated in European readers came from the fact that these same Brazilian folks who had no guile also practiced cannibalism—an activity that Europeans placed completely outside the pale of social mores and ethics. How could European readers reconcile such innocence and transgressiveness? The apparent incompatibility accompanied the recognition of real otherness. That is, the incongruity remained beyond comprehension—until readers saw in themselves that same incompatibility. Notice how Montaigne turned the shock effect to rhetorical advantage. He described Tupi cannibalism but then added:

> I am not sorry that we notice the barbarous horror of such acts, but I am heartily sorry that, judging their faults rightly, we should be so blind to our own. I think there is more barbarity in eating a man alive than in eating him dead; and in tearing by tortures and the rack a body still full of feeling, in roasting a man bit by bit, in having him bitten and mangled by dogs and swine (as we have not only read but seen within fresh memory, not among ancient memories, but among neighbors and fellow citizens, and what is worse, on the pretext of piety and religion) than in roasting and eating him after he is dead. (Montaigne, 155)

Brazilian cannibals and European citizens had this in common, that they indulged in types of inhuman behavior that their principles and values should preclude.

Setting aside the question of the accuracy of the reports Montaigne read and of his summary of them,[44] we might ask whether the Tupinamba did not have words for lying because they never lied, or whether they couldn't lie because they had no words for naming the act. These have very different ramifications. The first implies that the Tupinamba comprised a different kind of human creature, one who had by nature no disposition to misrepresent or one who had been tempered, educated, and governed so that dissimulation, which language by its nature makes possible, never actualized. A second view—that they could not lie because they lacked words for fraudulent concepts and for lying itself—implies a kind of linguistic determinism: no term, no concept. If the limits of one's language are the limits of one's world, then among the Tupinamba, the lack of words for deceit meant there was no deceit. The two visions of why the Brazilians did not lie reflect two versions of containing. In the first, moral training contains (in the sense of limiting and bounding) fraudulence, which language always makes possible. In the second, language itself contains (again, in the sense of limiting and bounding) lying.

Montaigne implies that a limited language blesses humanity. In saying that virtue, peace, and harmony existed among a tribe who lacked letters, trade, and numbers, Montaigne implied that letters—the writing and printing upon which Europe prided itself and which made his reflections on Brazil possible—had enormous human costs. They had either sprung from, or helped cause, the decay of a golden state of civilization. Hand in hand, language and civilization had destroyed an Eden from which no fall had been necessary. Montaigne reflected in his study on the possible connection between European animosity and the amount of writing: "When write we ever so much as we have done since our intestine troubles?" The greatest civilizations of the past and present appeared to him to be precisely those instructed in the "disesteeme of letters. I find Rome to have been most valiant when it was least learned."[45]

The discovery or imagination of linguistic paradises revealed a deep uneasiness over the fact that language made it easy to deceive and that Europe seemed unable to regulate deception in step with its many other putative cultural advances. Indeed, some linguistic paradises directly linked fraudulent language to those supposed advances. In the late seventeenth century, Aphra Behn's *Oroonoko* depicted the Indians of Surinam as a people who used language minimally, as if Behn recognized the inherent links between the profusion of language and submission to language's power to deceive. When the Indians spoke, they did so only to communicate the truth: "And these People represented to me an absolute *Idea* of the first State of Innocence, before *Man* knew how to sin." Behn continued:

Religion wou'd here but destroy that Tranquillity they possess by Ignorance; and Laws wou'd but teach 'em to know Offence, of which now they have no Notion. They once made mourning and fasting for the Death of the *English* governor, who had given his Hand to come on such a day to 'em, and neither came nor sent; believing, when a Man's word was pat, nothing but Death cou'd or shou'd prevent his keeping it: And when they saw he was not dead, they ask'd him what Name they had for a Man who promis'd a thing he did not do? The Governor told them, Such a Man was a *Lyar*, which was a word of Infamy to a Gentle-man. Then one of 'em reply'd, *Governor, you are a Lyar, and guilty of that Infamy.* They have a native Justice, which knows no Fraud; and they understand no Vice, or Cunning, but when they are taught by *White* Men.[46]

Because Behn's Indians couldn't conceive the possibility of using language fraudulently, they also didn't differentiate between one who intentionally failed an obligation and one who was prevented from doing so. Behn's nar-rator, speaking with inside knowledge of European civilization, surely knew the difference. Nonetheless, she made a tidy distribution: white makes fraud. However, we can detect something missing in this distribution. Anyone deft enough to set the rhetorical trap into which the governor so eagerly stepped had a high potential to deceive. That is not to say they would deceive, but that they had the ability to do so. In *Oroonoko*, however, deceit is configured so that it thrives only in the world in which the narra-tor is an insider but not in the one to which she is an outsider. Knowledge is incompatible with exoticism.

Montaigne's cannibals, Behn's Africans and Indians, Swift's Brobding-nagians and Houyhnhnms, Montesquieu's Persians, and Diderot's Tahitians all inhabit linguistic paradises and demonstrate the pattern by which knowl-edge of an alien discourse, whether factual or fabricated, converts into self-criticism. Far more than any treatise, these narratives raised important and still unresolved questions about the relations between language and fraudulence.

Because I began the chapter with a reference to the Whorfian hypothesis, I will close by relating the question of what language contains to the question of linguistic relativism and determinism. Recent studies have demonstrated that language structures affect thinking patterns. However, they have done this by showing very slight differences in habitual responses to thinking problems, differences measured in milliseconds in response times or small variations in the amount of detail a person can remember from a scene. John Lucy, for example, studied the ways in which speakers of English and Maya responded to and recalled details in drawings they were shown.

English has more overt structures for marking the number of animate or inanimate objects, and English speakers had higher recognition and recall of the number of items in the drawings. Lucy's findings support a limited Whorfian hypothesis that focuses on the effect of grammatical structures on habitual thinking patterns.[47] However, the figurative wealth that Sahagún found in Nahuatl or that Navarrete and Magalhães found in Chinese leads to the conclusion that any language offers its speakers such a trove of alternate forms for conceiving and expressing a single thought that tiny differences in habitual responses are hardly limiting. Add to that discovery what the explorers and inventors of linguistic paradises found, and what language contains expands immeasurably in another dimension. Every language presents innumerable opportunities to misrepresent what is perceived to be true. If that is so, the constraining influence of language is very small.

Notes

1 J. S. Cummins, ed., *The Travels and Controversies of Friar Domingo Navarrete 1616–1686* (Cambridge: Hakluyt Society, 1962), 1:168–69.
2 The literature of linguistic relativity—pro and con—is vast. The classic formulation by Whorf, who drew on the work of the anthropologist Franz Boas and the linguist Edward Sapir, can be found in Whorf's essay, "Science and Linguistics," in *Language, Thought and Reality: Selected Writings of Benjamin Lee Whorf*, ed. John B. Carroll (Boston: MIT Press, 1956), 207–19.
3 Letter of Bernardino de Minaya to Philipp II, cerca 1559, Archivo General de Simancas, Sección del Estado, Legajo 892, fols. 197 ff., extracted and translated in Lewis Hanke, "Pope Paul III and the American Indians," *Harvard Theological Review* 30, no. 2 (1937): 83.
4 Gonzalo Fernandez de Oviedo, *Historia general y natural de las Indias* [1535] (Madrid: Real Academia de la Historia, 1851), 1:235.
5 Fernandez de Oviedo, *Las Indias*, 2:386.
6 Quoted in John Hale, *The Civilization of Europe in the Renaissance* (New York: Simon & Schuster, 1995), 154.
7 *The Diario of Christopher Columbus's First Voyage to America, 1492–1493*, trans. Oliver Dunn and James E. Kelley, Jr. (Norman: University of Oklahoma Press, 1989), 67, 73, 75.
8 Diego de Durán, *The History of the Indies of New Spain* [1581], trans. Doris Heyden and Fernando Horcasitas (New York: Orion, 1964), 31.
9 "cuando llegaron los doce apostólicos varones, que fué el de mil y quinientos y veinte y cuatro, viendo que los templos de los ídolos aun se estaban en pié, y los indios usaban sus idolatrías y sacrificios, preguntaron á este padre Fr. Juan de Tecto y á sus compañeros, qué era lo que hacian y en qué entendian. Á lo cual el Fr. Juan de Tecto respondió: 'Aprendemos la teología que de todo punto ignoró S. Augustin,' llamando teología á la lengua de los indios, y dándoles á entender el provecho grande que de saber la lengua de los naturales se habia de sacar [*sic*]." Gerónimo de Mendieta, *Historia eclesiástica indiana*, ed. Joaquín G. Icazbalceta (Mexico City: Editorial Porrua, 1971), 606. Author's translation.

10 José de Acosta, *Natural and Moral History of the Indies* [1590], Hakluyt Society Publications, 1st ser., no. 61 (London, 1880), 390–91.

11 Acosta, *Natural and Moral History*, 1st ser., no. 60: xxvi; no. 61:392.

12 Garcilaso de la Vega, *Royal Commentaries of the Incas and General History of Peru*, trans. Harold V. Livermore (Austin: University of Texas Press, 1966), 16.

13 Garcilaso de la Vega, *Royal Commentaries*, 18.

14 Ibid.: familial terms, 211; general language, 407–11; invalid beliefs, 80–81; meanings, 76–81, 211; pronunciation, 79; trinity, 682.

15 Donald Lach, *Asia in the Making of Europe*, vol. 2, *A Century of Wonder* (Chicago: University of Chicago Press, 1977), 500.

16 "Pues hemos visto muchos, alos quales paresciendoles aver aprovechado harto en la lengua con saver declinar bien los nomres, y con ester muy promptos en conjugar los verbos, y con tomar cada dia buen numero de vocablos: medraron tan poquito en saver hablar, por no aver querido enterarse mejor en los preceptos del arte, que no savian explicar sus conception, ni declarar lo que quirian dezir, o del todo en dudesuna, quando tenian necessidad de hablar algo en la lengua, en lo qual no se perdiera mucho, si el daño fuera solamente el no salir con la lengua bien savida, si no se siguiera tras esso el daño de muchas almas hablando delos que tienen obligacion de saverla por tener a coargo algune dotrina." Ludovico Bertonio, *Arte y gramática muy copiosa de la lengua aymara* (Rome, 1603), 14–15. Author's Translation.

17 John V. Murra, "Waman Puma, etnógrafo del mundo Andino," introduction to *El primer nueva corónica y buen gobierno por Felipe Guaman Poma de Ayala*, ed. John V. Murra and Rolena Adorno (Mexico City: Siglo Veintiuno, 1980), 1:xviii.

18 Robert Ricard, *The Spiritual Conquest of Mexico: An Essay on the Apostolate and the Evangelizing Methods of the Mendicant Orders in New Spain, 1523–1572*, trans. Lesley Byrd Simpson (Berkeley: University of California Press, 1966), 21–25, 46–54.

19 John H. Rowe, "Sixteenth- and Seventeenth-Century Grammars," in *Studies in the History of Linguistics: Traditions and Paradigms*, ed. Dell Hymes (Bloomington: Indiana University Press, 1974), 361–79.

20 Mariano Cuevas, comp., *Documentos inéditos del siglo XVI para la historia de México* (Mexico: Editorial Porrúa, 1975), 159. I have followed Lesley Byrd Simpson's translation as found in Ricard, *Spiritual Conquest*, 50.

21 Citations *FC* refer to the Florentine Codex. Bernardino de Sahagún, "Introductions and Indices," in *Florentine Codex: General History of the Things of New Spain*, trans. and ed. Arthur O. Anderson and Charles E. Dibble (Santa Fe: School of American Research and the University of Utah, 1950–1982), no. 14, pt. 1, p. 50.

22 Mendieta, *Historia eclesiástica indiana*, 1, 82.

23 Luis Nicolau d'Olwer, *Fray Bernardino de Sahagún, 1499–1590*, trans. Mauricio J. Mixco (Salt Lake City: University of Utah Press, 1987), 28.

24 *Cédula* dated San Lorenzo, July 3, 1573, in *Ordenanzas y cédulas de Indias*, fols. 275 ff., Biblioteca Nacional, Madrid, MS, sig. no 3045; quoted in Arthur O. Anderson, "Sahagún: Career and Development," in Anderson and Dibble, *Florentine Codex*, introductory volume, 35.

25 Anderson, "Sahagún," 36–37.

26 Bernardino de Sahagún, *Colloquios y doctrina christiana con que los doze frailes de San Francisco embiados por el papa Adriano sesto y por el emperador Carlos quinto convirtieron a los Indios de la Nueva España*, ed. Vargas Rea (Mexico: Biblioteca Aportación Histórica, 1944).

27 Nicolau d'Olwer, *Fray Bernardino de Sahagún*, 134, 137.

28 Juan Lope Blanch, "Los Indoamericanismos en el *Tesoro* de Covarrubias," *Nueva revista de filología hispánica* 26 (1977): 296–315.

29 H. G. Rawlinson, "India in European Literature and Thought," in *The Legacy of India*, ed. G. T. Garratt (Oxford: Oxford University Press, 1938), 27.

30 "De la hebrea; los misterios, i preñezes. De la Griega; los articulos, i distincion; no solo en los nombres apelativos, mas también en los propios. De la Latina; la copia, e elegancia. I de la Espanola; la buena criança, comedimiento, i cortesia." Pedro Chirino, *Relación de las Islas Filipinas i de lo que in ellas añ trabajado. Los Padres de la Compañia de Jesus* (Rome, 1604), 35. Author's translation.

31 "idiotismos de las lenguas."

32 "pues cada lengua para sus naturales tiene su hermosura, i elegancia, que no luze en ojos estrangeros."

33 Quoted in Michael Cooper, *They Came to Japan: An Anthology of European Reports on Japan, 1543–1640* (London: Thames and Hudson, 1965), 176.

34 Luis de Guzman, *Historia de las missiones* (1601).

35 As quoted in Cooper, *They Came to Japan*, 171.

36 Gabriel de Magalhães [referred to as Gabriel Magaillans in the English translation], *A New History of China*, trans. Bernou (London, 1688), 72, 75, 77.

37 D. E. Mungello, *Curious Land: Jesuit Accommodation and the Origins of Sinology* (Honolulu: University of Hawaii Press, 1989), 77.

38 Mungello, *Curious Land*, 79.

39 See J. W. Bennett, *The Rediscovery of Sir John Mandeville* (New York: Modern Language, 1954), 65–66.

40 Angel Rubio, *De la obra cultural de la antigua españa: Trabajos filológicos en Indias durante los siglos XVI, XVII, y XVIII* (Panama, 1939). For other representative inventories the reader should consult the appendix "Native-Language Works," in Ricard, *Spiritual Conquest*, 406–14; Robert Streit, *Bibliotheca Missionum* (Münster and Aachen, 1916–1959), 2:287–330; and Victor Hanzeli, appendix, "Bibliographical List of Unpublished Manuscript Grammars," in *Missionary Linguistics in New France: A Study of Seventeenth- and Eighteenth-Century Descriptions of American Indian Languages* (The Hague: Mouton, 1969), 125–28.

41 Jean de Léry, *History of a Voyage to the Land of Brazil, Otherwise Called America* [1578], trans. Janet Whatley (Berkeley: University of California Press, 1990), 141.

42 The passage is in Francisco López de Gómara's *Historia general de las Indias* (Saragosa, 1554), bk. 4, chap. 108. Léry knew this work in its French translation of 1569.

43 Michel de Montaigne, "Of Cannibals," in *The Complete Works of Montaigne: Essays, Travel Journal, Letters*, trans. Donald M. Frame (Stanford: Stanford University Press, 1958), 156.

44 Tzvetan Todorov writes that Montaigne's list of Brazilian virtues proceeds mostly by negatives, identifying as virtues those European vices Brazilians lack or do not practice. Montaigne got his catalog not so much from the eyewitness reports he claimed to have, of course, but from his perceptions of his own society. Todorov, *On Human Diversity: Nationalism, Racism, and Exoticism in French Thought*, trans. Catherine Porter (Cambridge: Harvard University Press, 1993), 266.

45 Quoted in Hale, *Europe in the Renaissance*, 369.

46 Aphra Behn, *Oroonoko, or The Royal Slave*, ed. Lore Metzger (New York: Norton, 1973), 3–4.

47 John A. Lucy, *Grammatical Categories and Cognition: A Case Study of the Linguistic Relativity Hypothesis* (Cambridge: Cambridge University Press, 1992).

5 Philosophical Grammar, or Language and World in Stasis

Great Bacon's Soul, my Friend, divides with thee,
He found the Plat, and Thou the Husbandrie.
More there have talk'd on't too. So I hear say
Of the North passage. But who cuts the way?
Nature, that fram'd so rare an one of thee,
Thought thee most fit for this Epitome:
The Galaxie of Languages; where pack
A thousand lights of words all in one track.

—Joseph Waite to Cave Beck [1]

Universal Languages and Real Characters

The seventeenth century voiced its increasing frustration with the barriers that languages created and the impostures and deceptions that words made possible. John Wilkins's long critique of language made plain why new experiments with alternatives to natural language were imperative: Present languages brimmed with words that misled and deceived, they changed and decayed, their alphabets were either redundant or deficient and in either case were ordered in a confused manner, single words had several meanings, vulgar idioms couldn't be made sense of, figurative language created ambiguity so that a single word like *draw* or *pass* had thirty or forty senses, synonyms created superfluity, grammars abounded in anomaly, and languages generally reflected a lack of careful design and art, having been developed in a haphazard fashion before written grammars could regulate and refine them.[2] By contrast with Francis Bacon, who wanted to sift through languages and combine the best of them, the group discussed in this chapter had largely given up on natural languages. John Webster pointed out, to the chagrin of those who still dreamed of language as a route to nature, that one could name a certain tree or bird in twenty languages yet still know only one tree or bird: acquaintance with languages yielded no gain in understanding.[3] Isaac Newton captured the point in his 1661 manuscript "Of an Universall Language," in which he observed that because dialects of languages were so diverse and arbitrary, a "general Language cannot bee so fitly deduced from them as from the natures of things which is the same in all Nations & by which all language was at the first composed."[4] The key, of course, was to know "the natures of things."

With its increased awareness of the multiplicity of languages and confidence in rational and empirical approaches to knowledge, the seventeenth century saw a flurry of language projects to repair Babel. Some projectors set out to create a language that would be more rationally planned than natural languages and which could be learned everywhere, but this planned language would not claim to have special insight into the essences of things. Some wanted to see only a standard set of characters used in all languages; perhaps those characters could even refer directly to things and not to sounds. The more ambitious designed languages that, by conforming to the organization of nature or to the human mind's grasp of it, would convey either the nature of things or their place in the network of knowledge. Comenius (J. H. Komensky) trumpeted the idea of a "Pansophic language, the universal carrier of Light" as the one means by which "the commonwealth of men, now torn to pieces, [would] be restored, a single speech be granted again to the world, and the glory of God increased by so splendid a method."[5] Imagine a language in which the sounds of an unfamiliar term would reveal the very nature of the thing it named and locate its place in the tables of knowledge. Or imagine a language in which one could discover new knowledge simply by performing logical operations on its signs. Mathematics is such a language, and in combination with physics it has led to a table of elements wherein elements were predicted to exist even before they were discovered. What if one could, by manipulating biological taxonomies, predict as yet undiscovered species of plants and animals, or, by analyzing the terminology of social conflict, arrive at proper solutions? What if one could begin with root ideas in politics and religion and show by logical compulsion which beliefs and propositions are true or false? This was the world into which those who planned philosophical languages believed they were opening a door. They undertook these projects with extraordinary effort and great confidence in the outcome.

Almost all these projects assumed stasis in nature and a corresponding stasis in knowledge which language would both reflect and govern. Their proposers wanted usually to comprehend in one rational plan all the distinctions and divisions that nature could offer and all the mind could meaningfully devise. Then, assuming symmetry or conformity or isomorphism between nature and the best scheme the mind could devise, language would enforce the designed order, accommodate modest growth where needed, and facilitate communication between China and Peru. Language would blanket the world. It would fill all the available space and, like a Portolan map, indicate the bearings from one concept to another. They neglected what Wittgenstein could call "seeing as,"[6] the mind's reliance on context and point of view to make knowledge of objects and situations.

Proposals for a universal language came from the most diverse ideological perspectives, whether from new science, religion, or mysticism. They came from those who desired simply to enable nations to communicate; from those who were frustrated by natural languages' ambiguities and lack of economy; from those who saw a single language as a means of religious unification; from those who longed for what they thought they had found in Egyptian hieroglyphs and Chinese characters, a system of signs that could be read across language barriers and designate the referents of discourse in a less arbitrary way; from those who saw that as vernaculars supplanted Latin, no common means existed in the commonwealth of learning; and finally, from those who wanted to advance scientific knowledge by creating a language that was organized according to the structure of nature and the rational thought processes that were thought to give best access to it.

In France a certain lawyer by the name of Vallées claimed to have stumbled on a matrix language by which all others could be understood.[7] Having been denied the pension he wanted as a condition for disclosing the language key, Vallées never revealed it. However, the idea intrigued Descartes, who in 1629 exchanged letters with Father Marin Mersenne over its likelihood. Descartes desired a language of pure philosophy and speculated on what it would require, namely a type of rational grammar without the anomalies so common in known languages, a foundation philosophy of clear ideas, and a writing system for recording ideas.[8] Comenius and Leibniz voiced similar wishes. Descartes doubted it could be achieved.

Where earlier schemes concentrated on character systems, later schemes aimed at a philosophical language. This transition is perfectly understandable in retrospect. Inspired largely by Chinese writing (in which one character stood for one object or idea and could be read by Chinese or Japanese equally), language projectors such as Francis Lodwick and Cave Beck created writing systems that represented ideas rather than sounds. As they did so, however, they wanted to avoid the need for tens of thousands of characters (such as the Chinese writing system required), and that meant creating a system in which the same marking would always carry the same meaning, say for gender, size, quantity, quality, animate or inanimate, or some other division. To find the radicals, or root objects and notions, and the qualities and relations in which discourse would represent them, required an exhaustive analysis of all facets of nature and experience. That project therefore transformed from one simply of new character systems into one knowledge system with corresponding writing systems that could modify radical signs to signify their accidents and relationships to other ideas. Francis Lodwick's *A Common Writing: Whereby Two, Although Not Understanding One the Others Language, yet by the Helpe thereof, May Communicate Their Minds One to Another* (1647) provides an example of how the search for real characters led inevitably beyond character and into the study of the entire range of ideas. Lodwick's method interested him more than the writing form. He fell short of a full graphology and gave only illustrations of how actual characters might appear. He would assign individual signs to root concepts or objects and then mark their various derivatives with distinctive strokes. Of course, Lodwick was first compelled to divide his radicals into various classes. There were actions and nonactions, and the latter appeared as substantives, pronouns, adjectives, or other basic concepts.

In retrospect we can see the crux. As character schemes gave way to philosophical languages, they required profound understanding of at least one, and in some cases several, of the following components of understanding: the structure of nature and indeed of all aspects of experience, independent of our ways of speaking about them; the faculties and processes of the human mind by which that nature is understood; the nature of language or signs by which the mind preserves, manipulates, and communicates understanding; and the possible correlations among all these. The type of character system to which some of these men aspired was, in Eco's terms, *conformal*; that is, each inflection, suffix, or other change in a word's characters corresponded progressively to discrete differences in words' referents. Thus, the items named by the words *cat* and *car* would relate analogously to those named by *bat* and *bar* or *mat* and *mar*.

A number of thinkers had tinkered with possible designs for systematically arranging root ideas. Cave Beck tried to circumvent the challenge of designing a new script by assigning numbers to key ideas and then using letters of the alphabet to indicate person, number, and case. George Dalgarno recognized that a coherent writing system would need a combination of primitive ideas which could be progressively divided and refined by species and accidents, and a system of recording amenable to it. Dalgarno observed, "One who would impose the names of things rationally must first introduce into that chaos the form, beauty, and order of an ideal world existing in the mind, by a sort of logical creation."[9]

Sir Thomas Urquhart's *Logopandecteision, or An Introduction to the Universal Language* (1653), makes the spatial conception of root ideas overt.

Urquhart, a Scot by birth and royalist during England's civil wars, confidently announced that "this world of words hath but two hundred and fifty prime radices, upon which all the rest are branched."[10] His world of words would, he hoped, not only map all existing space but provide bearings as well:

> I have before my lexicon set down the division thereof (making use of another allegory) into so many cities, which are subdivided into streets, then again into lanes, those into houses, these into stories, whereof each room standeth for a word; and all these so methodically, that who observeth my precepts therein shall at the first hearing of a word know to what city it belongeth, and consequently not to be ignorant of some general signification thereof, till after a most exact prying into all its letters, finding the street, lane, house, storey and room thereby denoted, he punctually hit upon the very proper thing it represents in its most specifical signification.[11]

Urquhart's plan accomplished in the intellectual sphere what had not been done even in cartography. Perhaps more importantly, it conveyed the static conception of ideas as locations that don't change regardless of the use to which one puts them. No matter what route one takes to the lane, house, and room in Urquhart's map of ideas, one at last arrives at a one-and-only location.

Wilkins and a Philosophical Language

John Wilkins, who invented the most thorough and ambitious character and language system of the century, admitted the great difficulties facing him but had a tremendous sense of the need for it and great confidence in its benefits. His tabular displays of knowledge, and his classifications and divisions would logically order "all things, notions, and words."[12] Wilkins, a founding member of the Royal Society who was keenly interested in advancing experimental science through the aid of a language that conformed to nature, had assisted Dalgarno in developing a universal language but had offended Dalgarno by pressing for a more rigorous classification of knowledge as a first step. He was convinced by Seth Ward that a real character's starting point should not be "a Dictionary or Word" but "the nature of things, and that common Notion of them, wherein Mankind does agree" (Wilkins, Preface). Wilkins solicited the help of leading men of science such as John Ray to ensure that his underlying scheme properly reflected notions and things.

One of his purposes was to obviate change in language. In a section on language change, he traces the radical alterations that had made the English of six or seven hundred years earlier seem a foreign tongue, completely unintelligible. It was most unlikely, he observed, that any of the mother tongues issuing from Babel remained, a sad fact since "every change is a gradual corruption" (Wilkins, 8). Oddly, Wilkins pinned his hopes for freezing language on first making learning complete and stable. Yet the last hundred years in England, a period of increased learning, had seen the most rapid change of all as the transformation of Renaissance learning gave way to the beginnings of new science and, in the linguistic realm, old words were refined, foreign words assimilated, and new words coined.

Wilkins's *An Essay towards a Real Character and a Philosophical Language* (1668) contains three related components: a skeletal encyclopedia containing tables of "all things and notions that fall under discourse" (Wilkins, Dedication), a real character, and a "Natural Grammar" that eliminated "those many unnecessary rules belonging to instituted language" (Wilkins, Preface). Together these comprise a philosophical language that modeled itself on knowledge of external nature and, by implication, yielded the proper organization of ideas in discourse. Working by division and hierarchy, Wilkins ranked radicals or basic ideas under forty general heads or "transcendentals," including the common divisions of the natural world into classes of animals, plants, fish, and beasts; divisions such as parts, quantities, and qualities; ideas such as space and magnitude; and the most general classes of "general differences of things," actions, and relations. He then progressively subdivided each transcendental into two categories, "differences" and "species." Elements, for example, divide into simple and mixed, simple into real and apparent; real into lighter and heavier. By identifying a particular thing as a subset of a larger category, say flame as the first species of fire, which itself is the first division of simple, real, lighter elements, one could locate it in the complex grid of all knowledge. Wilkins reduced this grid to a table to provide a key to the whole system.

Wilkins next created the sound system. He assigned a distinct consonant and vowel sound to each general class (for example, *De* stands for *element*, *Do* for *metal*, and *Zi* for *beast*) and then assigned in sequence the consonants B, D, G, P, T, C, Z, S, and N to the differences under each genus and the vowels á, a, e, i, o, y, yi, etc., to each species of the genus in question. Following this procedure one could arrive at a word *Debá* for *flame*, which, as stated, is the first difference (signified by the consonant *B*) and first species (signified by the vowel á) of the genus *element* (Wilkins, 415). *Temptation* is written *bedodlq*, *be* for the transcendental category *action*, *d* for second difference or *comparate actions*, *o* for the fifth species of that, *trying* (in the sense of proving or testing), *d* again to show affinity, and *lq* for *corruptive*. And thus the words followed the course of natural divisions as Wilkins conceived them.

One cannot but admire his inventiveness. Wilkins meant every word: he cataloged "all such things and notions as fall under discourse" (Wilkins, 22). He also knew the difficulty. In classifying "transcendentals," or his most general categories, Wilkins found that little attention had been paid to these general classifications of ideas out of which others could be differentiated:

> There is so little assistance or help to be had for it in the Common Systems, according to which this part of Philosophy (as it seems to me) is rendered the most rude and imperfect in the whole body of Sciences; as if the compilers of it had taken no other care for those General notions, which did not fall within the ordinary series of things, and were not explicable in other particular Sciences, but only to tumble them together in several confused heaps, which they stiled the Science of Metaphysic. And this is one reason why the usual enumeration of such Terms is very short and deficient in respect of what it ought to be, many of those things being left out, which do properly belong to this number; which defects are here intended to be in some measure supplied. Tho it must be granted, that by reason of the exceeding *comprehensiveness* of some notions, and the extreme *subtilty* of others, as likewise because of the streightness of that method which I am bound up to by these Tables it will so fall out, that several things cannot be disposed of so accurately as they ought to be. (Wilkins, 24–25)

The last sentence offers Wilkins's concession to the fact that ideas shift their relation to a larger scheme of knowledge during actual discourse. However, he saw these shifts as minor nuisances, created but compensated for by the rigor of his method. Wilkins had confidence in the general plan and pressed ahead, striving for deep insight into the relations among the external world, human cognition, and the language by which that cognition meets the external world.

Wilkins's project seemed destined to succeed. He wondered why such a scheme had not been successfully launched ages ago, improved with successive generations, and transmitted to his own age with the authority of demonstration and to the benefit of all humanity. But why had it not been previously accomplished? This question raises several issues. One is whether knowledge can ever be one unified whole, or whether there are distinct kinds of knowledge (knowledge of the animal kingdom versus knowledge of how to construct fireworks or compose a sonnet) that relate to each other in different ways depending on the point of view of the observer and the purpose to which one puts the different kinds. Another issue involves whether knowledge is primarily an objective entity that has its own order, impervious to the purposes to which one puts it or the language in which one expresses it, or whether the organization of knowledge varies within the language that represents it for different purposes.

Regarding the organization of knowledge, Thomas Urquhart had complained that "no Language ever hitherto framed, hath observed any order relating to the thing signified by them: for if the words be ranked in their Alphabeticall series, the things represented by them will fall to be in severall predicaments; and if the things themselves be categorically classed, the word whereby they are made known will not be tyed to any Alphabeticall rule."[13] To come up with an arrangement that accommodated or circumvented both the topical and alphabetical was to struggle with the core problem. And the problem persists. Ask the academicians of different disciplines of today whether such a systematic, rational, exhaustive language would be possible and we would find a fundamental difference in their assumptions about language's relations to knowledge.

Wilkins's project, however, failed, as did every other universal or philosophical language. Why? Wilkins's attempt to create a language and its written form to circumvent all these flaws had one fatal flaw itself. We have access to that flaw through the spatial concept of language. He mistook a representation of knowledge for knowledge itself. Wilkins conceived of nature as a static entity which could be fixed in tables of knowledge. Language would then be created to mirror the static display, thus eliminating ambiguity. His was a brilliant project, but doomed from the start because the world doesn't hold still: it varies with the observer's position and attention. A single image or idea, say of a pair of scissors, can convey ideas of tailoring clothes, murder, fine workmanship, hair cutting, or editing a document, all depending on the context in which we encounter the image. Philosophical language, by contrast, was a language of stasis. Learning had reached a state at which it could be a model for language. Careful subdivisions of all existing things and all orders of ideas would now correlate to vocabulary. This conformity rested, however, on two different orders, one of existence and one of relation. Transcendentals of existent things provided the most general possible categories that could be rationally subdivided. Another set of transcendentals named relations; this set attempted to preserve something of the dynamic and shifting nature of ideas. By combining them Wilkins hoped to frame possible ways in which existent things could be perceived and understood.

The problematic relation between existential and relational transcendetals is mirrored in Wilkins's treatment of space. The corporeal (as divided from the spiritual) world consists of heavenly bodies and earth; the earth of water

III. By EARTH , *Land, World,* is meant the *habitable parts of this* III. EARTH. *Globe* ; to which may be adjoyned the more general name of the *Greater parts of the Earth*, denoted by the word COUNTRY, *Region, Land, Tract, Quarter, Coast.*

The most considerable Notions belonging to Discourse, which refer to this, may be distinguished *with respect to its*

Figure, || whether *equal* or *unequal, Convex* or *Concave.*

1. { PLAIN, *Champion, Level, Flat, Even.*
{ { MOUNTAIN, *Hill, Ascent, Rising, Upland, Downs, Knoll.*
{ VALLEY, *Vale, Dale, Bottom.*

Boundaries, or adjacent Waters ; which are either

On all sides, whether

{ Great, || *more* great, or *less* great.
} 2. { CONTINENT, *Firm-land, Main-land.*
} { ISLAND, *Isle, Insular.*
{ *Less,* || whether *roundish* and *high,* or *oblong.*

3. { ROCK, *Cragg.*
{ CLIFF.

On three sides, which, according to a higher or lower situation, as it is *conspicuous* || *more* or *less,* is called

4. { PROMONTORY, *Cape, Fore-land, Head-land, Point,*
{ PENE-ISLE.

On two sides, conspicuous, || *more* or *less.*

5. { ISTHMUS, *streight, Neck of land.*
{ BANK, *Shelf, Flat, Ridge, Shallow, Shole,*

On one side, either according to the more general name, or that particular kind which is *sometimes covered with Sea.*

6. { SHORE, *Strand, Sea-coast, Bank-side.*
{ WASHES, *Sands.*

Motion or Rest.

7. { QUICKSANDS, *Drift, Syrtis.*
{ OAZ.

Figure 5.1 Wilkins on Space. Wilkins's tables, "conteining a regular enumeration and description of all those things and notions to which names are to be assigned," provide these categories for the physical world. Compare these categories with those for abstract concepts for organizing space. Courtesy L. Tom Perry Special Collections, Harold B. Lee Library, Brigham Young University.

and land; the land of continents and islands; the land further of plains or mountains, hills, and valleys. The terrain consists of land and boundaries; and boundaries consist of rocks, cliffs, promontories, isthmuses, banks, shores, washes, and quicksands. A moment's reflection will show that this list is far from complete. It ignores types of terrain as well as boundaries (rivers, rifts, crevices, plant barriers, and ice). More to the point, a geological feature may well be conceived as either land feature or a boundary, depending on how we construe it. Deserts, valleys, and hills are types of land, but they are also just as easily categorized as boundaries, depending on one's location and relation to people occupying different spaces.

Wilkins provides another frame, that of abstract geometric space: "There is likewise consideration to be had of those Imaginary Circles by which men have agreed to divide both the Celestial and Terrestrial Globe, for the better explaining of the Distances and Motions of the Starrs, and the several Climates of the Earth; to which may be adjoyned for Affinity the Notion of Orbe or Sphere" (Wilkins, 55). Imaginary circles divide the outer surface of the globe from inner parts of the sphere that cannot be seen, horizontal circles like the equator and latitude facilitate finding location, oblique circles like the ecliptic and zodiac help determine the earth's relation to the heavens, and circles that intersect the horizontal such as the meridian are yet more arbitrary aids to cartography and navigation. The parts of the corporeal world correspond roughly to existential transcendentals, but the imaginary circles of abstract space are also treated as existential and not relational. They are roughly like Wilkins's total tables of knowledge in that they represent knowledge but don't exist in the same way as things named within the representation. Thus existentials already include relationals.

As Umberto Eco has perceived, the combination of real character, in which every change of character corresponds to a change in sense, plus an organized scheme of the world, meant finally that Wilkins's system could "name unknown things, but only within the framework of the system itself" and could therefore not serve as a basis for scientific discovery, part of its original purpose (Eco, 250-51). Eco posits another limit. The philosophical language purported to give information about the thing it communicated, but the sounds and characters meaning *wolf*, for example, gave only the wolf's position in a classification of animals "without providing information either on the physical characteristics of dogs or on the difference between a dog and a wolf" (Eco, 254). Restating Eco's observation in spatial terms, Wilkins's system is designed to define a word or concept's one location in a multidimensional grid, not to reveal essential information about the item named. Knowledge boils down to a location.

VI. Befides thofe General parts *into which* the World may be divided,
there is likewife confideration to be had of thofe Imaginary CIRCLES
by which men have agreed to divide both the Celeftial and Terreftrial Globe,
for the better explaining of the Diftances and Motions of the Starrs, and the
feveral Climates of the Earth ; to which may be adjoyned for Affinity the
Notion of ORBE, *Sphere.*

These Circles are either

Greater, *dividing the Sphere into two equal parts* ;

   Indeterminately ; namely that which *feparates the upper and vifible*
   part of the Globe, *from that which* by reafon of its being below us,
   we cannot fee, terminating our vifion.
   1. HORIZON -*tall.*

Determinately ; as to

   Northern and *Southern* parts ; whether

    Directly ; wherein the Sun makes every-where equal day and
    night :
    2. ÆQUATOR, *Æquinoctial, the Line.*
    Obliquely, namely, that Line wherein the Sun is fuppofed conftant-
    ly to move in its Annual courfe : to which may be adjoyned
    that *Circular fuperficies, on each fide of this,* which terminates the
    motion of the Planets ;
         ECLIPTIC.
    3.   ZODIAC.

   Eaftern and *Weftern* parts ; wherein the Sun makes mid-day or mid-
   night : to which thofe other *Circles* correfpond *which pafs through*
   the Poles of the Horizon, as the former do through the Poles of the
   World ;
        MERIDIAN, *Colure.*
   4.   AZIMUTH.

Leffer, *dividing the Sphere into two unequal parts* ; whether

   Polar defcribed by the fuppofed motion of the Poles of the Ecliptic ; ‖ either *Northern* or *Southern.*
        ARTIC.
   5.   ANTARTIC.

   Tropic, terminating the motion of the Sun in its greateft Declination ;
   ‖ *Northern,* or *Southern.*
        TROPIC of ♋ *Summer Solftice.*
   6.   TROPIC of ♑ *Winter Solftice.*

   Parallels, relating ‖ either *to the Æquator, or to the Horizon.*
        PARALLEL.
   7.   ALMACANTAR.

Figure 5.2 **Wilkins and Abstract Divisions of Space.** Courtesy L. Tom Perry Special Collections, Harold B. Lee Library, Brigham Young University.

Wilkins's system further tries to match the systematic order of things and ideas with a similarly systematic series of sound differences. Language denominates things by the use of sound differences: *cab* and *lab* use one sound difference to name two completely different entities. Things of all orders might also seem to array themselves in systems, but can the two be overlaid? In limited and particular domains, perhaps we could combine them, but only if the domains don't fundamentally change over time. And every field of knowledge has undergone tremendous changes both within itself and in responding to changes in other fields. However, in the realm of general knowledge the system wouldn't work even if time didn't alter the array.

Those who study language are deeply divided on this topic; those we might call *objectivists* hold that language functions to name ideas and objects that exist before language comes along to name them, while *experientialists* or *contextualists* hold that meaning is created within language by living speakers in specific contexts.[14] Both can deploy powerful evidence and arguments to make their cases, although they tend to use very different models of knowledge. The objectivists point to the success of scientific knowledge, which attempts to curtail as much as possible the effects of observer bias and language encoding. Contextualists point to historical, cultural, and social knowledge where the goal of objectivity approaches meaninglessness. With respect to Wilkins's philosophical language, the obstacle to complete success occurs in that facts, as well as the branches under which we might organize them, apparently exist on several planes at once, and their place in networks of knowledge is always a provisional one among other possible arrangements. The arrangements change over time, but they also change within the same time frame, and language must accommodate this fact. Encyclopedias wrestle with this problem and try to solve it with cross references and by using different principles of organization, say alphabetical in one part and topical in another. This is how the *Encyclopaedia Britannica* currently deals with this issue. Anyone who has tried to design a personal filing system has the same problem: the logic is equally strong for filing a given item by author, time period, topic, source, current interest in relation to a given project, or general category. This categorial instability results in language's ambiguity and also its richness.

There are signs that Wilkins recognized this problem. In a number of places, a term could easily have more than one home base. For example, Wilkins divides actions into corporeal and motion, and classifies staring, kissing, scratching, and writing as corporeal; yet he classifies bleeding, coughing, snorting, swallowing, belching, and chewing as actions of motion. Since many motions involve body parts, Wilkins cautioned that "many of the Species under this Head might, if there were convenient room for them, be reckoned under the former" (Wilkins, 239). In the tables of plants he confessed that "streining and force . . . must sometimes be used, to make things comply with the institution of these tables into which they are to be reduced" (Wilkins, 67). He then differentiated plants according to their leaves, flowers and seed vessels, but one quickly discovers that these classes start to overlap each other. Plants classed from the leaf standpoint are differentiated by flower and seed type, plants classed by flower are further differentiated by leaf and seed, and plants classed by seed vessel are further differentiated by leaf and flower. What appears to lie still in solitary unity when viewed within Wilkins's tables will shift to other locations and other frameworks as the purpose and occasion of communication change.

Finally, Wilkins's project ignored the fact that language is a creative and social as well as an intellectual product. It arises from people's need to communicate mutually, not from an isolated projector who sets out to revamp the relationship of knowledge to language. What Wilkins saw as a defect, that a single word such as *pass* or *draw* could have thirty or forty meanings, actually converts to a strength of language. The meaning only emerges in context as people communicate. Wilkins also objected to the fact that every language has "some peculiar phrases belonging to it, which if they were to be translated verbatim into another Tongue, would seem wild and insignificant" (Wilkins, 18). It takes speaker, listener, and the inference of context to determine which of its many meanings *pass* will take on. In its tangled slipperiness, language, used in a living way by real minds in the process of sharing ideas, is much more complete and fulfilling of the human need to hear and be heard.

For all his charges against language's ambiguity, deceit, disorder, and profuseness, Wilkins makes a circular journey to wind up close to where he started, showing in the process that language is an extraordinarily rich, flexible, and varied instrument. In Part III on natural grammar, Wilkins gave page after page of words which, by the addition of a simple mark to a root character, would carry a consistent change of meaning. Adding a mark that signifies "metaphorical" to the character for the word *straight* would change its meaning to *upright*. The same mark would change *element* to *principle*, *deformed* to *absurd*, *wrigle in* to *insinuate*, *suiter* to *candidate*, and *woo* to *canvase*. A mark signifying "armament or tackle" would change the character *horse* to *bridle*, *horseback* to *saddle*, *rider's foot* to *stirrup*, and *finger* to *thimble*. A mark signifying "vest or armour" would change *bishop's head* to *miter*, *votaries head* to *cowl*, *chin* to *muffler*, *chamber* to *hanging*, *belly* to *apron*, and *bed woolen* to *blanket* (Wilkins, 335). A mark for "officer" would change *city* to *mayor*, *money* to *bursar*, *poor* to *overseer*, *street cleansing* to *scavinger*, *pasture* to *hayward*, *conies* to *warrener*, *whipping* to *beadle*, and *fornicating* to *pander* (Wilkins, 338). I don't presume to guess what ideas might have occurred to Wilkins as he composed these lists, but the effect on me of scanning thirty pages of related words, a mere sliver of what any language contains, was to remind me what a panorama of word choices language provides for naming things, not only in multiple ways, but in multiple relations and connotations. Add the figurative layer, and the language makes accessible a near infinity of ways of apprehending, naming, and relating even the most quotidian reality. If natural language presented itself to Wilkins as a limit on communication and thought, it allowed him to produce a system that, while a mere shadow of the facilities of natural language (indeed, a system that attempted to reduce them), succeeded in making evident the mutable richness of language.

Leibniz's Monadic World

G. W. Leibniz's progressive speculations take the universal character project a step further than that of Wilkins. For Wilkins the problem was to locate knowledge in a world of both entities and relations, then to use language to signify that location. For Leibniz the problem was to combine a world understood as comprised of an infinity of indivisible monads—a spatial concept if there ever was one—with a character system so pure and congruent to nature that one could virtually calculate knowledge by manipulating the characters. The idea of monads gave Leibniz's world infinite combinations and perspectives, together with universal comprehensibility. The project could gradually reveal its impossibility, even though Leibniz himself seems never to have given up his belief in the possibility of a universal language.[15]

To grasp the great promise that Leibniz saw in a philosophical language and at the same time its enormous difficulty given his beliefs, we must address his theory of space and monads. Unlike his contemporary Newton, who posited an absolute space with its own attributes that conditioned reality, Leibniz for the most part denied the existence of space at all. He accomplished this by asserting that space is only what monads—which we can understand better as intelligences or souls—perceive. Monads construct ideas of space inasmuch as their percepts include ideas of distance and direction to other monads. Therefore space is ultimately relational. Leibniz goes further. What monads perceive is already intrinsic to monadic intelligence. Put differently, his position means that every monad has within it already the idea of other monads and therefore of spatial relations to those monads. So, space is partly an illusion, partly an idea necessary for perception, but it probably doesn't correspond to what is really there.

We understand Leibniz's language project by seeing that he wanted to achieve a language that would be the equivalent, simultaneously, of monadic intelligence (that is, knowledge assumed to derive from the outside is really derived from within each monad) and of the more global perspective that included the existence of all monads and therefore of the necessity of apparently sensory ideas by which relations among monads can be grasped. His universal language would allow one to calculate knowledge by manipulating signs, just as monadic knowledge can be calculated or manipulated within a discrete monad. And inasmuch as a language is a whole system and not just an expression of an individual point of view, a universal language would also include the useful but perhaps illusory concepts by which individual points of view take into account the existence of other points of view.

Two broad assumptions guided Leibniz in his proposals for universal characters and language: first, that language had a computational aspect that could make it a better tool for thinking if the right properties could be coaxed out and refined and, second, that the underlying logical form of language might be made to conform to the structure of the world. It should be apparent that if one could capitalize on both aspects, one could have arrived at a language that allowed one to compute knowledge along the lines of mathematics and thereby arrive at new discoveries, analogous to the way in which one arrived at an unknown but already implicit sum by adding a group of numbers. The beginning of Leibniz's *Dissertatio de arte combinatoria* (1666) had much in common with other projects. Acquaintance with the work of Dalgarno and Wilkins helped propel Leibniz forward. Leibniz notes that concepts could be broken down into their constituent ideas, and he proposes a character system whereby the written form of each concept signified the whole and all its associated constituents. If concepts were adequately analyzed and the sign system carefully designed, he reasoned, they could be made to express all ideas capable of expression, true or false, and since the range of true expressions must be finite it must lie within the reach of human capabilities. With his *Characteristica Universalis*, wherein he proposed a numerical coding system for ideas, Leibniz became convinced that with a lexicon of characters standing for the primitive ideas, the characters could be analyzed and combined to yield logical conclusions just as valid as those found in geometry.

The stumbling block, as we have seen in earlier cases, seemed to be the requirement for an exhaustive and systematic collection of human knowledge. Leibniz earned his living working for German nobility as librarian, archivist, historian, and diplomat, and these careers convinced him of the pressing need to integrate and catalog a chaotic and growing body of knowledge. He proposed an encyclopedia that would provide the data on all concepts and their constituent ideas. This encyclopedia would have to do two things at once: express in a rational order all ideas and concepts and, at the same time, make clear the relations that such ideas had under different points of view. As Umberto Eco has noticed, there is something incongruous in the fact that this project took shape in the same mind that viewed the universe as a collection of infinite individuals and indivisible monads, each generating in its own right a series of perceptive acts and capable of combining with others in a myriad of ways to yield the actual created world (Eco, 271). Using this principle as a true "alphabet of thought" meant resolving the problem of relation among possible points of view when each point generated a view. For Leibniz this mystery was not resolved, but he persisted in thinking that monads were harmoniously bound together. The articulation of that principle of harmony would later become one of the goals of scientific inquiry. Yet as a result of this kind of thinking, Leibniz came to imply, if not to realize, that most if not all concepts and objects of knowledge presented a different nature to inquiry depending on the kind of perspective from which the inquiry was undertaken.

Leibniz's encyclopedia proposals, in fact, seemed to obviate the possibility of a universal alphabet of thought and began to reflect the more practical problem of cataloging knowledge so that it could be usefully available and yet, at the same time, reveal its relational aspects. In the *New Essays concerning Human Understanding*, written in 1703 in response to Locke's *Essay concerning Human Understanding* (1689), Leibniz attacked Locke's tripartite arrangement of knowledge under three headings—physical or natural philosophy, ethical or practical attainment, and logical or the knowledge of communication by signs. Leibniz saw them as inextricable. He noted, for example, that the science of reasoning was quite distinct from the knowledge of words, but that one couldn't even pursue the science of physical objects without resorting to words and definitions, so therefore an unspecified relation existed between words and objective knowledge.[16] Then he continued to complicate the tripartite division by arguing that every particle of knowledge could be perceived from different points of view: the physical from the ethical or logical, for example, so that the three provinces of knowledge were "perpetually at war with one another because each of them keeps encroaching on the rights of the others" (Leibniz, 523). Items of knowledge, it seemed, were bound to appear as parts of interlocking branches and histories. The study of language, for example, must appear under all three headings. Generally, "a single truth can have many places according to different matters to which it is relevant" (Leibniz, 524). Thus he formally acknowledged what Wilkins saw as only a minor inconvenience. No system of branching trees or dichotomies could possibly comprehend all knowledge because it would leave out the crucial intersections, byways, and subtle reappearances of information when it was viewed by different minds and put to different uses.

It would be wrong to suggest that Leibniz discarded Locke's three categories, however; he merely reconditioned and renamed them as the theoretical or synthetic, the practical or analytic, and the inventorial or logical. These classifications served very well as long as they incorporated what Leibniz had said of their relational aspects, "not as distinct sciences but rather as different ways in which one can organize the same truths, if one sees fit to express them more than once" (Leibniz, 525). Eco argues that in fact the relational problems of organizing knowledge led Leibniz to the brink of celebrating the fall of universal tables of knowledge such as that of Wilkins. "Dimly shining from beneath the project of Wilkins," Eco says, "Leibniz has recognized the first idea of a *hypertext*" (Eco, 279).

Such an idea may be shining dimly beneath Leibniz's theories, but we must not forget that Leibniz insisted that it was the "same truths" that were being organized in different ways. Some order of knowledge existed apart from its different possible expressions and subordinations. The *New Essays* made this clear by repeatedly insisting on a universal harmony of all that was possible: "The universe contains everything that its perfect harmony could admit" (Leibniz, 307). The uncertain state of human knowledge within that harmony should not be read as a final statement about what was knowable. Far from it. "But our uncertainty does not affect the nature of things," he reminded Locke (Leibniz, 311). Therefore we must read Leibniz's encyclopedia ideas as provisional only, as a practical step forward in the accessibility of information, but not as a paradigm for the universe.

Another general problem, equally crucial, was the problem of divisibility. To ground his universal language Leibniz would need to arrive at the simplest set of ideas out of which all other concepts could arise. But if the world already were organized of infinite monads, and if monads were not simply identical duplications of each other, such that the only difference among them was position merely, might monadic intelligence not differ in perceiving which set of ideas was the prototype? Further, how was one to know whether one had in fact broken down an idea to its rudimentary constituents? After tracing Leibniz's quest for a full grasp of primitive concepts and for a number system to express them, Eco puts the issue this way:

> In fact, Leibniz was to advance a number of important philosophical considerations that led him to conclude that an alphabet of primitive thought could never be formulated. It seemed self-evident that there could be no way to guarantee

that a putatively primitive term, obtained through the process of decomposition, could not be subjected to further decomposition. . . .

If no one conception of things could ever count as final, Leibniz concluded that we must use the conceptions which are most general for us, and which we can consider as prime terms only within the framework of a specific calculus. With this Leibniz's *characteristica* breaks its link with the research into the definitive alphabet of thought. (Eco, 276–77)

Even though Leibniz continued in his conviction that a set of conventional prime thoughts could ground a discourse of calculation, the foundation for a truly real character and philosophical language had been sundered. One could overlay a language on reality, but there would always be distance at some nodes. Leibniz pursued his quest for a real character and a universal encyclopedia along different lines, which in their independence reveal that a universal language was a futile fantasy. More and more, Leibniz concentrated on a computational language that Eco calls "blind," that is, which promised in its formal application to lead one to valid discovery, even though the signs were not tied to any content. Unlike natural languages wherein errors can be concealed beneath ambiguity and equivocation, in a rightly designed calculus of thought "every mental error is exactly equivalent to a mistake in calculation."[17] In other words, the calculating language would have to be designed so that even when its characters were devoid of meaning, if one followed its syntactical rules, the characters guaranteed propositions that would be true when the meaning became known. With a language essentially divorced of content, we might consider Leibniz's calculating language more a method than a language, so it is no surprise to note that he came to view it more as a tool of scientific discovery than a means for expressing the full range of intellectual, moral, and psychological human thought.

George Steiner has characterized two approaches to languages in the seventeenth and eighteenth centuries. The first assumed an underlying structure common to all languages. The second, or "monadist," held that the universal, deep structures of language are either fathomless or so abstract and generalized as to be trivial. The systematic language projects of the seventeenth century, particularly universal grammar and philosophical language, had mixed success. Their failures didn't entirely eradicate the possibility of an underlying structure of language, nor did they demonstrate the validity of a strictly monadist constitution. Rather than sustaining either view exclusively, the mixed successes and failures of the two views point, I believe, to a third possibility, that of a dual process of mind working in language. This process uses both categories of apprehension. The particularized, position-bound, relational, monadist structure enables a multiple grasp of the world and communication about it. It deals in a world of fundamental ambiguity. But language facilitates a complementary apprehension that can reach across the multiple grasp of even particular languages, not only to assimilate its structures and categories into its own, but to make its own communicable to that other. Language may very well condition thought, but it does so by offering multiple points of view, multiple ways of naming similar information, and multiple ways of framing and ordering that information.

In retrospect, Leibniz appears to have demonstrated by his encyclopedia notions why it would be impossible to design a single exhaustive table of knowledge upon which a universal language could be based. Yet he retained an unshaken trust in the ultimate harmony of nature and an integration of knowledge in line with that harmony. On another side, partly by recognizing the relational aspects of knowledge and partly by extrapolating on the properties of a computational language, he gradually retreated from the connections of that language to the world of existence and concentrated on the language's formal aspects. It might be wrong to say that Leibniz proved his own project futile or that others saw his work as worthless, but we can view his work as brilliantly predictive of and paradigmatic for the lack of fruits produced by universal language schemes generally. After the seventeenth century, students of language were interested in discovering the causes and consequences of an intractable linguistic diversity. In a very real sense, they learned that the possibility of linguistic diversity was also the possibility of dividing up the world differently, of having not only different names for things, but different classes of things and especially different ideas not connected to the palpable realm of objects but to the social and moral universe. This possibility, seen as a problem by universal language projectors, was also the reason they couldn't succeed.

Notes

1   Joseph Waite, "To my intimate and ingenious Friend, Mr. Beck, upon his Universal Character, serving for all languages," in *Cave Beck, The Universal Character By which all the Nations in the World may understand one anothers Conceptions, Reading out of one Common Writing their own Mother Tongues* (London, 1657).

2   John Wilkins, *An Essay towards a Real Character and a Philosophical Language* (London: Gellibrand, 1668), chaps. 2–5, pp. 6–21.

3   John Webster, *Academiarum Examen . . .* (London: Calvert, 1654).

4   Reproduced in Ralph W. V. Elliott, "Isaac Newton's 'Of an Universall Language,'" *Modern Language Review* 52 (1957): 13.

5 Comenius [J. H. Komensky], *The Way of Light* [1668], trans. E. T. Campagnac (Liverpool: University Press, 1938), 8.

6 Ludwig Wittgenstein, *Philosophical Investigations*, trans. G. E. M. Anscombe (Oxford: Blackwell, 1953), 193–95.

7 Umberto Eco, *The Search for the Perfect Language*, trans. James Fentress (Oxford: Blackwell, 1995), 216.

8 René Descartes to Father Marin Mersenne, Amsterdam, 20 Nov. 1629, *Philosophical Letters*, trans. and ed. Anthony Kenney (Oxford: Clarendon, 1970), 3–6.

9 George Dalgarno, *Ars Signorum* (London, 1661), as translated by Mary Slaughter in *Universal Languages and Scientific Taxonomy in the Seventeenth Century* (Cambridge: Cambridge University Press, 1982), 143.

10 Thomas Urquhart, *Logopandecteision, or An Introduction to the Universal Language* [1653], in *The Admirable Urquhart: Selected Writings*, ed. Richard Boston (London: Fraser, 1975), 115.

11 Urquhart, *Logopandecteision*, 116.

12 John Wilkins, dedication to *Essay towards a Real Character*.

13 Urquhart, *Logopandecteision*, 2.

14 I use the terms Alan Melby and C. Terry Warner use, following Lakoff in *The Possibility of Language* (Amsterdam: John Benjamins, 1995).

15 I am not arguing for Leibniz's influence since, as Vivian Salmon has observed against those who make much of his place in the history of ideas, Leibniz's writings on universal language remained scattered and unpublished throughout this period. See Salmon's *The Works of Francis Lodwick: A Study of His Writings in the Intellectual Context of the Seventeenth Century* (London: Longman, 1972), 42. I am, however, following Eco's lead in seeing embedded in Leibniz the problems that were already obviating universal language projects and which therefore explain why their illusory promise was never fulfilled.

16 G. W. Leibniz, *New Essays on Human Understanding* [1703], trans. and ed. Peter Remnant and Jonathan Bennett (Cambridge: Cambridge University Press, 1981), 522.

17 Leibniz, *De Scientia Universalis seu Calculo Philosophico*, in *Die philosophischen Schriften von G. W. Leibniz* (Berlin, 1875), 7:198–203, as quoted in Eco, *Perfect Language*, 280.

6 Rhetoric and the Expanding World

Rhetoric is language in action. Because early modern Europe saw rhetoric as tightly bound to language itself, this chapter will show that a changing world dramatically influenced rhetoric in several important ways.

Eloquence and Space

Early modern rhetoric was largely spatial in its conceptual foundations. Speaker, audience, and topic were readily conceived as forces in various dispositions toward each other: opposition, complement, parallel. To sway an audience was to exert a force on it and move it in space. Eloquence, the power to accomplish this end, was proper elaboration or ornament on a base structure. So conceived, ornament could cover, conceal, or overweight the structure on which it lay. The common topics, or *topoi* of invention, were figurative places where one could find appropriate material for discourse. What may be less evident, many of the logical topics used to approach a subject matter, such as division, comparison, causality, and change, were also grounded in spatial experience. Divisions of whole into parts and of subject from adjunct are first spatial and then extended in a figurative manner to less concrete topics. Comparison is the act of setting two articles side by side and examining how the shape and parts of one correspond to those of another. Causal relations are conceived as chains of objects or as places or spaces seen before and after an event. The categories of change—addition, subtraction, transposition, and substitution—sound mathematical, but they represent operations on objects in a set field. Discovery, the act of uncovering possible arguments relevant to a topic, was crucial to persuasion and is, of course, analogous to terrestrial discovery. Even invention, which has higher overtones of originality, derives from the Latin terms for coming upon something.

Because eloquence was of such central concern in rhetoric, I will dwell briefly on it to show the problems involved in conceiving it spatially before turning in more detail to the disruptive influence that changing awareness had on two other aspects of rhetoric. One of the most central and nagging issues confronting rhetorical theorists involved how eloquence was to be conceived and limited. Did eloquence and its limits arise intrinsically from the skills and arts of rhetoric, or did they ultimately derive from the outside? Bounding and channeling eloquence was a concern that constantly arose among those who taught the arts of eloquence. Nearly all Renaissance writers on rhetoric expressed a double mindedness concerning the expert use of language. They held in awe the power of eloquence and at the same time registered a deep uneasiness about its use. Many harbored suspicions of what Debora Shuger calls the Classical grand style, which tended toward "the ostentation of the speaker, flattery of the audience, and emotional persuasion of a largely uneducated crowd."[1] Shuger gives many examples among church rhetoricians.[2] The controversy over eloquence centered on the relation of ornament to substance; on which kind of discursive force was appropriate, the kind that attracted the rational and emotive faculties to truth or the kind that pushed the feelings till they overpowered reason; and on the role of metaphor in both these areas. I hope to show that rhetoricians recognized the necessity and pervasiveness of metaphorical thinking and that they attempted to resolve the problems posed by eloquence by resorting to another spatial metaphor of relative distance, or near and far. As they did so they exposed the inherent limits and contradictions of such metaphors to give the appearance of a solution when none has really been found.

Metaphors played a vital role in differentiating plain from grand style, as well as in restraining inappropriate eloquence. In his 1593 edition of *The Garden of Eloquence* (1577, 1593) Henry Peacham voices caution about the misuse of stylistic devices to achieve a desired effect. Metaphors, for example, provided an infinity of places or perspectives from which to accomplish the "artificial translation of one word, from the proper signification, to another not proper, but yet nigh and like."[3] Adhering to proper significations brought with it many problems, however, since the act of translation—literally, moving from one place to another—achieves both its beneficial and pejorative effects by dislocating ideas from an original position and by playing between similarity and dissimilarity. Peacham attempts to resolve the attendant problems of metaphor by means of other metaphors of places and proximity. Seeing that an infinity of "places" offers various types of similarity to a given idea or object, he counsels those who cultivate appropriate eloquence to limit their metaphors' sources to that set of places which has proved "most apt, most usual, and most commendable" (Peacham, 4); he then lists and explains each one. These places include sight, hearing, smelling, and other senses; the likeness of body to mind, creature to human, and lifeless thing to living thing; and topics such as familiar substantives, the four elements, and deity. Thus, a finite cluster of places solves the problem of infinite possibilities. Yet this solution defers more to tradition and familiarity than to clear principles by which the vast possibilities of metaphor can be brought to yield the best. Peacham also employs another spatial concept when he cautions that metaphors should not be "farre fetcht, as from strange things unknowne to the hearer" (Peacham, 14). The neatness of the spatial concept—sticking close to what hearers already know—obscures the fact that the solution is superficial. One can stick with what an audience knows and still be far-fetched in other ways. Peacham also observes that judgment must constrain choice of resources that memory can provide (Peacham, 4). This solution merely admits the problem, and familiarity, tradition, and comforting spatial metaphors step in to make an apparent answer to the question that Peacham cannot otherwise resolve. Figures move constantly along the continuum of deficient or excessive, close or far-fetched, familiar or strange, mundane or learned, commonly accepted or shocking, and no one had a genuine solution. Peacham wrote in a time when the strange and literally far-fetched were becoming closer. Knowledge itself threatened the accepted boundaries of disciplines, of taxonomies, and of fact and opinion. Within the boundaries of the familiar one could find many degrees of appropriate and inappropriate likeness. The solution to the problem of metaphor, then, seems to come from another metaphor, which in turn duplicates the problem of using figures to convey thought. To limit the potential riot of figure, one had to master more than the devices; one had to have a wisdom that comes with practice—to some. How could that wisdom be codified? That was the problem.

The English clergyman Hugh Latimer illustrates the difficulty of locating proper boundaries on figures that contributed to eloquence. Latimer favored the most plain and direct language, but he chose, deliberately it would seem, extreme figures of speech to convey his points. In one of his best-known sermons, his 1548 "Sermon on the Plower," he calculated his main figure and theme—minister as plowman—to connote the hard labor and level social status of the preacher and thereby to unsettle those who preferred lordly churchmen. He hoped his flock would not be "offended with this my similitude," he said, "for I have been slandered of some persons for such things."[4] Latimer refers here to those who charged him with having used excessive metaphors, as in likening "Our Blessed Lady to a saffron bag" to connote that Saint Mary had given birth to the Christ child but had no more special office with him than did any other woman. While denying that he had used this specific figure, he claimed that such a similitude "might have been used without reproach":

> As the saffron bag that hath been full of saffron or hath had saffron in it doth ever after savor and smell of the sweet saffron that it contained, so Our Blessed Lady, which conceived and bare Christ in her womb, did ever after resemble the manners and virtues of that precious babe which she bare. And what had Our Blessed Lady been the worse for this or what dishonor was this to Our Blessed Lady? (Latimer, 30)

Latimer virtually baited his auditors by his daring metaphors, and in so doing raised the question, on what basis should the distinction between appropriate and inappropriate figures rest? On one hand, Latimer's figures suggest, in the manner of the metaphysical poets who would write decades later, that surprising and even disturbing figures of comparison have an advantage in surprise and newness but also in the propriety they reveal when we reflect upon them. That is, where conventional figures are appropriate for conventional relations between vehicle and tenor which they are designed to reveal, unexpected figures bring to mind hidden or neglected aspects. As a saffron bag inherits the smell of its contents, so the tenor of discourse inherits the qualities of the vehicle used to explain it.

In receiving and defending himself against the charge of offensive extravagance, Latimer revealed the volatility of figures and the difficulty of establishing real and general principles on which the volatility could be tempered. Figures involved too many planes of discourse at once to resolve: social, doctrinal, political, poetic, intentional, psychological, and metaphysical planes intersected. To simplify was to distort. Yet people, Latimer included, knew that speakers could go too far.

The roots of eloquence lay in the rich inventiveness of the mind that saw things from different angles and in different figurative lights, selected those most striking or appropriate for a given purpose, and then expressed them in language. To say that such figures should be close to the understanding of the audience really solved nothing, since the role of figure in the first place was to require the mapping of one concept on another in such a way as to provide novel insight related to the speaker's purpose. To say that figures should adhere naturally and closely to the topic also solved nothing, since one could only judge in retrospect whether a figure worked well. What eluded rhetoricians was the ability to state the principles behind what worked.

Another group offered a different solution, also with spatial underpinnings. Here, however, the spatial underpinnings involved a principle, not just a figure. The gift of shifting perspectives, with all its promise of new knowledge, could heighten rhetorical effect, but it could also lead to sterile permutations of erroneous opinion. Proponents of the new learning advanced a solution to the problems of sterile recombinations and inflaming eloquence by advocating that speakers follow the model of new knowledge, illustrated best in terrestrial discovery. Bacon was chief among these advocates. He divided invention into two branches: invention in the practical arts and sciences, which he vigorously promoted because he found it languishing, and rhetorical invention, or the search for arguments and appeals, which he vigorously discouraged because it had displaced the attention that should have been paid to the first: "The invention of speech or argument is not properly an invention," he insisted, "for to invent is to discover that we know not, and not to recover or summon up that which we already know; and the use of this invention is no other but out of the knowledge whereof our mind is already possessed, to draw forth or call before us that which may be pertinent to the purpose which we take into our consideration" (*Adv L*, 3:389).[5] From a rhetorical standpoint, eloquence was the appropriate use of resources. From a cognitive standpoint, it meant stagnation since it discovered—took the cover off—nothing. Rhetorical invention, etymologically to encounter or come upon, came upon no new territory but crossed and recrossed old terrain.

This debate didn't end soon, but by the middle of the seventeenth century, Thomas Sprat wished to ban eloquence, or at least he adopted the rhetorical pose of wishing so. First, he believed eloquence "fatal to Peace and good Manners."[6] He hedged, however, knowing that if only the good renounced rhetoric, "the naked innocence of virtue would be upon all occasions expos'd to the armed Malice of the wicked" (Sprat, 111). Second, he believed that eloquence blocked the path to new and useful knowledge by trapping the mind in an endless process of swapping perspectives and rehearsing old opinion. Rhetoric was not discovery. By contrast with the actual discoveries that voyagers announced year after year and the promise of experimental knowledge promoted by the likes of Bacon and Sprat, eloquence was a prison, a warfare over the same contested terrain, and a road constantly traversed but leading in a circle.

In endorsing the new rhetoric of science as sponsored by the Royal Society, Sprat used a language of closeness similar to that of Renaissance rhetoricians. Sprat promoted a discourse, which included "the primitive purity, and shortness, when men deliver'd so many things, almost in an equal number of words," together with a "close, naked natural way of speaking"(Sprat, 113). We see his difference from the rhetorician, however, in his conception of that to which language should have proximity. For Sprat, one measures that closeness to or distance from the benchmark of the behavior of nature one is describing. This manner would not only prevent discourse from forming too close an alliance with the passions, it would make discourse hew to its proper course, which is to assist people in the discovery and dissemination of knowledge. In that enterprise, "if but one link in the whole chain be loose, they wander farr away, and seldom, or never recover their first ground again" (Sprat, 18). Sprat questioned whether eloquence had any but a parasitic relation to knowledge and a poisonous relation to the advance of knowledge. Although many studies of Sprat delight in pointing out that he, too, uses figure and eloquence to achieve his purpose, they miss the point if they see no further. Sprat attempted to redefine effective discourse by using the familiar spatial figure in a new way. Old rhetoric gave lip service to "closeness" but defined it, as did Peacham, as closeness to the opinion and experience of others. Sprat and the new rhetoric defined closeness as a relation in which subject matter governed, and subject matter was also newly defined to mean the behavior of nature, not the accepted body of opinion about humans and the world in which they lived. By constant recourse to that behavior of nature and a persistent determination to observe and understand it, those who sought knowledge could make language serve a new master.

The actual discovery of new terrain therefore offered radical opportunities to assess the traditions of rhetoric. When missionaries and soldiers confronted foreign learning and eloquence, they constantly construed native rhetoric in two corresponding ways. They heard the indigenous hosts speaking a simple, truthful language, which they simultaneously admired and saw as evidence of the ingenuous and childlike nature of the native mind. Contrastingly, missionaries and travelers construed a native people's rhetorical skill and intellectual sophistication as evidence of devilish cunning and contamination. Montaigne's cannibals give us the simple, truthful language; the Jesuits in China and Landa among the Mayans perceive the demonic cunning. Construing the speech of alien others in these two ways came all the easier because the root problems of using and interpreting eloquence had not been resolved at home. Quite the reverse: the lack of resolution to the problems of eloquence guaranteed that travelers would project these concerns onto those they encountered.

It was quite natural that cogent criticisms of European rhetorical practices would come from new territory. European writers would adopt the figure of the exotic Other to expose the driving forces of artful rhetoric: malice, guile, and selfishness. Montaigne's cannibal (discussed on page 124) was a creature of pure simplicity who had no words for the cunning constructs of Europe:

> This is a nation . . . in which there is no sort of traffic, no knowledge of letters, no science of numbers, no name for magistrate, no riches or poverty, no contracts, no successions, no partitions, no occupations but leisure ones, no care for

any but common kinship, no clothes, no agriculture, no metal, no use of wine or wheat. The very words that signify lying, treachery, dissimulation, avarice, envy, belittling, pardon—unheard of.[7]

Nakedness corresponded to truth and simplicity, and European discourse suffered from too many terms, ideas, and practices that grew not from nature but from perversions of it. Of course, one wants to know whether to rely on Montaigne's report or whether it was a fantasy bred by the promise of the far-off. If so, the far-fetched came home as the simple and close.

As we will see, real discoveries and real spaces would contribute further to the unraveling of the old and the emplacement of a new rhetoric.

Exploration and the Disruption of Rhetoric

In the late sixteenth and seventeenth centuries, the wider world challenged and disrupted the ability of rhetorical theory to contain and systematize the practice of effective speech. The act of transplanting European rhetorical learning from one site to another would seem straightforward enough. We have already noted some of the problems of transplanting and translating religious knowledge into languages with no coherent lexicon for Christian doctrine. The same difficulties applied in rhetoric. In this section I examine a rhetoric using European terms and standards but written for the Americas and show how the new place and people changed apparently universal rhetorical distinctions and practices into something new and hybrid.

Diego Valadés, author of the *Rhetorica Christiana* (1579), was one of the most remarkable products of the military and spiritual conquest of Mexico. Son of a native woman of Tlaxcala and a father who had come to the Americas as a soldier and served in Pánfilo de Narváez's expedition to intercept and defeat the unauthorized foray of Cortés into central Mexico, Valadés enlisted as a Franciscan friar in Mexico and spent his last years in Europe in the top ranks of his order. After Narváez's defeat, Valadés senior joined Cortés and took part in the siege of Tenochtitlan, now Mexico City. He then remained in Mexico to serve in various civil and military offices. Born in about 1533, his son Diego Valadés grew up in the two cultures of his mother and father. He admired the indigenous peoples in almost every way, except for their practices of human sacrifice and idolatry, but his education and life unfolded more along the path of the ruling Spaniards. He knew personally several of the original "twelve apostles," the twelve Franciscans sent after Cortés's victory to begin the spiritual conquest of New Spain. He joined the Franciscan order shortly before a decree banned Indians and mestizos from the priesthood and then spent a good twenty years as a missionary among the peoples of Mexico, mastering not only Nahuatl, Tarascan, and Otomí, but Spanish and Latin as well.

Valadés traveled to Spain and Rome to represent his order's interests. While in Europe, reflecting on the problems that European missionaries and priests faced in teaching the people of New Spain, he compiled a treatise on rhetoric to assist the clerical orders in their preaching duties. The resulting *Rhetorica Christiana*[8] combined the classical and Spanish Renaissance traditions of rhetoric, Valadés's knowledge of the native peoples and customs, his experience preaching among the indigenous, and his personal grasp of the power of the spoken word to convert, teach, persuade, and motivate. Indeed, he viewed the principles of classical rhetoric as so many excellent human instruments waiting to be used in a cause much higher than any conceived by Aristotle, Quintilian, or Cicero. So far he had much in common with other Christian rhetoricians and particularly Friar Luis de Granada and his *Rhetorica Ecclesiastica*, which was published in 1578, just a year prior to Valadés's treatise. What sets Valadés apart is the *Rhetorica Christiana*'s additional richness of information on non-European languages, viewpoints, gods, and customs. That inclusion reflects a conception of rhetoric as context rich and audience driven. Although the *Rhetorica Christiana* pays ample homage to traditional rhetorical techniques, Valadés's attention to the people who were the recipients of the instruction, and who therefore should help shape those techniques, implies that techniques are not truly universal and therefore do not translate smoothly from an Old-World to a New-World setting.

Valadés describes many indigenous customs at length. He does so partly to show the benefits of applying the principles of rhetoric. Christian preaching, he gives evidence, had transformed a people. Valadés cites Cicero, who taught that humanity, once ferocious and savage, became calm and gentle under the guidance of a gifted thinker and orator. "The admirable effects of this influence appear nowhere more clearly than in the pacification of the Indians of the new world," said Valadés (Valadés, Pref/29). In spite of his soaring confidence in the power of persuasion, however, he knew that maladroit communication had equally disastrous effects on character. He had witnessed ample occasions of ineffective rhetoric, perhaps especially in the formal instruction of the large groups that one of his engravings depicts (Valadés, 211/478). He believed that the change brought about by the teaching and preaching of the missionaries would proceed even more effectively if those who taught first mastered the devices for elocution, memory, and argument that the rhetorical arts had long offered. The end of rhetoric, as implied by his treatise, was not simply to train people to speak well, but also to cultivate priests who could be "spokespersons of God, instruments of his divine goodness and criers of the Lord" (Valadés, Pref/27). To so culminate, rhetorical craft required both a knowledge of the arts of eloquence and a knowledge of the peoples who were converting to the faith outside Europe, as well as of the means by which they were brought to adopt that faith.

Insofar as it pertained to defining the purposes and categorizing the methods of effective communication, Renaissance rhetoric was a totalizing project. Nothing pertaining to these topics could lie outside its scope. However, Valadés's inclusion of New-World history and ethnography created ruptures in the rhetorical scheme that was to accommodate them. Valadés inserted ample material into Part Four of the *Rhetorica* for the immediate purpose of discussing the three types of oratory, which Valadés defined as demonstrative (praising or blaming an individual or action—in most classical rhetoric referred to as ceremonial), deliberative (persuading and dissuading from a course of action), and judicial (accusing or defending in a tribunal of justice). Learned rhetoricians already recognized that these three types notoriously overlapped each other. Indeed, the classification might well be considered more of a heuristic device to focus the mind on specific purposes than a rigorous division of discrete rhetorical types. The confusion persists in the *Rhetorica Christiana*, but the ethnographic and historical material aggravates the confusion. Valadés's primary purpose, to define the types of oratory and show how to apply them, becomes complicated and obscured by his second purpose, to illustrate the types of oratory through the description, history, and praise of the indigenous of New Spain and the three missionary orders who had the charge to convert and care for them. Notably, of twenty-five chapters in Part Four, Valadés devoted all or part of eighteen to the customs of the Indians or to the chronicles of the conquistadors and missionaries. This amount outweighed the requirements of Valadés's stated purpose. In fact, the ethnographic and historical material threatened to overturn the purpose. That is, although Valadés included the material to show how to apply the principles of rhetoric to proselyting, the radical difference of the customs, gods, and peoples further upset the already untidy scheme of rhetorical causes inherited from classical tradition and made it difficult for him to maintain any rigor of classification. While all three divisions appear in the treatise, each with a definition, the deliberative and judicial types receive short shrift and are eventually swallowed up in the demonstrative type, not because the demonstrative served the Christian minister any more than the other types (indeed, the deliberative would seem most useful), but because it served Valadés's secondary purpose most readily.

On the surface, that secondary purpose was, as noted, to inform priests in Mexico and superiors in Spain of the virtues of the Mexicans. Valadés had an ulterior purpose that emerges on closer study: to defend the Indians against the charge of incomplete conversion by showing their innate and post-conversion virtues. In treating specifically of the demonstrative genre, Valadés wanted to show that the Indians were true Christians, contrary to the attacks of detractors who viewed them as inferior humans and perpetual infidels. Nothing could be less true to those who knew the Indians, Valadés argued, but to see that, one must know them in a particular way. Therefore Valadés felt compelled to give extensive background information on the indigenous people and how they regulated their lives. What I am arguing is that the solution to the question of Indian virtue is provided not by recourse to the classification of rhetoric causes, not by a display of proper techniques for sustaining such an argument, though Valadés certainly included that, and not by the demonstration of proper logic or appeals or commonplace perspectives. The solution is to know the Indians better, and that means knowing them to some degree as they know themselves. Valadés's strategy implies that those Europeans who held the Indians up for praise or blame could not reasonably do so without immersing themselves in the differences between Indian and European customs and ways of seeing things. This strategy is bound to create problems in a handbook that purports first to teach rhetorical techniques because at one point the treatment will shift emphasis from technique—knowing *how*—to knowing *about* something quite specific and in a certain light.

One can see Valadés's purposes start to change even as he introduces the demonstrative genre. That type, he says,

> is additionally useful for praising or condemning things themselves, such as when one's purpose is to expel or wipe out the rites or customs of some nation as, for example, if one wants to accuse the Indians of infidelity. To accomplish such a task, we should be advised that not everything can be made as obvious and explained as clearly as we who treat of them desire, or as the mind conceives them. All the worse if one aims for brevity. For this reason, to avoid confusion and to accommodate those who have not witnessed such things, I take this opportunity to append some items that will help us perceive more properly the material on the Indians that will be presented later, along with all their rites. (Valadés, 167/387)

Notice how an example of a demonstrative topic turns into an occasion to consider what would be required to develop the topic, and what is required is a subtle and intimate acquaintance that can't be accomplished under the

Ad sensus aptat coelestia dona magister,
Aridaq; eloquij pectora fonte rigat.

Figure 6.1 Missionary Teaching an Indigenous Audience. Note the use of illustrated panels on the life of Christ. From *Rhetorica Christiana*, courtesy Bancroft Library, University of California Berkeley.

constraints of brevity and precision. To treat certain kinds of knowledge, especially those that deal with the customs of a foreign people as they relate to Christian principles, one must fathom first the ideas of the people and then recognize the difficulty of making ideas that are clear in one setting clear in another, and this requires a consideration of "how the mind conceives them"—a tidy shorthand phrase for an enormously difficult problem. Rhetoric turns into a psychology of cognition and communication. Cultural understanding precedes rhetorical analysis and requires something that rhetoric rarely addressed, a contextual understanding of the people given in terms close to those in which they see themselves.

The passage just quoted falls at the end of part four, chapter two. The opening of chapter three reveals yet another important reason for dwelling on the Indians:

> Since among all the accomplishments and happenings of the Christians since God created the world, there is none other so worthy of eternal memory, and in which His Majesty has manifested such clemency, as the conversion, pacification, and subjection of the lands of New Spain, I have determined to insert here a narration of the customs and ceremonies of the Indians so that, from the effects, their causes may more clearly be known. (Valadés, 167/387)

Here, the *Rhetorica* confronted its readers with an additional problem of synthesis. It sought to combine the sacred tradition of Holy Writ and divine providence with the secular heritage of rhetoric. It offered a systematic coverage of the discipline of rhetoric as applicable to the religious orator, but that synthesis was overshadowed by a providence that rhetoric might discuss or even promote, but which stood outside its bounds and made practiced rhetoric a puny instrument of response.

Underlying the role of rhetorical training in conversion was the vastness of miracle. Valadés did not seem to aim for hyperbole in declaring that the subjection and conversion of the native peoples of Mesoamerica stood as the greatest spiritual wonder since the Creation. And accompanying that wonder were other, lesser wonders: the European discovery of the Americas, the Christians' inhabiting a strange land and conversing with people with alien histories and beliefs, and the mystery of conversion from one religion to another. These were beneficial prodigies. What allowed them to come together was not rhetoric in the technical sense in which Valadés used the word, but an overarching divine will and a series of lesser interventions that helped those involved to wrest the most possible from their participation in the unfolding of divine will on earth. For example, how does one in a rhetorical treatise—manifestly a work of human design fitted

Figure 6.2 Instruction by Missionaries. In an open-air setting, missionaries carry out activities of baptism, marriage, and direct instruction on doctrine, creation of the world, penitence, and writing. From *Rhetorica Christiana*, courtesy Bancroft Library, University of California Berkeley.

for human capabilities—treat the gift of tongues? Valadés said that certain missionaries received this gift so fully that the Indians marveled at it (Valadés, 226/511). How did one integrate that into a treatise on rhetoric? In retrospect one might ask whether the *Rhetorica Christiana* strove to teach rhetoric using New Spain to illustrate its principles, or whether its ultimate purpose was actually to awaken the European church to the faithful conversion of the Indians and the divine force that was guiding the missionaries who preached to them, all under the cover of a rhetorical treatise.

It might be argued that the so-called incongruities in Valadés's rhetoric, which I trace to his birth, his intimate acquaintance with the peoples of Mesoamerica, and his desire to elevate Europe's opinion of these peoples, reflect merely his clumsiness and not any inherent incompatibility between the European discipline of rhetoric and the study of non-European peoples and customs. It might be argued that a more sophisticated mind might have produced a more rigorous rhetoric. This we can grant. In fact, Valadés had considered calling his book "Sum of All Sublime Learning." However, in response to his superiors, he had called it a rhetoric so it would be known that it contained nothing contrary to the church's teachings. Yet something about Valadés's treatise goes beyond clumsiness. A product of two cultures himself, he could not set aside his own rhetorical purposes in composing a treatise. His case typifies the challenge that the non-European world presented to the disciplines. It shows the effect that close contact with the new had on received knowledge, and it shows how difference could upset learned systems that reached out to assimilate it.

The Topics of Discourse: Exploration and the Decline of the *Topoi*

We will now see that world exploration and developments in concepts of space overturned some of the core tools of rhetorical training. This section will summarize the doctrine of the rhetorical commonplaces, or *topoi* (in English, topics), stressing the static, contained conception of space this doctrine invokes. It will then trace changes in concepts of space and place and finish by suggesting that these changes nearly eradicated one of the foundational principles of Renaissance rhetorical study.

The *topoi* comprised a mental technology of rhetorical invention and amplification. Topics, from the same root as *topography* and therefore denoting places, served the orator by functioning as so many figurative sites from which to view a subject and gather information and arguments, thereby creating meaningful matter for a speech or composition. For example, one could gather material about language by viewing it from places of logic and asking what it was, what class of thing it belonged to, what types it could be divided into, what caused it, what parts it contained, and what effects it had. Or one might view language from figurative places as a kind of hunt, garden, voyage, or book. Through such means one generated and then imparted plentiful and, it was hoped, valid information on the subject.

The question of this section is: What would happen to the important role of these metaphorical places by the time the actual world had become so large and varied that the ample but finite rhetorical places seemed paltry and inadequate? To a person on the surface of a spherical planet that rotates and revolves, what would fixed perspectives come to mean? By the mid-seventeenth century, leading thinkers had reversed the poles of traditional training: rather than the mind drawing cognitive advantage from the variety of stable viewpoints, stable viewpoints would draw their usefulness from cognitive activity in a world of flux, a world wherein common sense and ordinary perception might harbor as much prejudice and error as truth. The new doctrine declared that the places from which one takes those perspectives are not in reality fixed: they are movable and relative. By the later seventeenth century, ideas of space and place had altered drastically. Correlating to these changes, the rhetorical places dropped from sight. The locations idea had become a contingent one, subject to change and related to other planes along new axes.

The figurative places where one could find and store sufficient material for a given discourse have old roots in both philosophy and rhetoric. Aristotle posited epistemological places, where knowledge on particular subject matter resided. Wishing perhaps to avoid becoming entangled in debates on whether space was a void, a nothingness, or something that existed in its own right, he set aside the notion of space in favor of that of place. The latter notion made it possible to speak of the space an object fills without immediately having to explain what surrounds objects. One effect of this move was to make place a more finite, accessible idea, at least by contrast to metaphysical space. Aristotle saw connections between place in his philosophical and rhetorical speculations. He saw knowledge as organized on a spatial model, with *topoi* as sites where a person will find the appropriate information and arguments. Topics are thus mental places where knowledge is stored, properly manipulated, and even discovered. Some topics or locations are universal to all types of knowledge, some relate only to a specific subject matter. His *Rhetoric* states that because logic and scientific information fail to persuade some people, "the speaker must frame his proofs and arguments with the help of common knowledge and accepted opinion" and then refers us to his *Topics*, which is an example of that spatially conceived storehouse of common knowledge and approaches.[9]

Rhetoric treatises from classical antiquity through the sixteenth century continued to teach that one of the best ways to discover relevant things to say on a particular topic was to have a set of commonplaces in mind—a set of questions, points of analysis, and bits of wisdom. Cicero explained that his *Topica* "contained a discipline invented by Aristotle of inventing arguments so that we might come upon them by a structure and a path (*ratione et via*) without any error."[10] Quintilian, from whom Renaissance rhetoricians derived much of their material, stressed that by studying the commonplaces an orator "will be better able to expatiate on such as admit of excursive discussion and will be prepared for any cause whatever. All causes indeed rest on general questions."[11] Cassiodorus describes this storehouse of sayings and distinctions as

> a remarkable species of achievement—the fact that there could be assembled in a single place everything which the mobility and variety of the human mind has been able to discover in seeking the meaning of various situations! This achievement confines the free and voluntary intellect; for, wherever the human mind turns, whatever thoughts it considers, it refers of necessity to one of the commonplaces named above.[12]

It was as if the human mind had discovered all the fundamental intellectual places from which knowledge was produced. In the twelfth century John of Salisbury commended Aristotle's *Topics* "because of the abundance of commonplaces (from which arguments may be drawn) that are therein contained" and cited Isidore, who called them the "foundations of arguments, fountainheads of meanings, and sources of expressions."[13]

Edgar Mentner notes that in the Renaissance, given the "enormous increase in material discovered as a result of more intensive study of classical antiquity and the Bible," humanists sorely needed ways to order and classify their material. *Loci communes* were so many common places—places common to all—relating, as Rudolf Agricola stated, "everything that can be said about a particular subject as well as all the relevant arguments."[14] In the era's drastic expansion of knowledge and opinion, the commonplaces received a new impetus as a safe paradigm in which to assimilate the new. For example, Erasmus Sarcer, a German reformer who attempted to adapt the traditions of classical rhetoric to the proclamation of reformed religion, advised pastors to learn a method for collecting and inventing arguments so that "one has at all time sufficient material to talk or preach about and thus less need of labour and work."[15]

Aristotle's place theory, reinforced over the ages by medieval authority, came to comprise what we might call a finite dynamics. Although full of marvels and requiring movement, the medieval cosmology ultimately held many points of view repeated endlessly in a bounded space. Even when Christian theologians became comfortable thinking about nothingness and the vastness of space—because God created the world from nothing and would not be all-powerful if he couldn't create nothing as well as something—their expanded, intellect-teasing universe was confined pretty much to the superlunary sphere, which was outside humanity's normal area of concern, while rhetoric and knowledge had their application in the sublunary world which, for all its complexity, was held to be only a static and degraded image of God's infinite creation. Medieval thought generally presumed a world of finite spaces that contained, at least in form or essence, all that had been or could be thought. It implied a world of appearances and partial knowledge because it held that to understand an object, event, or issue, people had to contemplate it from several vantage points. One was unlikely to face radically new problems or confront masses of new information that might overload the powers of commonplaces to sort and relate. Rhetoric assumed that processes of mutability, decay, and regeneration bred new combinations of problems. But the theory of rhetorical invention assumed that one who knew the patterns underlying such disparate phenomena and who had training in delivering the products of topical analysis would be best able to understand the many faces of existence and thus influence opinion and action. In a sense, place theory tied human discourse to one of the most fundamental of all human experiences, that of location, and implied that by approaching knowledge and discourse from that metaphor, almost all that humans considered essential could be imagined, understood, stored, and recalled. Essentially, cognition was situation and choice.

The places brought with them many problems. They were ambiguous in Greek as well as in European languages and, not surprisingly, "underwent degradations and criticism" (McKeon, 25, 27). Places threatened to proliferate till each item of knowledge or memory had its place. The spatial metaphors embedded within the concept of topics offered no means of limiting the accretion of new topics. Studies could "spawn a seemingly unlimited number of related or subsidiary metaphors."[16] Place theory always suffered from a need for containment. Users of place needed what Bacon called "prenotion," or some idea of what they were looking for in the first place before the search began, to provide "a kind of cutting off of infinity of search" (*AL*, 5.5). Also, as Quintilian advised, "not every kind of argument can be derived from every circumstance, and consequently our search requires discrimination."[17] Quintilian barely registered the possibility that would become the hallmark of both fictional and real travel narratives—that extremely different places might offer such unfamiliar species as to resist conventional interpretation. To think in such terms would be to raise the possibility inherent in the place metaphor all along—that the sense of place itself is convention-shaped. What counts as a place? Even within a small patch of ground, an infinity of places can be specified. When one moves from the small patch to all the earth, what does he or she encounter? Infinity on infinity of places and, in nature and human society, extreme difference, disconnectedness, separation.

Joan Marie Lechner summarizes other limits of the topical approach to rhetoric. Rhetoricians had few compelling grounds for some of their most frequently stressed distinctions between general and specific or between rhetorical and dialectical (logical) places. Rhetoricians differed in classing ideas as categories on the one hand and sources of rhetorical amplification and embellishment on the other. Some proponents recognized the "ambivalent function" and "intermediate position between dialectic and rhetoric" (Lechner, 60) that the places held. Finally, place theory was better adapted to the preservation of knowledge than to the discovery of knowledge. When rhetoricians used the term *discovery*, they did so in a very different sense than that entailed in the new learning. Place theory implied that all had been collected, inventoried, and stored; one only needed a method of remembering and gaining access. Such a method of storing, as Lechner acknowledges, "excluded anything like the invention of new science as Bacon described it" (Lechner, 72).

Lechner notes that the places are, of course, not real but metaphorical. People used them as practical means to ends, not as paradigms for reality. Topics were thought to offer the mind advantages such as adaptability, fullness, and ease of memory, however problematic from a theoretical standpoint. At first glance, it does not appear that the metaphors used to suggest the places of argument and memory—hunting, forests, storehouses, gardens, landscapes, mountains and plains, rivers and tributaries, and rooms in a mansion—suggested a connection with the earth itself as a vast place to seek undiscovered lands and islands, treasures, knowledge, and points of view. But the metaphorical use of place had to keep pace with the literal sense of place. Soon the metaphorical began to collide with the literal places of a vast, varied earth that was moving through space.

The emphasis on the topics, which survived for over a thousand years of great cultural upheaval, nearly disappeared from rhetoric treatises by the mid-seventeenth century. As far as I know, no one has suggested that the changing sense of literal place in an expanding and more complex world had anything to do with this significant change. I will suggest it. I also suggest that this transformation related to the problem of systems and method in the seventeenth century.

Changes in ideas of place and space were part of the revolution in method. Wilbur S. Howell, a historian of rhetoric, has observed:

> A theory of communication is an organic part of a culture. As the culture changes, so will the theory change. The scholastic logic and the traditional rhetoric of the early sixteenth century were an expression of late medieval times, and were suited to those times. Had those times continued without change, scholastic logic and traditional rhetoric would not have come under attack by the Ramists, and would not have emerged from the collision with Ramism as modified versions of their former selves.[18]

Howell names three forces at work in the sixteenth century that changed theories of communication. These are the failure of deductive science to "offer a sufficient explanation of a world discovered through observation of nature," the loss of political power of the aristocracy, and the Reformation (Howell, 10).

Howell does not name another force often associated with cultural change in the sixteenth century and specifically with the failure of deductive science—the expanding knowledge of the Americas, Asia, and Africa. Perhaps we can consider this knowledge a special category of what Howell refers to as "a world discovered through observation of nature" (Howell, 10). Keeping in mind Howell's view of the organic relation between culture and a theory of communication, I submit that place theory nearly disappeared because it failed to explain and assimilate new information and new kinds of knowledge. This is not to say that place theory had no value but that it lost value. It simply declined and was replaced by a hardier, more robust approach to the relations among different kinds of knowledge. By robust, I mean that with care a certain method could be applied by anyone and lead to similar results, whereas place theory relied explicitly on the creativity and judgment of the person using it.

If the theory and practice of rhetoric in the sixteenth and early seventeenth century can be seen as one kind of system, the move from traditional rhetoric to what Ramus and Descartes would call *method* involves a radical change in the idea of system. The term *method* did not enter the Latin vocabulary as "methodus" until Aristotle's *Topics* had been translated in the twelfth century. Interestingly, the "Method (*methodos*) was used by Aristotle to signify a 'path to' the investigation of a scientific subject matter," and Aristotle differentiated this from the "paths or ways (*hodos*) constructed in universal arts for the statement of arguments or descriptions or accounts applicable to any problem or subject matter" (McKeon, 29). So although both method and commonplace are conceived spatially, they relate to a very different approach to knowledge. The commonplace system entailed a coherent arrangement of knowledge that facilitates comprehension and rhetorical discovery. This complex set of mutual relations for understanding, remembering, and applying both subject matter and the skills of communication gave way to a simpler, leaner set of principles, tools, and procedures—a method—whose purpose was to guide the mind through a world of knowledge that had become more complex than the arts of rhetoric could manage.

As philosophers contemplated empty space, sixteenth-century rhetoricians were already trying to resolve the problems of linked finite places by stressing that the dialectical places—the fundamental distinctions to which logic continually returned—had to prevail over the elaboration, amplification, and adornment that rhetorical places provided. Peter Ramus, the influential sixteenth-century grammarian, logician, and rhetorician, objected to the fact that places of invention and arrangement occurred in both logical and rhetorical writings. Not only did he see redundancy, but the redundancy created indecisiveness. Everyone had different versions of how invention in logic related to invention in rhetoric and how many places were involved. Ramus proposed separating logic, or dialectic, from rhetoric so that less ornamented but more certain and therefore compelling arguments would result. This gave rhetoric a ground on which to build appropriateness, something rhetorical theories had some difficulty achieving from within.

At the same time Ramus limited the number of places to eliminate the problem of endless mazes of ornament, amplification, and invention to which place theory often led. Ramus reduced to ten in his logic the large and indeterminate number of places of invention and amplification, and of these he was conscious of their necessity and relations. As Howell writes, "The ten basic entities in Ramus's theory of logical invention are in reality the ten basic relations between predicate and subject in the logical proposition, or the ten basic relations among the objects of knowledge in the human environment" (Howell, 156). They are cause, effect, subject, adjunct, opposite, analogues, name, divisions, definition, and witnesses.

I would like to suggest that this simplification resulted not from the recognition that knowledge was reducible so much as from the recognition that with expanding knowledge and with the growing recognition of the dangers of dispute inflamed by rhetoric (Ramus converted to Protestantism and was murdered during the St. Bartholomew massacres in 1572), traditional methods of creating, relating, and storing knowledge would fail. Ramus's lean rhetoric was therefore more able to accommodate, evaluate, and integrate new knowledge. One might even say that the program of

Ramus and his followers became imperative because the unity of knowledge was already threatened. A different kind of unity would be required. What Ramus offered was a new paradigm, that is, not just a new set of common-places, but a new way of conceiving of the intellectual order upon which knowledge and therefore rhetoric depended.

Walter Ong held that Ramus organized knowledge spatially; I would add that his spatial arrangement differs from that of the rhetorical places. Rather than organizing knowledge in a series of sites that contained, or allowed perspective on, a subject matter, Ramus arrayed knowledge in branching dichotomies. A subject is initially separated into two subdivisions, which are then further subdivided, and so on. "The resulting structure somehow corresponded both to the extramental actuality and to the contents of the mind."[19] Ramus's method seeks to escape the spatial paradigm of most rhetorical theory of his time and is itself spatial only in a far different sense. For him the branching lines of knowledge followed a structure far too subtle and elusive for normal rhetoric to discover. Once guided by his method, however, a mind could follow the traces of nature and make them yield up more of their organization. Thus Ramus emphasized a method, at once more certain and flexible, for proceeding by reasoning from things known to things less known.

Until his time, Ramus was convinced, rhetoric had concerned itself with that species of invention and discovery founded on opinion among the uninformed and not the type founded on logic and truth. He sought a way of proceeding that would apply to any topic, and he found this in method:

> The methode is a disposition by which amonge many propositions of one sorte, and by their disposition knowen, that thing which is absolutely most cleare is first placed, and secondly that which is next: and therfore it contynually procedethe from the most generall to the speciall and singuler. By this methode we proceade from the antecedent more absolutely knowen to prove the consequent, which is not so manifestly knowen: & this is the only methode which Aristotle did observe.[20]

Ramus stressed that this method could apply to any topic: "We doo not only use this methode in the declaration of artes and sciences, but in the expounding of all things which we woulde plainely sett forth."[21] He illustrated with an example from grammar. Confronted with confused divisions and rules of grammar, how should one proceed? One needed no topics of invention, said Ramus, only the method. One started with a general class, then took up the succeeding divisions with their definitions, then the subordinate parts and forms of the major divisions.

Descartes made similar criticisms of logic and of the topical method of arguing. His reflections effectively struck a blow against the possibility of commonplaces. For one thing, argued Descartes, that which one people generally approved might be held extravagant among another, and uncritical attachment to the practice might inure a people to its own error. In his *Discourse on the Method*, Descartes expressed his belief that these types of approaches "are of less use for learning things than for explaining to others the things one already knows, or even, as in the art of Lully, for speaking about matters of which one is ignorant."[22] He also remarked that although he had once "valued oratory, and was fond of poetry," he came to see both as "gifts of the mind rather than fruits of study" (Descartes, 114).

Descartes founded his "method" in response to a world that was less transparent in its organization and meaning than learned traditions had advocated. Indeed, Descartes held that uncertain knowledge was, if anything, more probable than the certain, that little in life was fixed, that the world and knowledge of it offered too many places from which to view things, and that these could never be fully categorized. One then required (1) an approach to knowledge based on minimal certainties from which one reasons and (2) the thorough organizing and dividing of the phenomena under study so that, whatever doubts, difficulties, and unexpected phenomena were encountered along the way, one didn't overlook anything. Through this method, one achieved maximum certainty while at the same time missing no possible branch of knowledge. If this procedure sounds reminiscent of Ramus, we must recall that Descartes studied logic under the Jesuits at the college of La Flèche, where the logic textbook was influenced by Ramus and featured a section on method.

An equally drastic blow to the *topoi* came from changes in the concept of space itself. In *The Production of Space* Henri Lefebvre presents a great shift in spatial thinking in the sixteenth century as Europe valorized urban existence over that of the countryside. His images of the new space include the facade that arranges space in pleasing and even eye-tricking ways and the tower, which allows the city dweller to survey one's surroundings from inside a space protected from whatever lies outside, where outside is divided physically by tower or city walls or culturally by taste, fashion, education, and politics. This move toward the mastery of terrestrial space might be perceived to strengthen the idea of orderly, finite space that the rhetorical topics exploited, were it not for accompanying changes in the epistemology and metaphysics of space.

If we ask, what lies in the areas between the rhetorical places, we can tease out these connections. One can answer "nothing." Or one can answer that the area between the rhetorical places is partly occupied by the subject of discourse, about which an orator seeks inventive information, and partly by ideas that have not been assimilated into the place frame. This mental game actually relates to one of the great splits in space theory, between those who conceive an absolute space that, although apparently empty, exists in its own right, and those who conceive only a relative space, which exists only in the sense that some factor makes possible the distance lying between entities that really do exist. We remember that Aristotle attempted to exclude infinite nothingness from philosophy and favored a relational conception in which places, as occupied by matter, exist, but in which space itself merits little thought.

Space as void had less impact in philosophy, even though Democritus had posited an absolute unfilled space, or void. The main impetus toward empty space came from Euclidean geometry, which, as F. M. Cornford explains, offered a mathematical conception of continuous and unending space that would be eventually identified with the space the physical world occupied. Cornford insists that these two ideas were available separately in ancient Greece but were not connected until the fifth century B.C. He explains that the numerous axioms of geometry that Euclid arranged into a coherent string of proofs required a space (not physical, but purely mathematical and conceptual space in which parallel lines could extend infinitely without crossing). However, Aristotle's "immense authority, fortified by ecclesiastical prejudice, held atomism at bay until physics began to move forward again at the Renaissance."[23] The Catholic Church resisted Copernicus's sun-centered universe and Galileo's observations of the earth's motion and imperfections, such as sun spots, in the heavenly spheres. In spite of opposition from the church, some Christian philosophers warmed to the idea of infinite nothingness. They saw any limit on God's power as a challenge to his existence, and they believed that church doctrine had already validated the creation *ex nihilo*, from nothing. If *nothing* did not exist, then God would have had to reduce himself to arranging what was already there, and where did that come from? Instead of recurring to an infinite regress, Christian philosophers chose a regress to infinity with their doctrine of creation from nothing. This infinite nothingness was pretty much confined, however, to spheres of existence beyond the earth, moon and stars.

Copernicus toppled the Ptolemaic cosmology when he put forth his heliocentric universe and at the same time shattered that separation between super- and sublunary existence by showing that the heavenly bodies all obeyed the same laws (Akhundov, 102). Copernicus's universe was still finite and fairly contained. Its counterpart rhetoric would be what we know as the medieval and early Renaissance version: dynamic, allowing movement from one position to another and entailing reference points and points of view, but still finite, with the possibilities for motion limited as were Copernicus's concentric spheres around the sun. Galileo's celestial mechanics further subjected all heavenly bodies to the same laws. His telescope revealed mountains on the moon, another uniformity between earth and heavenly bodies. Galileo wanted more to work out the calculations involved in his heliocentric cosmos than to trace out the implications of his discoveries in cosmology. However, his theory of gravity reinforced the concept of the void.

Others eagerly performed the task of sorting out the wider implications of the Copernican cosmos. Already in the fifteenth century Nicholas of Cusa had propounded the infinity of the universe. Inspired by Copernicus, Giordano Bruno practically taunted those who would eventually persecute and execute him for heresy as he wrote and lectured his way through France, Italy, Britain, and Germany on the beliefs to which the Copernican revolution led—namely, that we dwell in a universe of infinite space and plurality of worlds. He wrote:

> Space is a continuous three-dimensional natural quantity, in which the magnitude of bodies is contained, which is prior by nature to all bodies and subsists without them but indifferently receives them all and is free from the conditions of action and passion, unmixable, impenetrable, unshapeable, non-locatable, outside all bodies yet encompassing and incomprehensibly containing them all.[24]

It is not hard to see how these ideas impinged on space as most medieval minds thought about it, and from that, to see why Bruno alarmed his contemporaries. First of all, in an infinite universe, there can be no center, no privileged reference point. Second, a plurality of worlds made certain, portable knowledge, the kind that pertained regardless of location, less tenable.

Descartes rejected the reality of empty space. Space to him was non-material extension, whereas only matter had true extension. However, Descartes contributed to the study of space through proposing the coordinate system that could map an object's length, breadth, and depth along intersecting axes. The axes, which still bear his name, provide the geometry which is the graphic representation of the space in which objects have extension. Descartes even formulated two laws of motion in space that parallel those of Newton: things in themselves remain in the same state, whether in motion or at rest, and things move along straight lines.[25]

Descartes's geometrical mathematics helped Newton derive the laws of gravity and motion. By 1660 when Newton attended Cambridge, attention to space was "rampant."[26] Not only did Newton devise a mathematics that reinforced the concept of empty space, since gravity was shown to work immediately, that is, with no time intervening, across distance so large that it was difficult for the human mind to grasp. Newton also foregrounded the very idea of space, perceiving that space evaded the traditional distinction of entities into substances and attributes, having "its own manner of existence."[27] Space existed, but not in the same manner as objects do. Another aspect of Newton's explanation had impact on the sense of place and space. In order to measure the motion of objects in accordance with the laws of motion, one had to think in terms of an inertial system, that is, a system in which motion could be measured by reference to fixed axes or points. Yet, as we have already mentioned, in an infinite expanse there can be no center. Furthermore, depending on which motion one is seeking to chart, the axes must shift. Translated to the earthly frame, the fixity of the finite is illusory, revealing that our senses are adapted to the locale in which humans exist and not to the more vast setting in which our locale exists. We are only a few steps away from Kant's revolutionary insight, that space is in fact a pure form of intuition and a necessary condition of perception.

In light of his critique of the rhetorical training of his time, consider the implications of Descartes's remark on the difficulty of achieving a stable sense even of place in its most literal sense:

> To determine the position [or place or space], we have to look at various other bodies which we regard as immobile; and in relation to different bodies we may say that the same thing is both changing and not changing its place at the same time. For example, when a ship is under way, a man sitting on the stern remains in one place relative to the other parts of the ship with respect to which his position is unchanged; but he is constantly changing place relative to the neighboring shores, since he is constantly receding from one shore and approaching another. Then again, if we believe the earth moves, and suppose that it advances the ship the same distance from west to east as the ship travels from east to west in the corresponding period of time, we shall again say that the man sitting on the stern is not changing place; for we are now determining the place by means of certain fixed points in the heavens. Finally, if we suppose that there are no such genuinely fixed points to be found in the universe (a supposition which will be shown below to be probable)[28] we shall conclude that nothing has a permanent place, except as determined by our thought.[29]

One might say that with this stroke, Descartes toppled a system of thinking on which the *topoi* were built. I don't argue that historically Descartes had that effect on rhetoric, but that the entire movement I have been outlining, and which Descartes expresses, overthrows the world of the *topoi*. With Descartes, boundaries moved and places became unfixed. In that New

World, what one needed was not memory devices to help retain twenty probable kinds of arguments, but one method that would steer through unknown and exceedingly complex cognitive terrains.

Recognizing the movability of all places and even most points of thought, Descartes offered a method at once skeptical and thorough, decentered and systematic. His method relied precisely on the recognition that true knowledge was sparse, that it happened in the individual mind, and that if one could only isolate the few points of certainty, from these points one could also build a system for attaining knowledge in any of its branches. If anything, his method was like that of a man lost in strange terrain who resolved to arrive somewhere rather than remain where he was:

> In this respect I would be imitating a traveller who, upon finding himself in a forest, should not wander about turning this way and that, and still less stay in one place, but should keep walking as straight as he can in one direction, never changing it for slight reasons. . . . In this way, even if he does not go exactly where he wishes, he will at least wind up in a place where he is likely to be better off than in the middle of a forest.[30]

We find similar passages on place in Locke and Leibniz. Leibniz took a more relational view of space, considering it but an idea of coexisting things and one of the ways by which the mind thinks about empty place. That is, space is an idea of the mind and not a source of a thing's identity.[31] Locke called place "nothing but a relative position" which requires two other fixed things to ascertain. Consequently, we have no idea of place in the universe, only in the human sphere where we can locate objects in relation to each other. Even then place shifts its meaning in relation to that which we think fixed. Pieces on a chessboard may remain in the same place even though the chess board is carried from room to room, and a chessboard may remain in the same place in a room on a ship even though the ship moves, and the ship may remain in the same place even though the earth has moved a thousand miles in space. In a slightly different sense, Locke said, we would mistake if, when someone asked us where a certain passage in Virgil was located, we said it was in the library.[32] Place had, it seems, become an icon for the way the mind organizes ideas in complex relations to each other.

We have moved away from rhetorical studies to consider the epistemology of Descartes's method and its implications in light of the sea-change that occurred in other branches of discourse in the seventeenth century. But what actually occurred in treatises on rhetoric? The places of invention and memory were disappearing. In a characteristic treatise of the late seventeenth century, The *Art of Speaking* (1675), Bernard Lamy criticized the study of topics as a source of rhetorical invention. Granted, he said, "it is not to be doubted but the helps accrewing from it are of some kind of use. They make us take notice of several things from whence Arguments may be drawn; they teach us how a subject may be vary'd, and discovered on all sides."[33] They give fecundity of thought and grant to orators plentiful "matter of discourse, even on Subjects on which they are entirely ignorant."[34] However, Lamy called this kind of fecundity trivial and inconvenient. "The Art of *Topicks* furnishes nothing that is fit for us to say." The speaker who relies on them will find that they are "unable to supply him with necessary knowledg[e] for decision of his Question." Topics gave a person "infinite Arguments that defend and fortifie one another," but what a person needs is usually only one telling, perspicuous argument.[35]

Perhaps equally persuasive evidence of the decline of the *topoi* came from those who noticed and contested its fall. Writing in *On the Study Methods of Our Time* (1709), Giambattista Vico attacked the new methods of study and philosophy, calling them "critique" not simply because they left behind long-valued, humanistic knowledge-stores, but because their assumptions failed to coincide with the world as humans experienced and discoursed of it. Vico based his view on an assessment of the instruments, complementary aids, and aims of learning. By instruments Vico meant both mechanical devices and the measures for collecting knowledge that were antecedent to a discipline; by complementary aids and procedures he meant those measures concomitant with the search for knowledge. Chemistry was an instrument of medicine, and the telescope one of astronomy. Learned societies and universities were complementary aids. Many of the instruments of modern knowledge surpassed those of the ancients, Vico agreed. However, the moderns ignored some instruments of the ancients that still offered extraordinary benefits. The topics were among these:

> In our days, instead, philosophical criticism alone is honored. The art of "topics," far from being given first place in the curriculum, is utterly disregarded. Again I say, this is harmful, since the invention of arguments is by nature prior to the judgment of their validity, so that, in teaching, that invention should be given priority over philosophical criticism.[36]

Vico's admiration for the old arts expressed more than mere nostalgia, more than a wish for refinement and elegance, and more than a logical distinction over whether invention or critical analysis should be prior.

> Nature and life are full of incertitude; the foremost, indeed, the only aim of our "arts" is to assure us that we have acted rightly. Criticism is the art of true

speech; "ars topica," of eloquence. Traditional "topics" is the art of finding "the *medium*," i.e., the middle term: in the conventional language of scholasticism, "medium" indicates what the Latin call *argumentum*. Those who know all the *loci*, i.e., the lines of argument to be used, are able (by an operation not unlike reading the printed characters on a page) to grasp extemporaneously the elements of persuasion inherent in any question or case. (Vico, 15)

We can see that both Vico and Descartes were motivated by incertitude and by a desire for knowledge congruent with the actual nature of humans and the physical world they live in. But they meant very different things by these terms. Vico accepted incertitude as a given in all human endeavor: "No doubt all that man is given to know is, like man himself, limited and imperfect" (Vico, 4). Within that imperfection, the humanistic arts offered a way of communicating, speaker to listener, that bound them in their mutual humanity, acknowledged their limits, beautified the realm in which the limits operated, and still guided people to right action. For Descartes, limits and imperfections offered obstacles that must be overcome. Perhaps nothing irritated Vico more than the presumption that the impediments of human understanding could be eliminated. Vico saw Bacon as an originator of that dehumanizing confidence.

> While he discovers a new cosmos of sciences, the great Chancellor proves to be rather the pioneer of a completely new universe than a prospector of this world of ours. His vast demands so exceed the utmost extent of man's effort that he seems to have indicated how we fall short of achieving an absolutely complete system of sciences rather than how we may remedy our cultural gaps. (Vico, 3)

Vico believed that Bacon behaved like "the potentates of mighty empires, who, having gained supremacy in human affairs, squander immense wealth in attempts against the order of Nature herself, by paving the seas with stones, mastering mountains with sail, and other vain exploits forbidden by nature"(Vico, 4). These hyperbolic figures express the core of Vico's concern for the dangers of critical philosophy. This philosophy was out of step with living in the world, with humans as they really interacted. Instead of pioneering new universes, Vico suggested, human beings should be prospecting this world of ours. The disagreement between Vico and the science that toppled the topics is mirrored in their approach to space. Vico wanted to reinstate our experience of familiar space. He would urge that when we walk down a lane or through a door, our senses orient us quite well and allow us to arrive at our destination. Those he opposed would agree but insisted all the same that if one wanted to understand more than the neighborhood, one had to bring to bear concepts of space that, although perhaps foreign to common sense, would accommodate the information that the instruments Vico despised were providing.

Notes

1 Debora Shuger, *Sacred Rhetoric: The Christian Grand Style in the English Renaissance* (Princeton: Princeton University Press, 1988), 73.
2 Philip Melanchthon, an early Protestant rhetorician, warns in *De modo et arte concionandi* (1537–39) against "solicitude for eloquence and figural ornament; these distract from the sincerity of the preacher and the power of the Spirit" (Shuger, 67). William Perkins, a Puritan theorist, agrees in *The Art of Prophesying* (1607, 1592 in Latin), in which he urges others to "dismiss or ignore rhetorical eloquence in favor of a plain and spiritual preaching" (Shuger, 69). The French Jesuit Nicholas Caussin, in his huge work *De eloquentia sacra et humana* (1617), launched an "attack on florid, artificial preaching equal to any English Puritan's. Christian oratory should be sublime, agonistic, and passionate, not ostentatious and ornamented with pseudo-Classical frippery" (Shuger, 88). Samuel Ward, a Puritan, in "A Coale from the Altar," condemns "witty and ornate preaching" (Shuger, 94–95).
3 Henry Peacham, *The Garden of Eloquence* [1577] (London, 1593), 3.
4 *Selected Sermons of Hugh Latimer*, ed. Allan G. Chester (Charlottesville: Folger Library and the University of Virginia Press, 1968), 30.
5 Unless otherwise noted, subsequent quotations of Francis Bacon are cited in the text according to the abbreviations listed below: Each citation will include the abbreviated title followed by the volume and page number as given in *The Works of Francis Bacon*, ed. James Spedding, Robert Ellis, and Douglas Heath, 14 vols. (London: Longman, 1860).

Adv L	*Of the Dignity and Advancement of Learning*
GI	*The Great Instauration*
New O	*The New Organon or True Directions Concerning the Interpretation of Nature*
NWS	*The New World of Science or Desiderata*
IN	*Of the Interpretation of Nature*

6 Thomas Sprat, *History of the Royal Society of London, for Improving of Natural Knowledge* [1667], ed. Jackson I. Cope and Harold W. Jones (St. Louis: Washington University Press, 1958), 111.
7 Michel de Montaigne, "Of Cannibals," in *The Complete Works of Montaigne: Essays, Travel Journal, Letters*, trans. Donald M. Frame (Stanford: Stanford University Press, 1958), 153.
8 Diego Valadés, *Rhetorica Christiana* [1579], ed. and trans. Esteban J. Palomera, Alfonso Castro Pallares, and Tarsicio Herrera Zapién (Mexico: Universidad Nacional Autónoma de México, Fondo de Cultura Económica, 1989), Praefatio Auctoris. In subsequent references, page numbers before the slash refer to the original Latin edition; those after refer to the Spanish translation in this cited edition.
9 Aristotle, *The Rhetoric of Aristotle*, trans. Lane Cooper (New York: Appleton, Century, Crofts, 1932), 6.

10 Quoted in Richard McKeon, "Creativity and Commonplace," in *Rhetoric: Essays in Invention and Discovery* (Woodbridge, CT: Ox Bow, 1987), 26.

11 Quintilian, *Institutes of Oratory, or Education of an Orator*, trans. John Selby Watson (London: George Bell and Sons, 1909), 10.5, 12–13.

12 Cassiodorus, *An Introduction to Divine and Human Readings*, trans. Leslie Webber Jones (New York: Columbia University Press, 1946), 172–76.

13 John of Salisbury, *The Metalogicon of John of Salisbury: A Twelfth-Century Defense of the Verbal and Logical Arts of the Trivium*, trans. Daniel D. McGarry (Berkeley: University of California Press, 1955), bk. 3, chap. 9, pp. 186–87.

14 Edgar Mentner, "Topos und Commonplace," in *Strena Anglica: Fetschrift für Otto Ritter*, ed. G. Dietrich and F. W. Shulze (Halle: Niemeyer, 1956), 195.

15 Quoted in Joachim Dyck, "The First German Treatise on Homiletics: Erasmus Sarcer's *Pastorale* and Classical Rhetoric," in *Renaissance Eloquence: Studies in the Theory and Practice of Renaissance Rhetoric*, ed. James J. Murphy (Berkeley: University of California Press, 1983), 221–37.

16 Joan Marie Lechner, *Renaissance Concepts of the Commonplaces* (New York: Pageant, 1962), 131.

17 Quintilian, *Institutes of Oratory*, 5.10, 19–23, as quoted in Lechner, *Renaissance Concepts*, 144.

18 Wilbur Samuel Howell, *Logic and Rhetoric in England, 1500–1700* (Princeton: Princeton University Press, 1956), 9.

19 Walter J. Ong, "Peter Ramus," in *The Encyclopedia of Philosophy*, vol. 7 (New York: Macmillan, 1967).

20 Peter Ramus, *The Logike of the most excellent Philosopher P. Ramus Martyr*, trans. R. MacIlmaine (London, 1574), 94.

21 Ramus, *Logike*, 97.

22 René Descartes, *Discourse on the Method*, in *The Philosophical Writings of Descartes*, trans. J. Cottingham, R. Stoothoff, and D. Murdoch (Cambridge: Cambridge University Press, 1985), 1:119.

23 F. M. Cornford, "The Invention of Space," in *Essays in Honour of Gilbert Murray* (London: Allen & Unwin, 1936), 222.

24 Giordano Bruno, *De Immenso et Innumerabilibus* [1591], in *Opera Latine Conscripta . . .* (Naples: Morano, 1879), 1:8.

25 Murad D. Akhundov, *Conceptions of Space and Time: Sources, Evolution, Directions*, trans. Charles Rougle (Cambridge: MIT Press, 1986), 110.

26 Roberto Torreti, "Space," in *Routledge Encyclopedia of Philosophy*, ed. Edward Craig, vol. 9 (London: Routledge, 1998).

27 Isaac Newton, "On the Gravity and Equilibrium of Liquids," in *Unpublished Scientific Papers of Isaac Newton*, ed. and trans. A. R. Hall and M. B. Hall (Cambridge: Cambridge University Press, 1962), 92.

28 The French translates *demonstrable* more properly than "probable."

29 René Descartes, *Principles of Philosophy*, in Cottingham, Stoothoff, and Murdoch, *The Philosophical Writings of Descartes*, 1:228.

30 Descartes, *Discourse on the Method*, 1:123.

31 G. W. Leibniz, *New Essays on Human Understanding* [1703], trans. and ed. Peter Remnant and Jonathan Bennett (Cambridge: Cambridge University Press, 1981), 127, 221, 230.

32 John Locke, *An Essay concerning Human Understanding*, ed. Peter H. Nidditch (Oxford: Clarendon, 1975), 2.8; 7–10; pp. 169–71.

33 Bernard Lamy, *The Art of Speaking, written in French by Messieurs Du Port Royal, in pursuance of a former treatise intituled The Art of Thinking, and rendered into English* [French 1675] (London, 1696), 279.

34 Lamy, *Art of Speaking*, 272.

35 Ibid., 280–81.

36 Giambattista Vico, *On the Study Methods of Our Time* [1709], trans. Elio Gianturco (Ithaca: Cornell University Press, 1990), 14.

7 Locke and After: Language as the Mind's Space[1]

Although the inhabitants of Europe . . . are constantly publishing new collections of travels and reports, I am convinced that the only men we know are the Europeans.

—*Rousseau*[2]

The same upheavals in space and place theory that toppled the *topoi* from their high role in rhetoric also gave rise to a revolution in theories of language. This revolution occurred because of John Locke. Locke aimed to explain how human understanding arises from simple ideas that our minds combine, manipulate, and reflect upon. Language was vital to this process, and Locke's ideas on mind and language utilized both conventional spatial ideas and new conceptions of space. The chief conventional use occurs in his navigational metaphors, the need to compare the points of view that different locations offer, and his overall conception of the "way of ideas," a spatial metaphor of a path or route that explains the process of assembling simple ideas into more complex ideas. The new conceptions, which relate directly to his spatial metaphors, are reflected in his analysis of our ideas of place and space, an analysis that makes these much more contingent and conventional than his contemporaries had thought. I will explore these metaphors and ideas and then trace the consequences of the spatial treatment of language in the way his followers dealt with the problem of abstraction. Together, these thinkers treated language as a cognitive map—something far beyond a mere lexicon the mind uses for objects in the world. Language provided an architecture with its own structure which, like the conventions of mapping, allow us to represent the world in a different medium. Language is the mind's space. Just as objects exist in space in the world, certain ideas exist only in words and can be located and related to other ideas only through language. Understanding language in Locke and his followers resembles understanding a system of navigation. We have our familiar locales wherein we move comfortably, but moving from a familiar locale to a strange one far away requires arbitrary reference points and compass directions. Locke showed that to go from ordinary knowledge to foreign perspectives, or to understand the ways in which the mind creates knowledge, entails a similar need for a system of points and directions. His exploration of language comprised the epistemological equivalent of terrestrial navigation.

So radical was Locke's *Essay concerning Human Understanding*, and particularly its language theory, that Hans Aarsleff has written, "The *Essay* was literally epoch-making, and such works never fail to efface their own past; in fact, one can almost say that the *Essay* has no other history than that which was its own future."[3] In a study of seventeenth-century language thought which repeatedly calls Locke's theory "radical" and a "pivot" in the "revolution in semantic theory," Lia Formigari succeeds in identifying precedents only for those parts of Locke's theory that were not radical or pivotal.[4] Part of the problem of defining the past for pivotal texts may lie in where we look. The *Essay*'s past has often been sought in seventeenth-century language study or in the philosophy of rationalists and proto-empiricists. Yet there may be elements of culture not immediately associated with the issues Locke wrote about, but which conditioned his thinking about them.

Spatial models, including those found in travel narratives, are such elements.

Spatial Metaphors and Travel Literature

Locke collected and read voyages omnivorously. Peter Laslett calls this a "perpetual preoccupation" and believes that in applying his wide reading, "Locke may be said to have done more than anyone else to found the study of comparative anthropology."[5] John Harrison and Laslett show that books of travel and geography comprised the fifth largest category in Locke's library, ahead of works of philosophy, natural science, modern literature, and history. And he would have owned more had more been available. Evidence that Locke actually read what he owned also appears most frequently among this class of volumes, and citations to them occur more frequently than citations to other types of literature in the *Essay*. In the 1706 edition, the first book alone has sixteen citations, fifteen of them travel books.[6] By examining these travel books and the way the *Essay* uses them, we better understand how Locke's reading led to his revolutionary language theories.

Travel literature helped Locke escape the condition that Rousseau would later define and which I quote as the opening epigraph to this chapter, that even travel literature may only yield closer acquaintance with Europe. The trick was to read them looking for the absolutely foreign. Travel literature expanded intellectual boundaries that most thinkers considered fixed and well marked, making the familiar appear strange and altogether less certain than before. In travel books Locke confronted humans who thought and behaved so differently from Europeans that seventeenth-century linguistic conventionalism—the principle that sounds applied arbitrarily rather than naturally to the things named—was insufficient to explain how such variety could occur in ideas as well as words. As Locke worked to develop a theory that could account for both European and non-European ways of thinking, he turned English thought into a topic of study that could be viewed with objectivity—something that could be seen with some separation between it and the subject. Travel literature thus helped Locke confront the foreign just as literal travel, especially to distant and unknown places, brings with it a sense of geographical dislocation and new places in which to locate oneself and view others.

As travel books triggered this shift, they also provided Locke with linguistic information to use as evidence for his idea–language theories. The linguistic material recorded in travel books required careful scrutiny, however; it was often incorrect and had usually been gathered to support erroneous ethnocentric assumptions. But once Locke read that information in light of his theories, he could understand it more thoroughly than did those who recorded it. His theory turned anomaly into coherence and thus into evidence for the theories that made anomaly comprehensible. In brief, Locke saw that as they assemble complex ideas from simpler ones, individuals and peoples collect under single terms very different combinations of ideas, that terms from one language do not coincide neatly with those from another, and that to understand what a term means requires not that we grasp an innate concept or an essence but that we analyze the combination of ideas those who use the term have in their heads when they use it.

Locke casts much of the *Essay* in metaphors of travel and discovery: "Every step the Mind takes in its Progress towards Knowledge, makes some Discovery, which is not only new, but the best, too, for the time at least." Speaking of successive versions of the *Essay*, he records how an initially modest text grew as "New Discoveries led me still on" (Epistle to the Reader).[7] The *Essay* would "search out the Bounds between Opinion and Knowledge" (1.1.3) and map out those areas where truth was vital. A navigational metaphor conveys a major point, that to ascertain what we know we must also understand the means by which we know: "'Tis of great use to the Sailor to know the length of his Line, though he cannot with it fathom all the depths of the Ocean. 'Tis well he knows, that it is long enough to reach the bottom, at such Places, as are necessary to direct his

Voyage, and caution him against running upon Shoals, that may ruin him" (1.1.6). Until such work was done, Locke feared, we "in vain sought for Satisfaction in a quiet and secure Possession of Truths, that most concern'd us, whilst we let loose our Thoughts into the vast Ocean of Being, as if all that boundless Extent, were the natural, and undoubted Possession of our Understandings." Consequently, many thinkers were "extending their Enquiries beyond their Capacities, and letting their Thoughts wander into those depths, where they can find no sure Footing" (1.1.7).

Voyages, possessions, sure footings, discoveries—these figures are also germane to his methods. In case after case, he reaches to "remote ages and nations" to achieve in the domains of human understanding a task similar to that performed in navigation by map makers. By figuratively journeying in space and time, Locke increases certainty and clarity as he gives multiple viewpoints on difficult-to-grasp topics: "Some objects had need be turned on every side" (Epistle to the Reader). His topic being not merely British, but human, understanding, Locke saw that he could not content himself with viewing his object only as seen by his predecessors and colleagues. Viewing the marvelous phenomena that even an increasingly mapped and rationalized world contained also helped him to turn European ideas on different sides. Shaftesbury and Voltaire jested over Locke's credulous use of travelers' tales,[8] but their jests say less about his credulity than about the complacency of Europeans who mistook their own ideas for universal truth. Neal Wood records the following vignette: "A dozen years before his death the long-suffering Locke, embroiled in an extended controversy with a tenacious Jonas Proast, caustically replied to his learned critic who had confessed ignorance of the ways of the West Indians: 'But whatever you may think, I assure you the world is not Mile-end.'"[9]

Locke's procedure increased the challenge of describing and encompassing human nature and ideas within a theory. He met the challenge not by offering a catalog or encyclopedia of ideas but by elucidating the process by which ideas come into being in the mind. The *Essay's* successive drafts evolved as Locke kept before him the task of representing the expanding world. Locke first thought of writing the *Essay* in an entirely domestic setting. He had been disputing with a small circle of friends when it occurred to him that their dispute had as much to do with the meaning each person gave to key terms as with the nominal topic of discussion. Locke thought he would clarify this matter in a page or two, but the project grew from within, as he saw the need to bring the implications of his ideas clearly to view, and from without, as he regulated his speculations by way of his knowledge of the beliefs and mores of far-flung peoples.

In his earliest drafts of the *Essay*, Locke weaves the strands of a rudimentary comparative anthropology. His first (1671) makes few specific references either to travel books or to the ideas of different peoples. But already he can be seen deliberating on the difficulty of integrating his awareness of what we call cultural conditioning into a broader theory of knowledge. After he ponders how Jamaicans might name ice or what an English child might call a mandrill, Locke observes, "Nor is it soe easy as we imagin to destinguish things precisely into species, though for discourse & our ease sake & to serve the common affairs of life we confidently give names or receive the names commonly given though confusedly as if they were destinguishd, because it is very hard to set downe or collect that precise number of simple Ideas which doe necessarily goe to the makeing up any one species" (*Drafts*, 9).[10] If species are harder to establish than previously thought, Locke argues, then one path to certainty requires wide sampling of the opinions of humanity: "The first therefor & highest degree of Probability is when the general consent of all men in all ages as far as it can be knowne, concurs with a mans constant & never faieling experience in like cases, to confirm the truth of any particular proposition" (*Drafts*, 63).

After this beginning, it is not surprising that the second draft (also 1671) makes an early appeal to those readers who have "looked abroad beyond the smoke of their own chimneys" (*Drafts*, 104–5) and refers regularly to the peoples of Brazil, Africa, North America, Asia, and the West Indies. Sometimes Locke hypothetically places the reader abroad to convince of the contextual nature of language and ideas: "Had you or I been born in Soldania" or "had Tottepottemay been educated in England," he begins one conjecture, "our thoughts and notions had not exceeded those . . . of the savages there," and Tottepottemay "had perhaps been as zealous a Christian & as good an Architect as any." In either case, "the exercise of their facultys was bounded within the ways modes & notions of their owne countrys" (*Drafts*, 120). Locke's recognition that ideas and customs develop in accordance with, and are hedged and constrained by, different situations and needs would be further elaborated, with profound implications, in the published *Essay*.

Equally important, in the second draft Locke perceives that, insofar as morality is concerned, no opinion can be shown to meet the test he had earlier seen as yielding the highest probability of truth, the test of universal acceptance: "He that will carefully peruse the history of mankind & looke abroad into the severall tribes of men & with indifferency survey their actions will be able to satisfie him self, that there is not that principle of morality to be named nor that rule of virtue to be thought on, which is not some where or other slighted & condemned by the general practise of a whole society of men, governd by quite opposite practical opinions & rules of liveing" (*Drafts*, 110). As an empirical, inductive, and negative universal, this assertion implicitly calls for a new theory of knowledge. Such a theory would have to circumscribe the actual variety of notions that humans hold, without committing itself to the truth or falsehood of any particular set of beliefs. This theory would also have to take into account the positionality of much knowledge. The theory also runs counter to much seventeenth-century linguistic conventionalism, which assumed that while sounds could be arbitrarily assigned to name objects and ideas (or "notions" as the latter were usually called), the objects and ideas themselves were stable, natural, and universal. It is as if the nations offered different vantage points from which to view the world.

Locke seemed to find the geographical metaphor increasingly productive. As he prepared the *Essay* for the public he incorporated more and more references to travel literature. His first published version of 1690 makes more references to specific travel narratives and more allusions to others' beliefs and customs, and more citations to works of travel are added in the subsequent revised editions. The first book of the 1690 edition has only two citations; the fifth edition (1706) has sixteen, counting in-text references and footnotes—all but one to travel texts. Fourteen of the fifteen footnotes in the entire 1706 *Essay* cite travel books. The lone exception, which treats of recent European wars and politics, Locke connects with an anecdote of a Brazilian talking parrot.[11]

By presenting shifting viewpoints—places from which actual people see things differently—Locke more certainly established what is and is not humanly true, what is possible and impossible, what is known and unknown. He draws attention to "remote Ages, and different Countries" (3.9.10), "different Countries, and remote Ages" (3.9.22), "Languages of remote Countries or Ages" (3.11.25), "Children, Ideots, Savages" (1.2.26), and numerous monsters, brutes, prodigies, and borderline cases such as the child born "with a Man's Head and a Hog's Body" (3.6.27). To illustrate a hypothesis about the naming of complex ideas, he supposes "Adam in the State of a grown Man, with a good Understanding, but in a strange country, with all Things new, and unknown about him" (3.6.44). With this move Locke creates a hypothetical scenario of travel in space and time. In displacing Adam he has him follow his own path, one he makes explicit in his analysis of reflection. That is, he exercises judgment and comparison within matrices of the familiar and unfamiliar, known species and borderline cases, the present and past, the here and the far away. Locke makes comparison so central to his theory of knowledge that we can easily overlook it. Despite his frequent characterization as an empiricist, Locke considers the senses to give access only to simple ideas—data streams of touch, smell, sound—which the mind assembles into complex ideas. He continually returns to comparisons, contrasts, and relations to clarify ideas. "Unless the Mind had a distinct Perception of different Objects, and their Qualities, it would be capable of very little Knowledge. . . . On the faculty of Distinguishing one thing from another, depends the evidence and certainty of several, even very general Propositions" (2.11.1). Comparison is "the Prerogative of Humane Understanding, when it has sufficiently distinguished any Ideas . . . to cast about and consider in what circumstances they are capable to be compared" (2.11.5). Upon these operations depend the compounding, relating, and abstracting by which the mind creates knowledge.

Locke's views on place and space set the stage for his language theories. Locke treated these ideas to show how fundamental ideas occur to us in different modes, whether the mind derives the ideas from existent things or makes them within itself. Take space. We have ideas of space through touch and sight. Most immediately, it is the distance between two things. It can next be a bounded area. It can next be immensity, either finite or infinite (2.13.2–4). It is not one thing but several things extended and elaborated from a simple idea as the need arises and held together by one term, even though separate terms could be given to each mode. Space as immensity has no marks or variety (2.13.10). It is a blank three-dimensional continuum and therefore offers no bearings. If someone were to ask him to define the nature of space, however, Locke would reply, "I know not," and "I will tell him, when he tells me what his Extension is" or "when they that ask, shew me a clear distinct idea of Substance" (2.13.15, 17). Ideas exist and function without our knowing their exact nature.

Whereas he viewed pure space as a somewhat abstract notion, a space without solidity and resistance in and out of which one can move an object while leaving all others at rest (2.13.10), he treated place as simultaneously relative and determinate. Place is nothing but a relative position, he states, requiring at least two other fixed locations to ascertain. This is an important point. As we negotiate a room or navigate an ocean, we know our place by its relation to other things that are at rest. We apply the same technique as we attempt to fix ideas in an intellectual activity. In order to do so, we must either find several other items that are, so to speak, at rest, or we must determine to treat them as if they were. Defining is a way of stabilizing in relation to other ideas.

In going from physical position to "place" in discourse, I am leaping from an ordinary to a metaphorical sense of place. That is precisely what Locke does. His discussion of place assumes that there are different orders of place according to the nature of the reference points that ascertain it. Locke notes that, in answer to the question, In what place do those verses telling the story of Nisus and Eurialus occur in the *Aeneid*? it would be improper to say, "They were in such a part of the Earth, or in *Bodley*'s Library" (2.13.9). The idea of "place" in a text, or, by extension, in a discourse, means something quite different from a physical location. The mind works through spatial ideas even of different orders quite comfortably, yet it is clear that ordinary place, or location, grounds the different senses.

However, even ordinary place is not as simple as a fixed location. One must know those things to which an object lies in relation in order to fix a place. It is not a fixed location but one determined in relation to other positions which are, for the moment, considered fixed: "Our Idea of Place, is nothing else, but such a relative Position of any thing" (2.13.10). Location is not absolute but relational. Locke observed that chess men may remain at rest in relation to each other while the chess board is moved, and the chess board may remain at rest in a ship's cabin while the ship moves through a harbor (2.13.8). Knowing a place requires a context in which place has meaning. Knowing place or position requires one to place it in relation to other things determined to be at rest. In a world in motion, that act of relating would be influenced to some degree by purpose and context. It could even be arbitrary. Similarly, in language, words are not fixed *a priori* but determined in relation to the component ideas to which they refer, and these ideas cohere in relation to other assemblages of ideas composed by the mind.

In parallel fashion, in the section on complex ideas of relations, Locke points out that many ideas exist only in relation to others. Fathers are so only by having children; wives by having husbands. All ideas of cause and effect, magnitude of any order, identity, and diversity are ideas of relation, as are most ideas other than those of objects as they appear to the senses. We can form direct ideas only of substances and, with some limitations, our own emotions and state of mind. Perhaps only by locating boundaries between knowledge and opinion do most ideas take on fixed and useful meanings and cease to be sounds "without clear and distinct Ideas" (3.10.2). For Locke language partakes in these limitations but offers, in tandem with the ideas of the mind, a complex means of organizing and constructing knowledge by combining and relating ideas. It aids us in distinguishing objects by beholding them from a proper distance and assigning names to them, and it composes more intricate ideas by relating single concepts and conjoining them into coherent, complex concepts. Since it organizes elements in one medium by a complex set of internal and external relations and maps these relations onto other domains in the external world, we might with little exaggeration say that language is the mind's space.

Language Information in Travel Literature

Locke found ample evidence for his theory of mind and language in travel literature. Language information in these narratives falls into four broad, overlapping categories: (1) word lists with their equivalents in European languages, (2) analyses of vocabularies, with comments on the presence or absence of terms important in European culture, (3) grammatical comparisons and analyses, and (4) descriptions of customs and ways of thinking which, to Locke, had linguistic implications. Occasionally, one finds an important fifth category: some writers protested the inaccurate linguistic information found in most travel reports and the invalid conclusions drawn from it.

Locke's overt citations of travel works nearly always relate to these four categories of information, especially to analyses of vocabularies and descriptions of customs and ways of thinking. In one paragraph on the lack of innate ideas regarding God, the treatment of children, and the kinds of virtue, Locke refers to eight travel accounts (1.3.9). In a similar section on people who lack an idea of God, he cites nine if we count a work on Chinese religion (1.4.8).[12] These two passages have an unusually high number of references; in the rest of the *Essay* Locke occasionally refers to the words or ideas of exotic peoples, but never so plentifully as here, where empirical evidence (or what could pass for it) seems to be imperative and decisive. It is not enough to argue that ideas can differ; Locke has to demonstrate that they do so. He accomplishes this by showing that certain ideas, believed to exist universally, do not occur in many nations. The lack of such ideas is, of course, not strictly a linguistic matter, but Locke shows that it was inseparable from language.

Having confirmed that ideas differ among peoples, Locke can later adduce general claims that will resist challenge, the implication being that he could cite facts abundantly if he wished to do so. When he asserts in Book 3 that every language has a "great store of Words . . . which have not any answer in another," his argumentation, together with passing references to the likes of the "Caribee or Westoe Tongues" (3.5.8), precludes refutation. When arguing for the semiotic contingency of ideas, Locke also makes reference to "Americans" and "Tououpinambos" to show that nations who have no specific word for a number such as one thousand have no fixed idea of it either. Or, in showing that species terms can vary as much as terms of measurement, he refers to the weights and measures of Japan and to the inhabitants of America who measure the year by the return of a certain bird.

Locke would have found several types of especially useful information in a work he refers to three times, Jean de Léry's *History of a Voyage to the Land of Brazil,* originally published in French in 1578. Léry provides not only word lists and rudimentary grammatical information but a colloquy between a Frenchman and a Tupi informant. Much of the vocabulary names simple objects, the least problematic kind of language for Locke. But Léry notes the lack of words for distinguishing between a village and a city, "because of their own customs: they have no cities." The Tupi lexicon for lineage makes it evident that peoples differ in the relations they name. The Tupi have separate names for older and younger brother and for mother and father's companion—that is, the wife of one's father, who is not one's own mother—but they use the same word for father and uncle.[13] As we shall see, this kind of information becomes highly relevant to Locke's theory that many complex ideas have an element of arbitrariness because they select, from myriad sets of possible notions, certain ones that then are preserved and distinguished by names.

Locke may also have confirmed his theories in a more negative fashion—in the course of studying reports on language and communication written by those whose language assumptions differed from his own. His developing views may have helped him to make better sense of the information he read than those who recorded it had been able to do. For example, the French Jesuit Gabriel Sagard, a missionary among the Hurons of North America in the early 1600s, describes conversations with the Indians as follows:

> They would explain as best they could what I wanted to learn from them. And as sometimes they could not make me understand their conceptions they would explain them to me by figures, similitudes, and external demonstrations, sometimes in speech, and sometimes with a stick, tracing the object on the ground as best they could, or by a movement of the body . . . rather than by long speeches and reasonings that they might have advanced. For their language is very poor and defective in words for many things, and particularly so as concerns the mysteries of our holy religion, which we could not explain to them, not even the *Pater noster,* except by periphrases; that is to say, for one of our words we had to use several of theirs, for with them there is no knowledge of Sanctification, the Kingdom of Heaven, the most Holy Sacrament, nor of leading into temptation.[14]

Sagard overlooks the evidence of the cognitive flexibility of the Indians, as seen in their many strategies for communicating the meaning of their words to an outsider, even as he records it. Instead he assumes he has the conceptual and linguistic tools for access to the Huron tongue and that any difficulty in communicating resides in its poverty. But implicit in Sagard's account are other possible explanations that a reader like Locke would perceive. First, the problem of translation affects the Huron and French speakers equally. Sagard, secure in his religious, cognitive, and technological superiority, ignores the fact that both groups—not merely the French—have to use paraphrase and imagery to convey what to them are simple ideas corresponding to single words. Second, the differences in Huron and French cannot be accounted for by their relative closeness to an already determined set of ideas and terms such as those represented in the Pater noster. Third, the Huron practice of drawing a picture is right in line with Locke's position on definitions of certain terms. In the *Essay* he proposes that picture dictionaries would be much more effective than lexical ones for accurately conveying notions of material things (3.11.25). Fourth, Sagard's passage can be read as confirming Locke's point that peoples' ideas develop not in reference to a set of universals but in reference to their circumstances and needs. Why, Locke might ask, should a missionary be surprised to learn that non-Christian inhabitants of a distant land do not have discrete terms for what are actually very complex doctrines such as "Holy Sacrament"?

Locke might also have arrived at his conclusions more directly through another author. Garcilaso de la Vega, the son of a Spanish soldier and a native Peruvian woman, wrote several works to correct the Spanish historians who distorted Peruvian languages and customs as they wrote so authoritatively about them. Garcilaso gave clear examples of several principles on which Locke would himself insist. One principle holds that every language has terms that cannot be translated into other languages by word-for-word substitutions into another language. For example, the Inca word *huaca* is a sacred term with no counterpart in Spanish; roughly, it means "divine," "wonder," "excellence," "prodigy," or "monster."[15]

Another principle holds that the meaning of words inheres in the idea-complexes they stand for, not in standard definitions. In his *Royal Commentaries of the Incas*, Garcilaso takes pains to point out "the wealth of meaning that the Indians are able to pack into a single word." The term *apachecta*, which the Spanish mistook as referring to the steep slopes where the Indians made their devotions, actually refers to the act of carrying offerings and was used only when one had reached the crest. The word denotes "giving thanks and offering something to the one who enables us to carry these burdens and gives us health and strength to scale such rugged slopes as this" (Garcilaso, 78). Here is an assemblage of ideas designated by a word whose meaning is synonymous with that assemblage and not with an abstract essence or single concept. Locke showed that a degree of arbitrariness appears in the ideas that people determine to fix in language. That being the case, what counts as knowledge shifts from one society to another.

Garcilaso's *Royal Commentaries* illustrates another principle, that the vocabulary of every language preserves complex ideas that have no referents in nature. A large number of these occur in moral discourse. They are "made by the mind, but made very arbitrarily, made without patterns, or reference to any real existence" (Locke, 3.5.3). *Apachecta* is an example. By "arbitrary" or "without pattern," Locke means to say that such words name only a few of the possible ways of assembling ideas in any set of circumstances. In the Inca language, many terms differ according to the gender of the speaker, including words for "child," "children," "spinning," and many other articles and activities:

> Those who are interested in philology may like to know that the general language of Peru has two words for children: the father says *churi* and the mother *huahua*. . . . The two nouns mean "child" or "children," each including both sexes and singular and plural. But they are strictly limited to either father or mother, and cannot be changed round without implying that the male is female and the female, male. . . . They have four different words to name brothers and sisters. Brother calls brother *huauque*, "brother." Sister calls sister *ñaña*, "sister." If the brother said *ñaña* of his sister, it would imply he was a girl. (Garcilaso, 211)

The Incas also used different verbs for "to tell," depending on whether one tells good or bad things. While an English person would see no need to differentiate such matters, these terms make as much sense as do English terms of familial relationships—as Locke shows by asking why we have terms for parricide, adultery, and incest, but none for the murder of, or sexual relations with, persons related to us in any number of other ways.

Since Locke took as a given that people differed in their ideas, for him the corrective lay not in simply accumulating more information but in examining things through more comprehensively conceived relations and comparisons. Before debating the validity of different knowledge, Locke urged that we pay attention to the process by which different opinions were formed. From the first draft of the *Essay* forward he showed a constant concern for making inferences based on wide and diverse knowledge. In his manuscript "Of the Conduct of the Understanding," which Locke composed as an additional book of the *Essay*, he defined one of the principal causes of error as narrow acquaintance and knowledge. "We are all short sighted," he observed. "We see but in part, and we know but in part, and therefore 'tis no wonder we conclude not right from our partial views." To remedy this situation, even the "proudest esteemer of his own parts" will find it useful to consult others, even those whose quickness and penetration fall short of his own. Those who neglect wide and diverse reading and conversation

> have a pretty traffick with known correspondents in some little creek: within that they confine themselves. . . . Those who live thus mued up within their own contracted territories . . . but live separate from the notions, discourses, and attainments of the rest of mankind, may not amiss be represented by the inhabitants of the Marian Islands; which being separated by a large tract of sea from all communion with the habitable parts of the earth, thought themselves the only people of the world.[16]

But understanding diverse phenomena was never a simple matter for Locke. True, he stressed the importance of reflecting upon what one saw or read and of drawing conclusions—"'Tis not enough to cram ourselves with a great load of collections, unless we chew them up again."[17] But the entire *Essay* presents evidence that many ideas—as well as inferences derived from them—depend on the use and convenience of those who construct them.

The Problem of Abstraction

Of the many influences of Locke on eighteenth-century language thought, I choose to concentrate on abstractions and general terms because they demonstrate how spatial models played a role in conceptualizing the underlying causes of language differences. Abstract and general terms demonstrate how flexibly and effortlessly—and how differently—our minds use ideas of the most abstract order, how we make them explicit as the need arises, and how contingent those ideas are upon the people, occasion, and purpose that call them into being. If, as I have analogized, language is the mind's space, abstract ideas provide the largest frame in which to locate other ideas and perceive the divisions and hierarchies in related ideas. Abstractions and generalizations provide an essential means by which we relate ideas in a total discourse because they belong by nature to the possible hierarchies of generality, gradually detaching from physical objects like pens and rocks to identify classes of things and then classes of ideas that relate ideas of things. Because such a process is integral to culture, the abstract terms of various peoples yield a window into their systems of ideas.

As theories developed, the problem became a puzzle: how could ostensibly universal processes of thought give birth to ideas that differed so demonstrably from one people to another that it became possible to question whether the thought processes were in fact the same? Or, to put it another way, if language constitutes or even just conditions thought, do not linguistic differences come to signify mental differences?

Given the influence of Locke on these speculations, it will be no surprise that spatial models continued to influence the discussion. Travel narratives also continued to provide the type of dislocation that fostered an openness to new ideas. Several figures to be discussed actually took part in expeditions to measure the curvature of the earth and returned with a keener interest in the mental and linguistic differences of humanity. Travelers had already paid close attention to the abstract terminology of languages, often measuring the stature of a society by its words, but Locke provided a new, less normative viewpoint. Abstractions and general terms differed drastically from people to people. Lacking innate ideas, nations and peoples chart their own physical and cultural worlds. A study of abstraction opens up to view how this charting is possible even when beings of a similar nature inhabit what are ostensibly different mental worlds. Étienne Bonnot de Condillac would eventually reason that to a large extent, thinking was language, and language was thinking.

Eighteenth-century discussions of difference in the naming functions of language inevitably created certain tensions in theory. One explanation for the tension is that universality and difference appear to be simple contrasting terms like motion and stillness, fast and slow, old and young, but they are not just contrasting terms. They are rather, like space and subject, a dialectical pair, existing only in terms of each other while not of the same order. Sameness is by its nature that which can be assimilated into systematic representation. True difference—not merely variation within a class or paradigm—can be more radical. Descriptions of difference often reduce it to known paradigms and thus reduce differences to distinct ways in which similarity manifests itself, but some types of difference defy such reduction. Difference can signify precisely that which cannot be systematized, domesticated, or assimilated. It is the remainder left over after we have explained something unfamiliar in terms of familiar knowledge. Thus, any description of what is universal and what is different in human nature or one of its manifestations—for example, language—will be problematic, however suggestive its articulation. Perhaps this fact explains why suggestiveness has often been the rule in discussions of linguistic relativism.

A more pointed reason for the theoretic tension exists. Any explanation of linguistic universality and difference will inevitably involve a complex and elusive fourfold relationship among mind, language, the Other with whom a subject communicates, and the external world. Most theories place one element prior to the others in the chain of causes that bring about language's development and traits. Discussions of linguistic universals naturally focus attention on the language component, but to isolate any element is a challenging task. These elements not only affect and are affected by each other; they paradoxically constitute each other. Neither language nor mind nor external nature can be isolated for its effects without first recognizing how each in turn exists only in conjunction with the other elements, yet without being reduced to the others. For example, to specify how mind can belong to and yet demarcate itself from an external reality is endlessly difficult. It becomes more so when we recognize that mind cannot so exist and differentiate itself without some sort of language in which to represent nature, itself, and even itself representing itself.[18] Nor can language exist without a mind which creates it and is created by it, an external reality that calls for naming, and social others to whom we communicate. The existence of others—non-selves who appear in the external world and call forth a response from the self—is another ingredient difficult to isolate because in some ways others exist in the world external to the subject; yet our sharing of language separates the Other from external nature in kinship with the subject. The very possibility of communication with others implies that an underlying sameness can be manifest through and in spite of the medium of different languages. The eighteenth-century fascination with natural language and gesture arose from this possibility.[19]

The subtle and complex problems that result from describing the influence of thinking (the mind) or culture (minds in collective activity) on language and vice versa usually stem from the assumption that mind or language exists independently and can be analyzed separately. But any analysis that identifies one element as prior to the others will inevitably reveal traces of the other elements. This is a problem inherent in analysis itself, but especially so in relation to language. In fact, the problem of abstraction is mirrored here: we can name mind, language, world, and the Other, but naming may not imply the discrete existence of the thing we name nor a knowledge of it even if it does so exist.

We must return briefly to Locke since he is the first to articulate how abstractions could differ radically from language to language. Most travel narratives presented linguistic similarity and difference in a grid of the familiar and the wonderful or the superior and the inferior. However, Locke saw in them something far more profound: the extraordinary range of naming that language made possible. He perceived that ideas differed from one people to another to such a degree that the vocabulary of one language often could not be translated directly into others and that behind differences in lexicon were differences in ideas:

> A moderate skill in different Languages, will easily satisfie one of the truth of
> this, it being so obvious to observe great store of Words in one Language, which
> have not any that answer them in another. Which plainly shews, that those of
> one Country, by their customs and manner of Life, have found occasion to make
> several complex Ideas, and give names to them, which others never collected
> into specifick Ideas. (3.5.8)

Linguistic differences, Locke could see, reflected different ideas—different
conceptions of the world assembled by reflection and association from the
simple data of sensory perception.

Because ideas vary, and because ideas and sounds are linked arbitrarily,
Locke could argue that language was ultimately private: "Every Man has so
inviolable a Liberty, to make Words stand for what Ideas he pleases, that no
one hath the Power to make others have the same Ideas in their Minds, that
he has, when they use the same Words, that he does" (3.2.8). This formulation may lead us to ask what conditions allow us to communicate at all.
Locke answers that various checks operate on language. We must distinguish in Locke, however, between the language of physical reality and that
of culture, value, and belief. Physical reality operates as a check on the way
individuals relate words to ideas of things, but when words name what
Locke called general, complex, and mixed-mode ideas—most of the ideas
by which we order and connect our raw sensations and simple ideas of physical reality—nature cannot provide a test or check because the mind makes
these ideas for its convenience, and no pattern for them exists in nature. At
the most, the external world and our need to communicate (the convenience
Locke refers to has a social dimension) merely limit the possible ways we
can order and relate ideas, but even within those limits the possibilities
appear nearly infinite.

Locke was emphatic that language required generalization and abstraction. Even in the modern period, students of language have been fond of
observing, as did E. J. Payne, that primitive peoples lack general terms and
"will have twenty independent words each expressing the act of cutting
some particular thing, without having any name for the act of cutting in
general."[20] Yet Locke's argument is conclusive: even to name different types
of cutting is to generalize, since it is impossible to name every particular
act of cutting, just as it is impossible, in Locke's example, for people to name
every "Crow that flies over their Heads" or "every Leaf of Plants, or Grain
of Sand" (3.3.2). As far as generalizations are concerned, then, Locke argues
that all language uses them but that external reality is not so clearly accessible as to require the same generalizations from everyone. External reality
constrains only as does a field of possibilities. Locke does not pretend to

solve the problem completely by specifying what the possibilities are and how reality constrains them.

Still more removed from the objects of the external world are mixed-mode terms, which include "the greatest part of those which make up Moral discourses" (3.5.8). These are made by the mind, but "made very arbitrarily, made without Patterns, or reference to any real Existence" (3.5.3). Locke asks, "And if it be true, as it is, that the Mind makes the Patterns, for sorting and naming of Things, I leave it to be considered, who makes the Boundaries of the sort, or Species" (3.5.9). The apparent answer to this question is not "nature," but "our minds." The only way to rectify or verify this kind of language is to compare carefully the ideas that speakers hold in association when they use a term and thus make certain that the terms mean the same thing to those who use them.

James Burnett, Lord Monboddo, working decades later on problems of linguistic similarity and difference, charged that Locke's position—that "all *generals* are creatures of our own understanding"—was tantamount to saying that "truth has no foundation in nature" and becomes a mere "agreement or disagreement of our ideas."[21] Locke's beliefs and principles, however, make his relativism more limited than the sections on language alone would lead us to think. Locke considered nature to be not a flux but a stable reproducer of itself: "I do not deny, but Nature, in the constant production of particular Beings, makes them not always new and various, but very much alike and of kin one to another" (3.6.37). In other words external nature is the same over time and distance, and in spite of the philosophical difficulty one has accounting for the way various individuals perceive and name it, nature does not trick us by changing. Also, Locke believed in the mental equality of humanity.[22] He affirmed that God had endowed humans with faculties sufficient to the business of their lives and to the discovery of the important truths of nature and religion. Although he acknowledged that people assembled and named different ideas, he implicitly affirmed that the processes of rational reflection by which they assembled ideas were the same in all humans. The association of ideas could operate more fancifully than rational reflection, and in fact Locke feared the unrestrained processes of association, but there is no evidence that he considered differences in language solely due to habits of association. Rather, differences were inherent possibilities in the play of reflection on the ideas of perception.

Locke can be said to have a double vision of relativism. He saw the world external to humans as already coherent and lending itself to the understanding. Yet he also saw that the human mind was partially alienated from nature in that the senses provided only the simplest direct perceptions. All the rest of the work had to be performed by the mind as it combined simple ideas and reflected upon and associated simple and complex ideas without prior patterns. The mind generated its own classes, divisions, abstractions, and generalizations, largely through the medium of language. Insofar as language is a cognitive tool that aids each person in constructing a different set of ideas, each person lives in a slightly different world. However, language also has social determinants. Once a word is spoken with the intention to communicate, that word becomes a social phenomenon as well.

Abstraction in Reports from Abroad

After Locke, those who wrote about language found it almost mandatory to consult reports on the ideas and terminology of other nations. However, there remained important differences in how people used such evidence, with the key differences hinging on how completely they understood Locke's model of ideas and language. We can see the sustained interest in abstractions in two reports from the Americas, one by Joseph-François Lafitau and another by Charles Marie de La Condamine. Lafitau, a Jesuit in Canada in the 1720s and a careful student of North American Indian customs, firmly grasped language's arbitrary nature. Whether he obtained his superficial understanding of the arbitrariness of language directly from Locke or indirectly through others is not clear; certainly he knew Locke's works.[23] If his ideas came from Locke, he did not grasp Locke fully. He did not trace arbitrariness into the different ways people assembled ideas in a world whose nature and order were not transparent.

Lafitau's respect for Indian languages came not only from firsthand familiarity with them but from his understanding of the vast diversity that language itself made possible, given the arbitrary relation between sounds and ideas: languages "could be so entirely different from each other that there would not be a single word or expression with the same meaning in two languages except through pure chance or communication."[24] But how deeply did such differences extend? For Lafitau, they extended to words and to surface variations in grammar and syntax, but not to ideas. In his *Customs of the American Indians* (1724) Lafitau cautioned those who wanted "to judge [Indian] languages by the European ones" and who imagined that inasmuch as Indians lacked words for the divisions and functions of government, religion, and the arts, Indians had no ideas of these orders of things, "neither in the thought nor mouth" (Lafitau, 2:266). Such people concluded that the lack of terminology revealed a lack of corresponding concepts, whereas Lafitau supposed that there were other ways to express ideas than to isolate and designate them by single terms. He saw, as above, that words did not translate from one language to another, but he believed that ideas may be embedded in structures and terms in less direct ways than in simple naming; therefore a fund of similar ideas could still be in the minds of speakers of nonrelated languages and could still be expressed. For Lafitau, linguistic differences were limited to the varied means of accomplishing similar grammatical functions, not to ways of thinking:

> Since language was instituted to express our thoughts and has an essential connection with the operations of the soul and the objects on which our thoughts turn . . . it is necessary for the bonds of society, for trade and the communication of our ideas which are everywhere almost the same for all men and have the same objects everywhere, it is necessary, I say, that every language have, like ours, some nouns of different kinds, adjectives, substantives [here he enumerates the necessary sorts of inflections, cases, etc.], or . . . an equivalent which can furnish as many signs as are needed to supply the lack of different parts of speech which since they are in one language, found another in which they are lacking, defective, if it did not have in its structure something to fulfill the end and goal of all language which consists in such a communication of our thoughts that there is nothing on which we cannot speak and reason. (Lafitau, 2:267)

Lafitau thus arrived at a principle of modern linguistics, that all languages are equally sufficient to express the needs and ideas of those who speak them.

Certain problems exist in Lafitau's manner of defining diversity and universality, however. In their ideas and the objects of their ideas, "which are everywhere almost the same for all men," and in the requirement society places on them to communicate their ideas, Lafitau believed societies far more similar than different. To communicate their ideas, he asserted, people use very different words and structures. Indeed, whatever is missing in one set of words and one structure will present itself in another. Lafitau's diversity is a kind with which most eighteenth-century thinkers were very comfortable—a surface variety, a thin veneer of linguistic options over a deep and solid layer of unchanging human nature. This diversity affirms the possibility of translation and therefore of communication, and it implies the ability of one human to understand another in spite of apparently deep differences. Ultimately, for Lafitau, the differences revealed in language are only apparent ones. Given a high degree of isomorphism between the operations of the soul and the objects we think about, there are no real differences, aside from those striking divergences from known customs and manners which Lafitau explained by the principle of degeneration.[25]

However, Lafitau's experience in North America did not bear out his trust in the uniformity of ideas as much as he seemed to think. Because North American languages lacked vocabulary to express knowledge of the arts and religion, missionaries "had to swallow insurmountable difficulties" to learn the languages and then "draw from the very depths of these languages, as it were, a new language, which serves to make known to the Indians matters pertaining to God and abstract truths." This new language of periphrases and compounds, even though it conformed to the "turn of their language," was so alien to the ideas of the Indians that "Europeans who have lived among them many years and learned their language in childhood avow ingenuously that they would not know how to tell them of God and instruct them as missionaries do" (Lafitau, 2:264).

La Condamine's report of South America, published twenty years later in 1745, contrasts with Lafitau's in purpose (Lafitau was committed to understanding and preserving the manners of the people he lived among; La Condamine collected cultural curiosities largely on the basis of what would interest readers in Europe). It differs also in its underlying assumptions about language and thought. La Condamine's reports illustrate the staying power of the view that attributed the real differences among languages of less polished peoples to the inferiority of their minds. A member of a French expedition sent out in the 1730s to measure the curvature of the earth, La Condamine spent eight years among the people of South America, returning to France to publish his report in 1745, on the eve of speculation on the origins of language which would be initiated by Condillac and Maupertuis. La Condamine reported:

> All the languages of South America with which I am acquainted, are very poor; ... they are universally barren of terms for the expression of abstract or universal ideas, an evident proof of the slight progress of intellect among these people. Time, duration, space, entity, substance, matter, corporeity; these are words which, with many others, have no equivalent in their languages. Not only metaphysical terms, but also moral attributes, require long paraphrases to be expressed, though with them, in but an imperfect manner. They have no words that correspond exactly with virtue, justice, liberty, gratitude, ingratitude; a fact with which it seems difficult to reconcile what Garcilaso related of the policy, industry, arts, government and genius of the ancient Peruvians.[26]

The implication here is hard to miss: without the abstractions sacred to Europe, no race could lay claim to civil, intellectual, or even moral advancements, even when such advancements are described by a native historian such as the Peruvian Garcilaso de la Vega. To La Condamine, if South

American peoples had thought about policy and arts, they would have words for them, words that he would readily recognize.[27]

Perhaps not far beneath the surface here is the assumption made by universal grammarians—that certain concepts and distinctions universal to human thought are reflected in words and grammars. Languages without similar grammatical distinctions and word forms would, of course, be considered incomplete. This view of linguistic difference reminds us of a tradition of language study whose assumptions contrasted sharply with those of Locke and Condillac. Many language theorists, especially those who founded their work in rationalism and universal grammar, assumed that the mind and the structure of nature were uniform, that nature's structure was apparent to the careful mind, and that the terminology of European thought expressed it. Adam Smith, to take just one example, believed that the process of making genus and species terms was transparently simple. Smith even ridiculed Rousseau for thinking the process was somehow mysterious and difficult. He observed, "What constitutes a species is merely a number of objects, bearing a certain degree of resemblance to one another, and, on that account, denominated by a single appellation."[28] Smith did not ask whether different peoples might see different clusters and degrees of resemblance and so derive radically different ideas of species. For universal grammarians, the differences were superficial; if not superficial, they resulted from error.[29]

Universal grammar tended to assume that the mind, language, and external nature are fitted to each other like hand, glove, and handle. Any supposed defects in barbarous languages were attributed to defective understanding of the world and, ultimately, to deficient minds. One way to avoid this difficulty would be to combine Locke's relativity of naming with the universal grammarian's linkage of grammatical structures and thinking. This is also one way to describe the contributions of Condillac and Maupertuis, who explored the possibility that differences in language and thinking were inherent not only in the complexity of external nature, but in the ways language conditioned the mind in its attempts to understand nature.

Condillac and Maupertuis

Étienne Bonnot de Condillac carried a step further the concept that, in discussing Locke, I called language as the mind's space. He did this first by suggesting a material image to assist in thinking about Locke's association of ideas. Condillac pictured associated ideas as a network of interlocking rings and chains; he then suggested that signs operate in tandem with the network to make memory and attention possible. Thus signs create an ability, akin to consciousness, that separates humans from animals. Abstractions attain importance not because certain sets mark the more advanced languages, but because a society's abstractions signal its ability to manipulate signs in a more or less sophisticated way. The most sophisticated societies have plentiful and even redundant abstractions, including those for ideas, knowledge, and thought processes. Progress, then, relates to the rich interaction of mental spaces and language.

In his *Essay on the Origin of Human Knowledge* (1746), Condillac analyzed the relations between signs and knowledge and deduced that Locke hadn't recognized an implication of his own theory: that thought depends on signs in general, and language in particular, to such a degree that without language, thought would not exist. Locke perceived that certain types of ideas, namely those abstract and complex ideas that we form without having patterns for them in nature, are held together because we assign words to them. However, Condillac accuses Locke of still supposing

> that the mind makes mental propositions, in which it joins or separates ideas without the intervention of words. He even pretends that the best way to arrive at knowledge, would be to consider the ideas in themselves; but he observes that through the prevailing custom of using sounds for ideas, this is very seldom practiced. (*EOHK*, 136)[30]

This thinking illustrates that "a very little thing is sufficient to retard the progress of even the greatest genius" (*EOHK*, 136). Condillac took the next step, holding that in most cases, it is futile to ask us to examine directly our ideas or discourse on their nature. We know them directly only in the sense that we experience them (have them) and can separate them from each other and from all that takes place outside ourselves. "If we go any further, we stray from a point which we apprehend so clearly, that it can never lead us into error" (*EOHK*, 14). Enormous errors had occurred, Condillac stated, because philosophers believed they reflected directly on their ideas when they were actually reflecting upon, and being propelled by, the signs they used to name them. What we can do is to gain knowledge of signs and the relations of ideas that signs make possible.

Condillac asserts confidently that our ideas area connected to such a degree that if the links between them were destroyed, we would cease to know the continuity of the self, cease to derive meaning from ideas, and be deprived of memory and imagination. Directed by our attention, as it is in turn driven by our wants, our minds erect chains of associations and forge connections like so many interlinked chains, until we create the entire network of ideas that is synonymous with our knowledge. Our wants constitute our most basic perceptions,

> and the perceptions of them might be considered as a series of most fundamental ideas, to which we might reduce all those which make a part of our knowledge. Over each of these series, other series of ideas might be raised, which should form a kind of chains. . . . Want is connected with the idea of the thing proper for relieving it; this is connected with the idea of the place where it is to be had; this, with the idea of the persons we have seen there; this in fine, with the ideas of such pleasures or pains as we have felt there, and with many others. We may even observe, that in proportion as the chain extends, it is subdivided into different and smaller chains; so that the farther we remove from the first ring, the more we increase the number of these smaller chains. A first fundamental idea is connected with two or three others; each of these with an equal, or even with a greater number, and so on.
>
> The different larger or smaller chains which I suppose to be over each fundamental idea, might be connected by a series of fundamental ideas, and by some rings which probably would be common to many; for the very same objects, and of course the same ideas are oftentimes relative to different wants. Thus all our knowledge would form only one and the same chain, whose smaller chains should reunite at particular rings, to separate at others. (*EOHK*, 46–47)

Several things should be carefully noted. One is the thorough-going spatial presentation of knowledge, conceived as building blocks, chains, and rings further associated with given places. One might say that Condillac anticipates cognitive science's view of thought as coordinated neural activations, clusters of neurons that fire and activate other clusters while our brains function. As such, he also anticipates the ultimate spatial configuration of language, seen as patterns of neural activation in different parts of the brain in response to what we experience as a single concept or mental task. Condillac's chains give us a static representation insofar as chains don't come into and out of existence as do brain activation patterns, but the chain image is dynamic in that it offers the possibility that rings unite at some points and separate at others as our attention shifts.

Nothing in Condillac's treatment yet indicates that we require words for the flux of ideas to link and break in series of chains. Indeed, as Condillac perceives this process, he sees nothing to separate us from animals. The network is, if motivated solely by attention and want, not only fairly capricious but mechanistic in its nature, metamorphosing as our needs drive attention from one chain to another to seek relief. What relieves it of brutish selfishness is an additional source of connection which Condillac calls "the analogy of signs."

Signs separate us from brutes because signs give humans the power to remember and imagine. Signs are the key to mental operations (*EOHK*, 51) and meaning (*EOHK*, 53) because they provide the means for manipulating ideas. The chain is there, perhaps in any animal. Signs give humans the ability to dwell mentally on the chain, to create new links, to dissolve others in order to analyze what signs make possible as discrete ideas, and to create new chains that equate with rational thought. "We cannot revive our ideas, but as they are connected with some signs" (*EOHK*, 130). Signs are also vital to knowledge in that they offer the links and relations by which attention may connect ideas to derive a more sophisticated knowledge than the kind that results from the order of our perceptions or the circumstances linked to them. Indeed, a great part of the strength of the network of ideas consists in "the analogy of signs" (*EOHK*, 46). By this phrase he seems to mean two things, first, grammatical and syntactical relations provide a kind of logic by which to connect ideas. A sentence is a chain of ideas linked by the relations among the signs. Second, signs lend themselves to analogy by sound, spelling, and word forms. The idea named by *justice* will be linked in the network of ideas not only by those simpler ideas it includes, but by the word's being a different form of the word *just*, which has links to *justify* and, through its Latin roots, to *jus* or *law*. Signs therefore impose an abstract organization upon the want-driven network of ideas. "If we recollect that the habit of imagination and memory depends entirely on the connexion of ideas, and that the latter is formed by the relation and analogy of signs, we shall be convinced that the less a language abounds in analogous expressions, the less assistance it gives to the memory and imagination" (*EOHK*, 287–88).

Signs, including words, operate both within and upon the chains of memories and impulses; signs therefore bestow the capacity for networks of ideas not possible in lower creatures. This concept led Condillac to believe that he had found the reason why some nations advance beyond others: not their ideas solely, but their ability to use signs. A well-developed language facilitates multiple relations among ideas and provides abundant opportunity for abstractions. A Corneille or a Newton, born before the language of poetry or mathematics had matured, might possibly have shown marked abilities but no greatness: "There can be no such thing as a superior genius, till the language of a nation has been considerably improved" (*EOHK*, 290).

Abstraction performs an especially vital role here. As Condillac defines it, abstraction separates those ideas most essential to a subject so that they can be considered in isolation from the subject itself. For example, *substance* separates all things that have extension and mass from the essence or quality of being such a thing. This operation is fraught with danger in that the careless philosopher soon mistakes his abstractions for existent entities and begins reasoning from principles rather than from the origins of ideas. Following Locke's nominalism in defining the role of language in mediating between mind and world, Condillac viewed general ideas and abstractions as mental associations, not names for objective reality. He also viewed them as "beyond all manner of doubt, absolutely necessary" to language and thought. "But," he continued, "we must observe that it is less in regard to the nature of things, than to our manner of knowing them, that we determine their genus or species, or to speak in a more familiar language, that we distribute them into classes subordinate to each other" (*EOHK*, 138–39). Condillac doubted the validity of many abstractions employed in European thought because their purveyors "realized" them—that is, they mistook them for entities of nature. "Notions arising from such an origin, must needs be defective," he warned (*EOHK*, 140).

In positing a level of sign that operates apart from, but in tandem with, the chains of material sensations, memories, associations, and desires, Condillac provides a concrete figure for the distinction that Locke made between ideas of the senses and understanding. Condillac's chains of sensation and associations link us to raw reality, but they do so in a manner we share with beasts. I said earlier that Locke's distinction between ideas of the senses and understanding resembles nothing so much as the distinction between knowing a familiar locale and having a navigational system to chart, and arrive at, all other locales, known or unknown. Condillac's figure of the two orders of chains—one of desire and memory and one of signs by which one can direct the attention, dwell on memory, and reflect on relations among sensations, memories, and places—makes this resemblance yet more to the point. Language is, for Condillac, nearly synonymous with thought just as navigaton, whether on land or sea, exists only to the extent that a person has a system of reference points, distances, and directions. Condillac's answer to the question, why do some nations progress further than others in knowledge, is that some nations have developed better sign systems, just as some nations, I suggest by analogy, had developed better navigational systems.

Having doubted the usefulness of many of the terms that dominated European philosophy, did Condillac afford a degree of respect to other languages that lacked these dubious terms? Yes and no. He regarded primitive languages as more poetic and more expressive of the imagination. On their categories of thought he was somewhat ambivalent. Because he mistrusted the empty abstractions that pervaded philosophy in Europe, he did not regard the lack of certain of them as a great flaw. As primitives moved from ideas of sensible things to general ideas, he speculated,

> they rose only by degrees to the most abstract ideas, and it was a long time before they had the terms of *essence, substance,* and *being.* Doubtless there are nations that have not as yet enriched their language with these terms [he cited La Condamine here]; and if they are more ignorant than we, this is not what renders them so. (*EOHK*, 250)

Note particularly the last clause in this passage. Condillac rejected the assumption that a people's lack of certain abstractions impoverished their thought.

Then wherein does the ignorance of these people lie? The answer involves his theory that language helps to constitute thought (*EOHK*, 102, 114–20).[31] In a simple-minded stab at this theory he asked, "Should we be capable ever to reflect on metaphysics and morals, if we had not invented signs to fix our ideas, in proportion as we formed new combinations?" (*EOHK*, 117). In a later work he said, "The art of reasoning began with languages; it could progress only insofar as languages themselves improved"; he further noted that individual languages inclined speakers to certain kinds of analysis inherent in their signs and therefore could, if poorly constructed, perpetuate error.[32] In the *Essay on . . . Human Knowledge*, he summarized: "By gestures, by signs, by sounds, by cyphers, by letters; by instruments so foreign as these from our ideas, we set them [ideas] to work, in order to raise ourselves even to the sublimest knowledge. The materials are the same in all men; but the art of making use of signs varies; and from thence the inequality which is to be observed among mankind" (*EOHK*, 122). What emerges as important, then, is not whether people have valid "archetypes" and "notions," but whether they have developed signs, or rather, the art of using signs, to a state at which they could become a platform for advancing knowledge beyond the rudimentary stage common to most societies. Ignorance and knowledge relate not so much to the terms a people use, but to their collective sophistication in creating and manipulating signs. Condillac thus raises the ante on humanity. He might as well be saying that no matter what abstractions a society had attained, until they began to reflect on abstractions themselves, see their array in discourse, and theorize about how they relate to objects in nature, that society would never produce a Locke— or, perhaps, a Condillac.

If language constitutes thought, however, how does one get enough purchase on language and knowledge to be able to talk *about* them or to pronounce a set of terms valid or erroneous? If sophistication in the use of signs is the hallmark of the advance of knowledge, from what vantage point does Condillac observe that some languages have too many general and abstract terms, and that philosophers in particular have perpetuated error?[33] Only if certain forms of thought are extra-linguistic—that is, if some thoughts occur without being heavily conditioned by language—can we reach such conclusions. Otherwise, such thought is nothing more than a manipulation of signs in a closed system. For Condillac this vantage point is reached partly by having signs for signs and partly by the proper application of the analytical method. This only pushes the problem back to another level, however, since it is clear in Condillac's discussion that analysis, too, is partly a matter of signs and partly above the conditionality of signs. Proper analysis is constrained by observation as it moves from what is known to what is unknown, as it recognizes that general and abstract ideas are only signs, and as it tests the results of thought against nature itself.[34] Yet to ascertain the truth of what is known is a major problem in a system that treats knowledge, analysis, signs, and language as nearly synonymous. Condillac clearly believes that the knowledge embedded in language, though conditioned by that medium, is about something external to signs and is testable by reference to that which it represents. Yet when he articulates how we come to know external nature more adequately, he generally reverts to an account made through signs, analysis, and language; and with this we return to the problem of truth to which the analysis of signs has led us. His extremely provocative treatment of language leaves us stranded between a conception of knowledge as manipulation of signs and a conception of knowledge as about something for which signs are only representatives and to which the mind has some other access apart from signs.

Pierre-Louis Moreau de Maupertuis's short work, *Réflexions philosophiques sur l'origine des langues et la signification des mots* (1748), followed Condillac's *Essay on . . . Human Knowledge* within a year and seems to have been suggested and influenced by it.[35] Interestingly, Maupertuis accompanied a French expedition to Lapland which left at the same time and had the same purpose as La Condamine's South American expedition. Maupertuis proposed that "a philosophical mind could infer much of great usefulness" from the study of other languages—not the ones close in structure to those of polished nations, but "those of distant people, which seem to have been formed on plans of ideas so different from ours, that one can barely translate into our languages what has once been expressed in theirs" (II).[36] The trace of Locke is obvious here. As does Condillac, Maupertuis crystallizes the differences in an image. His metaphor, that of the plan, differs from Condillac's chain and network image, however. It integrates the dynamic chains into a single overall lay-out characterized by another essentially spatial feature of language, that it functions by the composition and decomposition of ideas coming through the senses.

The issue of human mental differences is even more central to Maupertuis's treatise than to Condillac's. How can distant peoples who share the same mental endowment and sensory experience form ideas so different that one can barely translate them at all? The answer for Maupertuis is the very medium in which ideas are expressed and the effect that medium has on the minds of its speakers. Because of its analytical nature, language imposes such effects that otherwise similar minds become, through different lan-guages, the embodiments of different kinds of signs and their structuring. A particular language pulls the mind into the ideas that constitute its over-all plan. In a sense, Maupertuis argues that humans conform to their language, so much so that it is impossible to recover or remember that aspect of simple perception which early humans once shared and which infants must still, for a time, experience. The traces of natural perception have been erased as language has developed, since each language has selec-tively isolated and assembled different aspects and parts of that natural ex-perience. Even that which we call science depends so much on a certain way of designating perceptions that its "questions and propositions would be completely different if one had established other expressions of those first perceptions" (XII). One might hope to recover the condition of first per-ceptions in the memory of infancy, but even this is hopeless because the minds of babies are preempted by language: they are bombarded with words from their earliest moments of awareness (VI). Another way would be to find tribes so primitive that they have yet to develop language past its initial stage. Maupertuis doubted that any such tribes still existed. Thus conditioned by language, our knowledge has become one of signs and only secondarily one of reality.

Maupertuis demonstrates this conditioning by showing that language necessitates the composing and decomposing of ideas. Treating our percep-tions as instantaneous and whole, he notices that language can represent them by designating each perception by its own sign, which taxes memory exceedingly, or by progressively analyzing each perception. This analysis or decomposing makes knowledge and memory possible, but it also progres-sively misrepresents experience. What starts out as one single perception and a single utterance for it (for example, a single utterance meaning "I see a tree") must be broken into parts and differentiated as the "I see" is ab-stracted. One can then have not two completely different expressions for "I see a tree" and "I see a horse," but similar ones. Then, to say "I see two horses," or "I see two trees," one must formulate an additional linguistic entity to represent number. As the signs so develop, they make it possible to think separately about number, the objects of sight, and seeing itself. And so language is the condition of knowledge, but it takes us farther and farther from the immediate, undivided experience. And since each language develops signs for different parts of that immediate experience and separates even those parts differently, knowledge relates more to signs than to the external world or unfiltered, integrated perceptual experience of it.

Yet Maupertuis's emphasis on difference is undercut by the very possibility of his reflections. He proposes that we may not uncover the primitive simplicity of human perception, which for him seems to represent the universal experience, but we can grasp the nature of difference and abstract an idea of that universal experience by comparing languages from the standpoint of language's analytical nature. His "plan of ideas" offers a simple and useful image for thinking about linguistic and cultural differences, but the plan seems to insert itself between our experience of such events as seeing a tree, falling off a ledge, or drinking a tasty beverage. We now know that all these experiences are, in the brain, processed as distributed neural activations. Therefore Maupertuis had it right when he came at our ideas through both composition and decomposition. Not only language, but cognition in almost any form comprises an ability to perceive an event, scene, or concept as a whole or as a construct of parts. To notice that language also decomposes ideas is to see only half the process, and it attributes solely to language something that holds for all thought. I add a further complication. If, as Maupertuis conjectures, the philosophical mind can "learn much of great usefulness" from the languages of distant peoples, if one can posit the existence of "plans of ideas so different from ours," and if one can gain immeasurably from spending an hour with the tailed half-humans reported to exist in the Pacific, then the mind's structures are available outside the limits imposed by language. To say "I cannot translate" implies many things. It implies a recognition of the "genius" or characteristic imprint each language leaves on thought. However, to recognize that "plans of ideas so different" exist and that such differences may in fact be grasped would be impossible if our minds and perceptions had become strictly conditioned by the languages we used. To assert that our knowledge is of signs and not of reality is to make a distinction that signs make possible and at the same time to call into question the tyranny of signs. If one can discover the first vestiges of the human mind by comparing supposedly untranslatable languages (II), then one can, by the use of languages, transcend linguistic knowledge.

The study of languages, the development of language theory, and the theory of the dynamics of difference continued to be threaded together in the intellectual culture of the very late eighteenth and early nineteenth centuries. Monboddo and those who followed him wrote with a keen eye on the reports of new languages being discovered and newly studied around the globe, and they wrestled with similar problems of universality and diversity. The problem always was to articulate their theories with the increasing information on world languages. The proto-anthropologist Joseph-Marie Degérando, detailing instructions on the study of savages for a soon-to-be-mounted French expedition, offered unusually far-sighted ideas on the relation between culture and language. The grand synthesizer and theorizer Wilhelm von Humboldt drew on detailed studies of exotic languages and theories of language development to comprehend in a finite hierarchy of language types all the possibilities of better and worse, difference and universality, limit and growth.

Beginning with Locke, the problem of language difference became one of the most important issues of language study. In the eighteenth century and beyond, language differences became a sort of problem of problems, manifesting itself in studies of language origins, comparative linguistics, national character, and even political legitimacy. As I have attempted to show, the exploration of language difference, viewed even through the limited field of abstraction, exposes to view the way in which Locke and his followers tried to enter the mind and unfold its processes. They proceeded first by applying navigational and topographical metaphors to clinch the point that, in Locke's words, "the exercise of their facultys was bounded within the ways modes & notions of their owne countrys" (*D*, 120). Once they had convincingly established the differences between peoples, they used rudimentary spatial models to explore the way of ideas. Finally, they offered metaphors such as chains and rings and plans to tease out the role that language plays in channeling the minds of different nations down slightly different paths.

Notes

1 I originally published parts of this chapter as "'Adam in a Strange Country': Locke's Language Theory and Travel Literature," in *Modern Philology* 92 (May 1995): 460–81, and as "Language and Difference: The Problem of Abstraction in Eighteenth-Century Language Study," in *Journal of the History of Ideas* 54 (1993): 19–36. I am grateful to the editors for permission to include them here.

2 Jean-Jacques Rousseau, "Rousseau's Notes," in *The First and Second Discourses*, trans. and ed. Victor Gourevitch (New York: Harper & Row, 1986), 218.

3 Hans Aarsleff, *From Locke to Saussure: Essays on the Study of Language and Intellectual History* (Minneapolis: University of Minnesota Press, 1982), 43.

4 Lia Formigari, *Language and Experience in Seventeenth-Century British Philosophy*, Amsterdam Studies in the Theory and History of Linguistic Science, vol. 48 (Amsterdam: John Benjamins, 1988), 113, 117, 119, 133.

5 Peter Laslett, introduction to *Two Treatises of Government*, by John Locke (Cambridge: Cambridge University Press, 1960), 98. Locke's use of travel books has also been noted by Aarsleff (*Locke to Saussure*, 45 and 71–72 n) and Neal Wood (*The Politics of Locke's Philosophy* [Berkeley: University of California Press, 1983], 31–33 and 81–82). William Batz ("The Historical Anthropology of John Locke," *Journal of the History of Ideas* 35 [1974]: 663–70) is primarily interested in Locke's vision of the history of humanity in *Two Treatises of Government*.

6 John Harrison and Peter Laslett, *The Library of John Locke* (Oxford: Oxford Bibliographical Society, 1965), 27–28. In all, Locke cites eighteen texts of travel and geography, plus several works of comparative religion.

7 John Locke, "Epistle to the Reader," in *An Essay concerning Human Understanding*, ed. Peter H. Nidditch (Oxford: Clarendon, 1975). Subsequent citations to the *Essay* are made parenthetically to book, chapter, and section number.

8 Voltaire, *Le philosophe ignorant*, in *Œuvres complètes de Voltaire* (Paris: Garnier, 1879), 26:84. Earl of Shaftesbury, "Advice to an Author," in *Characteristics of Men, Manners, Opinions, Times*, ed. John M. Robertson, (Gloucester, MA: Peter Smith, 1963), 1:223.

9 Neal Wood, *The Politics of Locke's Philosophy: A Social Study of "An Essay concerning Human Understanding"* (Berkeley: University of California Press, 1983), 31.

10 John Locke, *Drafts for the Essay concerning Human Understanding, and Other Philosophical Writings*, ed. Peter H. Nidditch and G. A. J. Rogers (Oxford: Oxford University Press, 1990).

11 Sir William Temple, *Memoirs of What Past in Christendom from the War Begun 1672 to the Peace Concluded 1679* (London, 1692).

12 In 1.3.9 he cites Johann Gruber, *Travels from China to Europe*; Lambert; Isaac Vossius, *De Nili Origine*; Peter Martyr, *De Orbe Novo Decades*; Garcilaso de la Vega, *Historia de las Incas*; Jean de Léry, *Histoire d'un voyage fait en la terre du Brésil*; Martin Baumgarten, *Peregrinatio in Aegyptum*; and Pietro della Valle, *Viaggi*. In 1.4.8 he cites Thomas Roe, *The Embassy of Sir Thomas Roe*; Léry, *Histoire d'un voyage*; Pierre Martin de La Martinière, *Voyage des pais septentrionaux*; Edward Terry, *A Voyage to East India*; John Ovington, *Voyage to Surat*; Nicolaus del Techo, *Historia de la provincia del Paraguay*; Simon de la Loubère, *Du royaume de Siam*; Domingo de Navarrete, *Tratados . . . de China*; and *Historia cultus sinensium*. Lambert and Roe are cited in Melchisedech Thevenot, *Relations du divers voyages curieux*.

13 Jean de Léry, *History of a Voyage to the Land of Brazil, Otherwise Called America* [1578], trans. Janet Whatley (Berkeley: University of California Press, 1990), 186, 190–91.

14 Locke doesn't cite Sagard by name in the *Essay*, but he owned both *Histoire du Canada* and *Grand voyage du pais des Hurons* and made notes concerning the Huron language when reading Sagard. Aarsleff details this and other examples of Locke's travel reading (*Locke to Saussure*, 71–72 n). The passage here is from W. H. Langton's translation of *Grand voyage . . .* (The Long Journey to the Country of the Hurons) (Toronto: Champlain Society, 1939), 73.

15 Garcilaso de la Vega, *Royal Commentaries of the Incas and General History of Peru*, trans. Harold V. Livermore (Austin: University of Texas Press, 1966), 76–77.

16 *Posthumous Works of Mr. John Locke* (London, 1706), 8–10.

17 *Posthumous Works*, 60.

18 I don't mean to ignore completely the possibility that mind may operate without language. G. A. Wells reviews some formulations of this possibility in section 3 of "Herder's Resistance to Language as Invention," *JEGP* 86 (1986): 167–90. At stake here, however, is not whether the human mind can carry out some processes without verbal language (I think it can), nor whether aphasic people can perceive things and form ideas without using or understanding speech (I think they can), but whether we would, in any meaningful sense, be able to refer to or have within us the "human mind" without its ability to represent its perceptions symbolically.

19 Rudiger Schreyer, "The Language of Nature: Inquiries into a Concept of Eighteenth-Century British Linguistics," in *Progress in Linguistic Historiography*, ed. Konrad Koerner, Amsterdam Studies in the Theory and History of Linguistic Science (Amsterdam: John Benjamins, 1980), 153–73.

20 Edward J. Payne, *The History of the New World Called America* (Oxford: Oxford University Press, 1892–1899), 2:103.

21 James Burnett [Lord Monboddo], *Of the Origin and Progress of Language* (Edinburgh, 1774–1792), 5:357.

22 Neal Wood dates Locke's commitment to the idea of the mental egalitarianism of humanity, as expressed in the *Essay*, from the second draft in 1671. *Politics of Locke's Philosophy*, 33.

23 William Fenton and Elizabeth Moore, introduction to *Customs of the American Indians Compared with the Customs of Primitive Times*, by Joseph François Lafitau (Toronto: Champlain Society, 1974), 1:xcii.

24 Joseph François Lafitau, *Customs of the American Indians Compared with the Customs of Primitive Times* [1724], trans. and ed. William Fenton and Elizabeth Moore (Toronto: Champlain Society, 1974), 2:267.

25 Fenton and Moore, introduction, 1:xlvii.

26 Charles Marie de La Condamine, *Relation abrégée d'un voyage fait dans l'intérieur de l'Amérique méridionale* (Paris, 1745), 53–54; as translated in *A General Collection of the Best and Most Interesting Voyages and Travels in All Parts of the World*, ed. John Pinkerton (London, 1808–1814), 14:222.

27 Such reports even found their way into philosophy. Voltaire, for example, who ridiculed Locke for being too credulous in his use of travel accounts, observed that "there are some entire nations who have never been able to form a regular language." *La philosophie de l'histoire*, in *Œuvres complètes de Voltaire* (Toronto: University of Toronto Press, 1969), 59:97.

28 Adam Smith, *Considerations concerning the First Formation of Languages*, in *The Theory of Moral Sentiments* (1853; reprint, New York: Kelley, 1966), 509.

29 Many reports from distant corners of the world seemed to confirm what La Condamine had observed, but only by mistaking the nature of abstraction. The naturalist J. R. Forster, who sailed on Cook's second voyage in 1772 to 1775, stated in *Observations Made during a Voyage round the World* (London, 1778) that "the Taheiteans have no expressions for abstract ideas" (543), though page after page of his analysis of Tahitian manners implied otherwise. Side by side with such pejorative observations one finds much uncertainty over them. The journals of voyagers, especially of Cook, made clear that they were beginning to understand the subtle intricacies of behavior patterns, culture, and language and were consequently growing impatient with the simple-minded gathering of vocabulary based on the assumption that one could, by recording equivalents for English words, approach an understanding of a people's way of life (*The Journals of Captain James Cook*, ed. J. C. Beaglehole [Cambridge: Cambridge University Press, 1955–1967], 2:234 n; 3:166).

30 Étienne Bonnot de Condillac, *Essay on the Origin of Human Knowledge* [1746], trans. Thomas Nugent (London, 1756), 136, hereafter cited in the text as *EOHK*.

31 See also pt. 1, sect. 2, chap. 6, para. 107 of the French edition of 1746.

32 Étienne Bonnot de Condillac, *La logique, ou Les premiers développemens de l'art de penser*, vol. 22, *Œuvres de Condillac* (Paris: Houel, 1798), 109–10, 120–25.

33 Condillac, *La logique*, 40–43.

34 Ibid., 13, 101, 109, passim.

35 Hans Aarsleff has noted the highly probable connection. I am much indebted to his discussion of Maupertuis in "The Tradition of Condillac," in *Locke to Saussure*, 146–209, which treats the *Réflexions* and its relevance to the work of Condillac more fully than I am able to do here.

36 Pierre-Louis Moreau de Maupertuis, *Réflexions philosophiques sur l'origine des langues et la signification des mots* [1748], in *Œuvres de Maupertuis* (1768), 1:259–309; reprint in *Maupertuis, Turgot et Maine de Biran sur l'origine du langage*, ed. Ronald Grimsley and trans. Marie-Henriette Day into English (Geneva: Droz, 1971). Numerals in parentheses refer to section number.

8 Language as the Journey of the Human Mind: Typology, National Culture, and the Role of the Linguist

If the feeling truly awakens in the soul, that language is not just a medium of exchange for mutual comprehension, but a true world which the mind must insert, by its own inner labour, between itself and objects, then it is on the right road towards continually finding more and depositing more in its language.[1]
—*Wilhelm von Humboldt,* On Language

Locke thought of language as something like the mind's space—a sphere or realm which, however abstract or ideal, allowed the mind to assemble ideas, relate them to each other, move them with ease, and thus create a partial map of the world, the map of human understanding. His followers went further, concluding that all thought rising above brute levels took place in that mental space called language. In conceiving the history of language in accordance with these principles, late eighteenth-century thinkers provided an additional important development. Assuming much that Locke and his followers implied about the endless possibilities that the mind's interactions with the world created through language, they revived one of the most common space-related concepts of all, the journey. They used this commonplace, however, in novel ways and with profound implications. Rather than viewing humanity's journey to understand language, the theme of much of this book, they viewed languages themselves as branching journeys by which, as nations progressed through time and place, they fashioned their separate mental destinies.

The journey metaphor entails a structure that includes a traveler, a path, a destination, and often a narrative comprised of events along the way that may change the traveler. Thus the journey of language may constitute a narrative of consciousness. Johann Gottfried Herder and Wilhelm von Humboldt envisioned each nation or linguistic group as the traveler, the path as language, the narrative as each nation's progress as it communally exerts its mental force to make language serve its need for survival and intellectual mastery, and the destination as the unfolding and not yet completely known place to which humanity might arrive, once it sees the full potential in the interplay of language and mind. Although the precise destination may be unknown, Herder and Humboldt said that through careful study we might perceive something of the present location, and we might assure ourselves that as the journey unfolds, the possibilities will be constrained by the nature of language generally, the particular language of a nation under consideration, and the mental endowments of the nation applying language to move itself forward.

Longitude as a Language-like Problem

Locating a nation's position in the unfolding journey resembled navigation by dead reckoning, or the use of direction and distance to calculate an approximate position. However, using a larger framework, one could be more accurate, could determine relative positions of many nations in their various unfolding journeys, and could calculate the relative directions in which the nations were moving. That larger framework resembled the problem of fixing longitude. The eighteenth century achieved this great navigational feat for the first time in history when it produced methods of ascertaining east–west position, or longitude, even at sea with no landmarks. For centuries, mariners had been able to fix with some precision their north–south position by measuring the height of the sun or (if in the northern hemisphere) of the north star. However, fixing one's east–west location posed difficulties so great that the best minds of the early modern era could not crack the puzzle. The clockwork of the heavens promised a solution, but the stars' paths and the angles between them and the moon—both features that could be plotted—changed with latitude and longitude. Mapping the paths and angles required measurements more accurate and tables more exhaustive than technology could supply. Further, whereas there was a fixed zero degree of latitude (the equator), there was no such thing in longitude. Even the imaginary lines that mark latitude and longitude differ, with the latitude lines running horizontally east and west, exactly parallel to each other, and longitude lines converging at the poles and bulging from each other as they approach the equator.[2] As trade and military shipping increased, solving the longitude problem became more and more imperative. For a trading nation such as Britain, a simple error in calculation of longitude could mean stupendous losses in lives and commerce. A 1707 naval fleet, returning from

Mediterranean engagements with the French and prevented by fog and clouds from taking navigational readings, hit the small Scilly islands off Land's End and sank with two thousand hands. Seagoing European governments, including Great Britain, offered huge prizes for a demonstrated, reliable solution to finding longitude.

Oddly, it took accurate measurements from another dimension—time—to solve the longitude problem. As astronomers plied their telescopes searching for points and that could be of use in real time to ships at sea, others realized that a far less complex solution could be reached simply by having accurate timepieces on board. If sailors had a reference meridian—a north–south line arbitrarily set anywhere but whose position was exactly known—and knew the exact time at that meridian, no matter where a ship sailed, they could compare exact noon at their location at sea (obtained by measuring the zenith of the sun) to the current time at the meridian and then convert the time difference to the exact number of degrees east or west of the meridian. Since the distance corresponding to one degree differs with latitude (near the equator, a degree measures nearly sixty miles, but at the polar circle measures only about forty), sailors would also have to know their north–south position as well. Thus, only by combining abstract systems of location with the measurement of time could mariners fix their longitude. John Harrison, a Yorkshire clockmaker, earned the British award with a series of chronometers that measured time accurately even on board a ship rolling through heavy seas and subject to cold and hot weather.

I won't argue that the solution of the longitude problem led directly to new types of language philosophy or that new language philosophies were fashioned in an atmosphere of pressing political and economic necessity. But I will argue that developments in longitude and language thought were more than coincidence. Both required a global grasp of the factors involved, a confidence in order, confidence in an ability to derive systematic correspondences that would unlock the path to solutions, and similar types of cognitive stretch, in which one must coordinate different orders of experience to create a frame suitable to the problems they posed. And we want to note that language philosophers tied their theories to the current and potential status of nations and states, just as advances in navigation translated into commercial, political, and military advantage. In navigation, the problems were obvious (find the means to fix location on rolling seas when celestial sightings couldn't do the job), and the orders that needed coordinating were local position on land or sea, abstract systems for relating positions in a coherent pattern, and the new dimension of time. In language thought, the problems included history, or time, the cognitive dimensions of language, and typologies, or classifications of language groups, that could be used to coordinate languages' cognitive and historical features.

Languages are not as destructive as shipwrecks, of course, but far-reaching implications of language theories were not hard to seek. Theories of language and its relation to cognition were the maps coordinating linguistics, early modern anthropology, and epistemology. Students of language had spent volumes exploring the probable history of language on the one hand and the relations of language to cognitive development on the other. These two studies remained largely disconnected, however. Linguistic navigation, if I can call it that, required that the history and cognitive implications of language be integrated if linguists were to be able to determine where exactly, in the history of language, the nations and their languages stood and where they could still go.

In Locke, for example, one finds a predominantly synchronic treatment of the linguistic and cognitive differences among peoples. His study treats the relations of words and ideas and the means of improving communication among peoples by clarifying the ideas pertaining to a concept conveyed by a single word. One can extract implications for a history, but Locke paid little attention to how actual language communities arrived so far apart that many words in one language had no counterpart in another. Theories connecting cognition and language to the history of the species required coordinating the external world, the plastic human mental capacities, and the ability to represent phenomena in verbal signs. Such theories also required the dimension of time, not just as the chronological development that impinges on histories of language, but as a new measure, linguistic time, by which I mean the ongoing struggle of any community to make its language fully adequate to its experience and needs—a struggle, as conceived in the late eighteenth and early nineteenth century, never fully successful, and never entirely unsuccessful, either. By combining the spatial concepts we have seen in Locke, Condillac, and Maupertuis with the notion of a journey down alternate paths, the German thinkers Johann Gottfried Herder and Wilhelm von Humboldt were able to think about the relations among language, individual cognition, and national culture in a more comprehensive framework. Within this framework Herder and Humboldt explained linguistic variety as inherent to language and nature, posited typologies of language as the separate mental paths that nations took from past to present and into the future, specified linguistic forms as the essence of those typologies, and cast the linguist in a new role as the sage who charted humanity's present location and possible futures on its intellectual and spiritual journey.

Herder and the Journey of Language

Johann Gottfried Herder had read extracts of Maupertuis[3] and had certainly read Condillac, but he was unsatisfied with their theories on the relation between language and thought. Condillac and Maupertuis had drawn on travel literature to sustain their theories of the links that language provides the mind as it assembles ideas. Herder calls into question those conclusions about savage language which are based on "a host of half-true examples taken from savage life"[4] and shrewdly perceives the inconsistency in reports such as that of La Condamine. The reports invalidate their own assertions: they deplore the lack of abstract terminology among peoples such as the Peruvians yet prove in narration and description "that they draw conclusions according to these ideas and demonstrate by their actions, they possess these virtues" (Herder, 65). While Herder does not deny that some languages have more abstractions than others, he affirms that all languages have abstractions—just as many as the people have need of. Furthermore, "no language has ever been discovered to be wholly unfit for the arts and sciences" (Herder, 67).

More broadly, Herder was dissatisfied with the leading versions of linguistic history. Michael Morton observes that conventionalism, as Condillac advanced it, divorced language from reflection. Creationism, as put forth by Süssmilch, left too firm an imprint on language for it to develop as diversely as it had.[5] Herder wanted a model that explained not only how the mind uses signs and how diversities could occur in the operations of the human mind on nature, but how the nature of language and the history of humanity virtually guaranteed the known range of diversity while still drawing on similar powers of reflection. Two of Herder's writings that bear directly on this problem are *Über den Fleiss in mehreren gelehrten Sprachen* (On Diligence in Several Learned Languages) of 1764 and *Abhandlung über den Ursprung der Sprache* (Treatise upon the Origin of Language), his Berlin Academy prize essay of 1770, published in 1772. In these works Herder thinks of humanity's linguistic history as both one and many journeys down the branching pathways that the mutually constituting entities, reflection and language, make possible. To grasp the unity of human nature and human thought is to grasp an abstract entity, since any language and thinking process can actualize only the particular contours, strengths, and weaknesses of a particular stage and path in that great journey. Herder doesn't assume a harmonious fit of mind, language, and world. Instead he built into his theory the disjunctures and incompatibilities that helped to determine humanity's development as much as did the harmonies. Morton states that Herder's position in *On Diligence* entails the coincidence of opposites in experience. "Though organically conceived, reality is for Herder nonetheless not a seamless whole, but rather a fabric manifesting at once continuity and disjunction" (Morton, 17). An adequate comprehension of how language and culture interact will not simply "resolve what appear to be some very fundamental contradictions" but will "preserve within that synthesis precisely the element of tension between contraries that it at the same time overcomes" (Morton, 22–23).

Unlike Condillac and Maupertuis (and perhaps as a result of reading them), Herder was convinced that the human mind could not exist at all without language.[6] What distinguishes humans from all other creatures is reflection; language and reflection were born in the same instant and are mutually dependent. Reflection replaces instinct in humans. People require reflection rather than instinct because their increased span of attention and action brings with it the need for signs that facilitate the shifting of attention. Take a worm or spider whose spheres of action are tightly constrained. They have organs adapted to the micro environment in which they live, and such organisms react by instinct. There is no thought as we know it in a worm's burrowing.

Herder frequently relies on organic imagery to expound his ideas. What may be harder to appreciate is the role of space in his theory. Space, or the range of response an organism's environment makes possible, influences the capacities of the organism. Or, to turn the formula around, we could just as easily say that the organism's capacities for exploring space dictate its range of response, and thus the nature of the space it occupies. Each organism adapts to the amplitude of its spatial environment. Expand an organism's sphere of action, and the role of instinct decreases. "The more contracted, therefore, the sphere of the animal, the less occasion is there for language" (Herder, 18). Expand the sphere, and the organism must have a greater ability to select those aspects of its environment to which it will respond. In humans, this selectivity and range of response are so great as to bring with them the need for reflection and language. Reflection and language bestow an ability to live intelligently in the widest spatial environment. The ability to control attention is the ability to reflect, and reflection depends on language because language allows the mind to represent and hold in attention that which it dwells upon. Through the facility of language, therefore, the human space also includes themselves. Language makes it possible to reflect on the self:

Man must attain to greater clearness since he does not blindly fall upon one point, and blindly there remain, but stands free, can select his sphere, and contemplate in himself the nature of his own being. No longer an infallible machine in the hand of nature, he is the object, and aim for the application of his own powers. (Herder, 21–22)

However, language and reflection are capacities that can be realized in different forms. Inasmuch as language makes reflection, memory, and selective attention possible, linguistic diversity is inherent in language. To know the world's languages is to see the possibilities to which language opens the way. Herder's *Treatise* states that "the human race could not possibly continue only one flock, confined to one language; therefore, the formation of different national languages became necessary" (Herder, 99). Differences arise even at the level of pronunciation and increase through synonyms, varieties of grammatical relations, and figurative language. A principle of human nature aggravates the differences: humans innately suspect difference and thus develop "reciprocal family and national hatred" (Herder, 103). They emphasize that which unites the focal group, and in so doing they also accentuate that which separates the group from others. As language and reflection unfold in individuals and groups, linguistic choices begin to channel thought and feeling in each group and eventually each nation (Herder, 93–95). This channeling is absolutely necessary for the development of culture: culture cannot be anything and all things; it develops only by taking particular forms.

As the worm reacts by instinct to its neighborhood of dirt and grass, humans are equipped by language to range over the whole earth. The earth is, of course, the widest possible physical space in which people can reflect and act. And this partly solves the puzzle of the geographical dispersion of languages: "Language is a Proteus upon the round surface of the earth. Many modern philosophers have been so little able to fetter this Proteus and view him in his true form, that it has appeared probable to them, that nature should have created for every large tract a first human couple, the first parents of mankind as peculiar animals for each climate" (Herder, 101–2). Not so, says Herder. The potential for diversity lay dormant in any original language and continues in any present one.

To characterize the single origin, the evolution of diversity implicit in that origin, and the diverse destiny of humanity, Herder resorts to the image of the journey. He actually links two domains within the cognitive metaphor, one of the total human race and another of all language considered together, arguing that just as the human race is one large family moving forward, so is the development of language the project of humanity. His *Treatise* states: "In all probability, the human race constitutes one progressive totality, from one source, and forming one vast household. The same principle refers to languages, and with them to the whole chain of cultivation" (Herder, 107).

Individual, group, nation, and race are linked in this dynamic of similarity and difference. Just as our past decisions affect the course of our existence, so in language the steps of ancestors affect the course of the present generation, and that course is handed on to the next generation in turn.

Another cognitive metaphor of space, the figure of the chain, occurs again and again to express the concept. A person thinks "throughout the chain of his existence" (Herder, 107); such links are preserved in language which is shared, altered subtly in the present and, as the chain of the human race spreads in its diversity over the earth, "the chain is continually extending from its first link" (Herder, 115). Although from time to time all things seem to lie in ruin in particular nations, the human race moves forward in a "chain of certain progression" (Herder, 115) because the nations depend upon each other in this spiritual and intellectual exploration of the possible. The secret to progress lies only partly in exploiting the inherent possibilities in each language for intellectual probing of inner experience and outer reality.

The spreading chains image helps convey the paradox that the individual can contain the possibilities of the whole race, yet the race can comprehend more than any individual or nation. The possibilities do not develop best in isolation. Herder observes: "A society can discover more than an individual, and the whole human race, more than a single nation. And this is not merely according to the number of heads, but according to manifold internally increasing circumstances" (Herder, 113). The development of one culture, while in some ways the embodiment of a given people's brilliance, does not prevent or excuse the culture from the need for cross-breeding. If, from the range of possibilities, a nation or tribe is to unfold the most positive but as yet unrealized potentials in the totality of human nature—a human nature which, like the destiny of the race itself, we know only as an abstraction of many particulars, realized and unrealized—that nation or tribe must draw on the mental accomplishments of others. The process of sharing and learning from such differences is, for Herder, the revelation of the universal. Each group that participates in such interdevelopment helps to determine what form the totality of human culture will take now and in the future. For Herder, then, there is clearly a component of human intelligence that can operate outside the limit any one language places upon it, though it cannot perhaps operate outside the limit of language itself.

Cross-fertilization occurs when speakers of one type of language borrow ideas and words from those of another. Given that each nation enjoys only a limited range of "nature's gifts," each must exact an illicit "tribute from other peoples' riches." In cultural enrichments, nations grab what they need from others. Nations that cut themselves off from cultural commerce deprive themselves of the booty and commodities that will raise their intellectual standard of living.[7] Thus, he observes, "how little progress would we have made, were each nation to strive for learnedness by itself, confined within the narrow sphere of its language?" (*On Diligence*, 31). The Germans themselves "might still live tranquilly in their woods . . . or be merely warriors . . . had not the chain of foreign culture pressed so closely upon them, and, with the accumulated force of ages, necessitated them to general participation" (Herder, 114). This account denies to the Europeans the comforting illusion that they have single-handedly nurtured the branches of knowledge in which they take pride. Herder instead places the cause in the exchange among languages and cultures by which people discover and assimilate ideas that could not be easily reached within their own traditions.[8] Herder's position differs significantly from that of Condillac, who believed the most reliable languages would advance on their own principles and avoid the confusion that results when they incorporate forms from other languages built on different principles. To Herder, such linguistic purity would result in stagnation, since each language has only limited structures to stimulate thought and advance knowledge. Through this mutual exchange "language, in all its stages and variations, has been progressively cultivated with the human race" (Herder, 116). Interestingly, a universal language might kill the living exchange of mentalities; therefore, it belongs among "empty projects and journeys to the moon" (*On Diligence*, 31). Nor do translations alone lead a nation out of its confinement. Translations bring some of the ideas that shine through the veil of language, but they lose the core strength and fail to transplant the mind from one clime and time to another. Diligence in foreign languages allows a nation to bring in not only ideas but to plant in the mind the otherness of alien minds.

Alert to the contrarieties of his own ideas, Herder saw that the call to multilingualism could be mistaken for mere cultural relativism, which he likened to a voyage on a "limitless sea" (*On Diligence*, 32) with no home port. The antidote to relativity comes through one's native tongue, its forms, its sounds, its distinctive casting of reality. Deep study of one's native tongue provides the "bark which carries me" (*On Diligence*, 33):

> But what a limitless sea do I see here before me, where I do not dare to venture without a Polinarus of my own—a labyrinth of languages where, without a guiding thread, I lose myself! Very well, this guiding thread is my native tongue, to which I must therefore offer the firstborn sacrifices of my diligence. Just as the love of our fatherland binds us to each other by heartfelt bonds of affection, the language of our father holds attractions for us also, which in our eyes exceed all others. (*On Diligence*, 32)

Herder nods here to inescapable positionality. One must build a cultural home, and after doing so, one will never achieve universal scope. But one can venture into other languages and traditions, comparing and sampling from the deck of one's own vessel the best that nations have thought and created. He doesn't endorse jumping ship.

Typology as Pathway

Herder's vision of the single-origin, multiple-destiny journey of humanity called for a synchronic supplement in the form of typologies of languages. Only with these could the scholar give precision to studies of linguistic diversity, specify how linguistic borrowing affected deeper structures, and speculate in detail on how language differences influenced, or were influenced by, general cultural and intellectual developments. Typologies in turn strengthened the concept that humanity, in all its races and branches, participated in a grand, open-ended journey to unfold the potential of human nature as it molded and was molded by language.

A degree of circularity characterized the movement between classifications and histories of language. One could identify language families by defining their distinctive traits or by tracing their genealogy, and one method always demanded correlation with the other. A class of language such as Indo-European thus had both genetic and typological ramifications which depended on each other for full definition: language families immediately brought attention to the shared traits by which they could be recognized, and those traits in turn suggested histories that could be tested against the accepted histories of nations and regions. Further, as typology and history interacted in this way, stages of linguistic development seemed to offer convenient classifications, so that synchronic and diachronic ideas converged. They converged especially in the recognition that languages of a given type can so change character over time as to lose the level of commonality that would justify classifying them as the same type. That is, languages that appear to fall into one class today may have been transformed from an ancestor of a different class by natural change or by external forces such as mixing and borrowing. The desire to relate language classifications to historical stages, and especially to earlier-to-later and worse-to-better stages of language development, triggered far-reaching speculation into the relations between language and thinking in both its individual and group aspects.

As an attempt to name broad groupings of language, typology dates back at least to early observations of the kinship of Europe's languages. Arno

Borst names Archbishop Rodrigo Jimenez de Rada of Toledo as the first to classify languages empirically rather than genealogically in his 1243 list of European languages. Rodrigo lumped England, Germany, and Flanders as of the same tongue, which differed from other Germanic tongues spoken in Scandinavia.[9] Giuliano Bonfante chronicles many such attempts to classify languages from 1200 on.[10] In *Diatriba de Europaeorum Linguae*, written in 1599, Joseph Scaliger brought attention to the affinities among general groupings of European languages by classifying them as Romance, Slavic, and Germanic. Martin Fogel (1634–1675) and Johann Eberhard Fischer (1697–1771) sought to demonstrate the shared descent of regional languages such as Hungarian and Finnish. Vasilij N. Tatishchev (1686–1750) did the same for Slavic languages. These definitions and groupings stimulated others to think about broad classes of language and about their undeclared assumptions regarding what constituted families, but they didn't involve types in the more general sense.

A few eighteenth-century thinkers implied a need for more clearly defined and discrete language types without knowing exactly how to invent them. Closely examined, Adam Smith's conviction that rational grammar would provide at once the "best system of logic in any language, as well as the best history of the natural progress of the human mind"[11] correlated thought and grammar in a way that would reveal developmental stages as well as facilitate comparisons among current languages. The Scottish barrister James Burnett, Lord Monboddo, took a step in the direction of classification by posing developmental stages according to languages' degree of grammatical complexity. First, for him, came languages that aggregated simple ideas into single long words, with each long aggregate word corresponding to whole sentences in other languages. Then over time came languages in which individual words emerged for various objects and actions, and in which those words could be marked for case, gender, aspect, tense, and other qualities. For Monboddo, highly complex, inflected languages represented the highest stage of artfulness, but some of them gradually gave way to a third type, the regular, as their complex modes were simplified to achieve a balance of ease and sophistication. Monboddo's stages are types in one sense: even though they are phases, he found living samples of all of them, but he stopped short of suggesting what others in his age were starting to discover—that types of languages could be distinguished according to the ways their grammars embedded semantic distinctions.

Monboddo points to a puzzle in the relation between classification and historical development. If the types of language represent stages of development, why did Monboddo find current examples of all three types? Why did some languages stagnate in the first stage, some reach the second, or most artful, stage and then cease to develop, some attain the regularized stage, and some degenerate from that plateau? Did the causes of advance lie in external factors such as climate, conquest, proximity to other languages, and commerce? Or did they lie in the intellectual potential of individual populations? If external factors played much of a role, why did backward people not advance visibly when they borrowed supposedly superior linguistic structures from their neighbors?

Given all the information on languages then available, late eighteenth-century thinkers deemed it possible and desirable to produce more penetrating classifications. Their efforts to collect and classify culminated in three massive projects: Peter Simon Pallas's *Linguarum Totius Orbis Vocabularia Comparativa* [Comparative Vocabulary of the World's Languages] (1786–89), a collection of samples of around 700 known languages, Don Lorenzo Hervás y Panduro's *Catálogo de las lenguas de las naciones conocidas* [Catalog of the Languages of Known Nations] (1800–1805), and Johann Christoph Adelung's *Mithridates* (1806–1817), which presented samples and compared texts of nearly a thousand languages. None of these projects actually solved the deeper problem of providing an adequate basis for comparison, but their span focused attention on the need for an adequate basis.

The Spanish linguist Hervás y Panduro scorned the useless mystical penetrations, the catalogs proving a single primitive source, the voluminous polyglot vocabularies, and the deep-searching etymologies of former eras and even recent times. For example, the four quarto volumes of Antoine Court de Gébelin's ambitious etymological study *Monde primitif* (1774–1796) did not, in Hervás's opinion, advance linguistic knowledge. Besides Court de Gébelin's numerous mistakes in classification, affiliation, and etymological tracings, said Hervás, he had relied on sources who had no more knowledge of a region's languages than they did of the lunar world.[12] The critique of *Monde primitif* seemed to presage the long-awaited arrival at the proper foundations of language study. Yet Hervás balked. His own catalog classed languages not principally by type but by geography. Hervás knew that improved linguistics would depend on the degree to which accurate linguistic groupings could be discovered. For example, consider how much easier it would be to write a grammar of a newly encountered language if, early on, one could ascertain the family to which it belonged. One could then quickly differentiate the key and shaping structures from the accidental. Proper classes would also help to differentiate between those languages that were dialects proceeding from the same ancestry and those that became cousins by virtue of borrowing. They would help to distinguish those aspects of language most impervious to change from those most susceptible. They would help linguists discern the degree of mixing and borrowing in a particular language. And they would strengthen the ability to see affinities and differences among peoples of geographical regions.

Arriving at proper classifications entailed many difficult challenges, however. In many cases the knowledge that would proceed from valid classifications was also the knowledge needed to establish them. For example, it was difficult to determine what to classify—individual words, sounds, word order, the manner of forming words, verbs and the various ways of forming and conjugating them, and so forth. Which of these would prove most stable over time and therefore give the most reliable evidence of descent and point up the most essential differences among current languages? Also, would languages of the same type in fact retain the essential features on which the type was originally based? If they did not, typology would have to proceed on different assumptions for different classes of language and perhaps for different stages of their development. Needless to say, this prospect complicated the task immensely. Finally, certain cultural and political affinities at were stake. For example, European classifiers, who tended to admire the complexity of inflecting languages, seemed to enjoy thinking that "isolating languages" such as Chinese, which devoted a separate word to each item of meaning, were the least sophisticated and even posed obstacles to the intellectual advancement of those who spoke them.

Not all of these issues were apparent from the beginning. Only repeated efforts to establish typologies brought the problems and their possible solutions to the surface. I can best convey the predicament by analogy to another emerging discipline. When eighteenth-century scientists began to view invisible structures and organisms with the microscope, they seemed to have entered a world in which prevailing ideas on plants, animals, and tissues no longer held up. Barbara Stafford explains the problem of assimilating these anomalous organisms into current knowledge:

During the eighteenth century, microscopic organisms were perceived as being liminal entities. As literal pictures of ambiguity, they purveyed a new realm of equivocal biota. . . . Much of the Enlightenment understanding of the complicated processes of growth, nutrition, and reproduction depended upon kinetic and dynamic representations of tiny biological systems. These animated "no-bodies" could not be effectively described in words. The paradox posed by complex and contradictory "invisibles" was that their intricate, and obviously compounded, look rendered them apparently unclassifiable. This condition of unclarity, visible but difficult to explain or describe, meant that illuminating metaphors had to be drawn from supposedly demarcated epistemological areas.[13]

By contrast, students of language exuded greater confidence and less sheer wonder than did early microscopists, and no wonder: language was out in the open, not invisible. Enlightenment assumptions about the advancement of civilization, individual cognition, and even national character depended on schematizing knowledge of individual languages and their relations. Yet for all their apparent accessibility, many languages, intricate and compounded in themselves, resisted exact description and classification.

Stafford documents various trials by microscopists to overcome the apparent liminality. While some microscopists emphasized the strangeness of the newly discovered microbes and catered to public curiosity, others sought finer and more comprehensive renditions of this fascinating and unpredicted world. The Abbé Dicquemare, for example, proceeded on the conviction that the natural kingdoms did produce hybrids indiscriminately and that the equivocal would disappear with closer and more rigorous observation. But it was to be the Dutch jurist and theologian Pierre Lyonet, studying a single species of caterpillar, who solved the enigmatic and the neither/nor. The solution lay not in drawing or naming every minute fragment but in perceiving the ideal form, the *ligne ideale* shared by each sample of an organism or structure. As Stafford puts it, "Salvation from disorder was to be achieved through the external superimposition of regularity and symmetry onto internal animal complexity. Imaginary constructs tamed phenomenal wildness. They redeemed both the shortcomings of the observer and the uncontrollable excess of life."[14]

I am not trying to legitimize language study by painting it as an early modern science. It can stand quite well on its own history. What I do claim is that the model of ambiguous, neither/nor organisms made accessible through a new medium brings to light aspects of language study that might otherwise escape attention. Both fields depended on two types of information: first, increasingly detailed and accurate representation of particulars so subtle and minute that they resisted exhaustive depiction, and second, the formulation of generalized principles in terms of which the particulars had more than isolated, instantial meaning. Both these aspects are entailed in typology, precisely the field that sorts out complex particulars to discover relationships both vertical (genus and species, for example) and horizontal (items that relate as members of a single differentiated class or that occupy analogous positions in the hierarchy).

The student of languages faced complications more difficult than microscopists. We can see the difficulties if we analyze the elements of microscopy. They include the microscope itself and the object viewed, but they also include the eye and the mind that directs the eye. In microscopy the lens, eye, and mind are presumed to be reliable, transparent, and at rest, although some opponents of early modern science argued that a microscope lens simply substituted its own type of distortion for that of the naked eye.[15] In language study, the target of observation included not just liminal objects but the medium of observation, the faculty of observation, and the observer as well. If ideal forms could do for the chaos of tongues what they did for microscopic organisms, what ideas in the linguistic realm would clarify the analogous role of the microscope, the eye, and the mind that directed the eye to see through the instrument? Early modern science was attempting to exclude them from consideration in favor of the object itself. By contrast, in language study, what began as a project to focus only on the target of study quite necessarily refocused itself to include all four levels. The most advanced students of language believed that all four levels influenced each other in a variety of ways. Finally, we must note an important difference in the roles of *ligne ideal*—and that is what language typologies are—in going from natural science to language studies. Microscopists used ideal forms to represent the target of observation. As we shall see, students of language extended the ideal forms of typology to the domain of mental functions and operations, even down to the act of perception itself. They did so on the assumption that the two domains were so closely intertwined that what applied in one domain, even when rationalized and formalized, applied in the other.

Efforts to establish valid typologies in the eighteenth century began sporadically. Gabriel Girard distinguished "langues analogues" from "langues transpositives" in his *Les vraies principes de la langue françoise* (1747). Adam Smith admired Girard's work, and his own "Considerations concerning the First Formation of Languages" (1761) contributed another kind of language classification, "original" and "compounded." The first label referred to those languages that developed in isolation and that had simpler word bases but complex cases and inflections for all kinds of qualities and relations among words; the second referred to languages that mixed and borrowed and therefore had more extensive word bases but simpler means (such as prepositions) to mark relations among them. Smith also contributed the idea that verbs were among the first types of words to be created. J. C. Adelung in *Mithridates* (1806–1817) classed languages as mono- or polysyllabic, a useful if crude distinction based on words only and not grammar. A spur to typological study came from Sir William Jones's famous 1786 observations on the relationship between Sanskrit and the European languages:

The *Sanscrit* language, whatever be its antiquity, is of a wonderful structure; more perfect than the *Greek*, more copious than the *Latin*, and more exquisitely refined than either, yet bearing to both of them a stronger affinity, both in the roots of verbs and in the forms of grammar, than could possibly have been produced by accident; so strong indeed, that no philologer could examine them all three, without believing them to have sprung from some common source, which perhaps, no longer exists: there is a similar reason, though not quite so forcible, for supposing that both the *Gothick* and the *Celtick*, though blended with a very different idiom, had the same origin with the *Sanscrit*; and the old *Persian* might be added to the same family.[16]

Perhaps as important as his recognition of Sanskritic affinities, which others had noticed as well, Jones stressed that mere word similarities did not suffice to show kinship; one must study root verbs and forms of grammar.

The German poet Friedrich von Schlegel, influenced by reading Jones's observations on Sanskrit, in his *On the Language and Wisdom of the Indies* (1808), urged that the time had come to stop conjecturing on language origins and begin a proper historical study. As a step toward making this possible he more sharply distinguished two language types implicit in eighteenth-century classifications. Schlegel called these inflecting languages, which changed or added to a word's meaning by altering the word, and noninflecting languages, which changed a root word's meaning by adding a separate word or appending an affix.[17] Greek, Latin, and most European languages fell into the inflecting class; Asian and American languages generally fell into the noninflecting. Friedrich's brother August Wilhelm von Schlegel developed the twofold into a threefold typology by differentiating the noninflecting into the isolating type, in which discrete words are added to express time, quality, relation, and other categories of meaning, and the agglutinating type, which attaches affixes to existing words to change their meaning. Schlegel added the further qualification that in languages of this type the affixes have separate meaning in themselves. To express this differently, isolating languages devote one word to each element of meaning, while the other two categories pack more than one element into each word, with the distinction that inflecting languages modify the word, while agglutinating languages string separate unmodified elements together into longer units. A. W. Schlegel considered the isolating languages as older and less sophisticated, even though the Chinese, using an isolating language, had created a great civilization.

Johann Georg Hamann (1730–1788), a self-educated philosopher of mantic pronouncements, leveled much of his intellectual energy against Enlightenment philosophers who arrogated their position into a cultural pinnacle from which they could subject alien languages to critique. Hamann turned the tables, subjecting Enlightenment ideas to critique. He attacked the inconsistencies and mystifications of Herder's prize essay on the origins of language. While he accepted Herder's notion that language couldn't be separated from human nature, he saw language not as the companion of reflection but as inseparable from reason itself, indeed from any form of human thought, whether intuitive or rational. Hamann also quarreled with those who believed proper philosophy to be discursive and who implied that only unenlightened people reasoned imagistically and intuitively. Language, properly understood, included all the symbolic forms by which humans carry out all kinds of thinking, and some of these were as vital, if not more so, than rationality.[18] To talk about thought, whether in reference to mathematical discourse or the visions and premonitions of a bard, was to talk about language. The stress on reason had actually diminished humanity's ability to draw on the full range of its mental/linguistic powers. In several of his works, notably "Die Magi aus Morgenlande" and "Lettre perdue d'un sauvage du nord à un financier de Pe-Kim," Hamann counterposed Europe's rationalistic discourse against that of the Orient, wherein he found "natural language," together with magical worldviews, imagistic and holistic thinking, and poetic expression—modes of thought on which Europe and especially France had turned its back. In such contrasts he found evidence for his assertion that a people's language corresponded to their whole state of being. Equally, their history lived in their language. Every people's language blended and coalesced with its civilization and, in a dialectical process, was also shaped and influenced by it. Even economics corresponded to language. But Hamann didn't necessarily view the facts of this bonding as being open to rational scrutiny. Analysis would retrieve dead facts but would fail to register the aliveness of language in its past or present. Only an analysis that entered into the significant forms and symbols of each era and language would be useful. One would need to be a prophet and poet to write history and philosophy.

Typology and history coincided in eighteenth-century speculation on language and national character. Perhaps following the lead of Condillac, d'Alembert observed in the "Discours préliminaire" to the *Encyclopédie* of 1751 that language and thought are generated together. The title of Michaelis's Berlin Academy prize essay typified the current interest: *The Influence of Opinions on Language and of Language on Opinions*. If language conditioned or, more emphatically, constituted thought, then what did language differences reveal about the intellectual variety of humanity?

Wilhelm von Humboldt and Diverse Journeys

Wilhelm von Humboldt fixed his attention on the relations between languages and the intellectual stature of the nations. To this topic he brought a knack for sweeping speculation akin to that of Herder and Hamann, but he also brought a linguist's close knowledge of specific languages and their structures. In him the concepts of language as a journey and the linguist's role as navigator and scout reach culmination.

Humboldt produced an influential typology of languages. At work on an ambitious study in the first decades of the nineteenth century, Humboldt added to Schlegel's types one more, the incorporating languages, which assimilated into the verb other information not usually folded into the verb. For example, some languages incorporate what we isolate in pronouns into the verb, so that a verb expresses not only an action but the person who performs it. It was perhaps because of his close knowledge of languages that he regarded the process of classification as ever difficult: "Our present observations show at once what a *variety* of different structures man's language-making is able to embrace, and lead us therefore to doubt the possibility of an exhaustive *classification* of languages" (Humboldt, *OL*, 235). Yet many of his utterances rest on the possibility of perceiving the foundational structures of different languages and drawing inferences as to their general influence on cognition.

He thought that once the structures underlying the language types are perceived, even in the abstract, the cause of language's power to shape thinking emerges clearly. Herein Humboldt shows us both the creative aspects of his spatial thinking and its limits. Structure is, first and foremost, a spatial concept. Although our minds have many instantiations of the concept, they rest on prototypes, which are the architectures of natural and artificial objects. Knowledge of language structure builds on spatial architectures but derives its own special character from the sounds, words, and word orders that comprise language. Much progress had been made in specifying the structures of language. One need go no further than the continued development of grammars to see this progress. The concept of language types had contributed another dimension to the understanding of language structures. Yet to make the leap from language to the structures of the mind, one also needs to have ideas of the actual and possible constitution of thought. What is thought, how does it proceed, and upon what elements of the mind does it depend? Since these aspects of thought are not open to inspection but appear only in language or some other medium, our concepts of mental structures tend to be conjectural or derivative. Language structure becomes the analog to mental structure and the window through which the latter can be viewed. When we approach thought through language, we must not be surprised when thought appears to follow the contours of language. Humboldt, as we will see, seems equally confident talking about either, but he knows language structure the best, and he tended to view thought and language as nearly identical at the level of inner form.

Humboldt posited that language mediates—that is, it filters, embodies, and comes between—the external world of objects and the internal world of thoughts. Of this role of language Humboldt said, "If the feeling truly awakens in the soul, that language is not just a medium of exchange for mutual comprehension, but a true *world* which the *mind* must insert, by its own inner labour, between itself and *objects*, then it is on the right road towards continually finding more and depositing more in its language" (*OL*, 157). It followed that each language shaped and channeled its speakers' intellects differently. "Languages develop under equal conditions and together with intellectual power, and at the same time they constitute its stimulating, vital principle" (*LVID*, 24).[19] Elsewhere he noted that language "does not just passively receive impressions, but it selects from among the multiplicity of possible intellectual directions a single definite one and modifies internally every outside influence exerted upon it" (*LVID*, 21–22). In sum, "a unique cosmic viewpoint reposes in every tongue" (*LVID*, 39). It follows that when one language influences another through proximity, conquest, or commerce, it reconstructs a different language and outlook (*LVID*, 134). Since each language gives only a partial rendering of all that humans can potentially perceive and utter, Humboldt considered each language a trial or essay in how to experience the world.

For Humboldt, the types of language were firmly connected to humanity's developmental stages and to the increasing—or stagnating—mental proficiency of nations. Of these stages he said, "*Language* is deeply entangled in the spiritual evolution of mankind, it accompanies the latter at every stage of its local advance or retreat, and the state of culture at any time is also recognizable in it" (*OL*, 24). Hence the fact that humankind is divided into peoples and races is directly linked to the diversity of their languages and dialects, and both these "are also connected with, and dependent upon, a third and higher phenomenon, the *growth of man's mental powers* into ever new and often more elevated forms" (*OL*, 21). The advances thus produced do not occur in a smooth continuum but are "achieved only because an uncommon power has unexpectedly taken its flight thither; cases where, in place of ordinary explanation of the effect produced, we must postulate the assumption of an *emission of force* corresponding to it" (*OL*, 31). Thus Humboldt acknowledged the role of genius. But even without the genius who assists nations in making linguistic leaps, individuals ceaselessly employ the language-making power to bring out all they can according to their mental capacities and the demands that experience places on them (*OL*, 27). To some degree, therefore, all people share in the race's advances, and all nations can fulfill the drive to progress, albeit along different tracks.

As conceived by Humboldt, language and the mind interact to link the individual, the nation, and the entire race. Language first mediates between individual and individual. To exist as a conscious individual—to have language, that is—means already to exist in relation to others. Language proves

> that man does not possess an absolute, segregated individuality, that 'I' and 'Thou' are not merely interrelated but—if one could go back to the point of their separation—truly identical concepts, and that there exist, therefore, only concentric circles of individuality, beginning with the weak, frail single person who is in need of support and widening out to the primordial trunk of humanity itself. (*HWP*, 236)[20]

Self-development proceeds partly through language, and insofar as it does, it also proceeds in step with the shaping of the world that language brings (*HWP*, 265). So conceived, the relations between language and other human spiritual and mental endowments guarantee the broadest variety of language. Of the individual, Humboldt said, "Since all objective perception is inevitably tinged with *subjectivity*, we may consider every human individual, even apart from language, as a unique aspect of the worldview. But he becomes still more of one through language" (*OL*, 59). Elaborating, he said,

> Everyone uses language for the expression of his particular idiosyncrasy, for it always proceeds from the individual and everyone utilizes it for himself alone. Nonetheless, it suffices for everyone insofar as words, though inadequate, still satisfy the urge to express one's innermost feelings. It cannot be claimed that language as a universal vehicle will equilibrate these differences. It probably does build bridges from one individual to another and mediates mutual understanding; on the other hand, it rather enlarges the difference, since by its elucidation, distinction, and refinement of ideas it makes us more clearly conscious of how it takes root in the original intellectual foundation. (*LVID*, 129)

Or

> Only in the individual does language receive its ultimate determinacy. Nobody means by a word precisely and exactly what his neighbour does, and the difference, be it ever so small, vibrates, like a ripple in water, throughout the entire language. Thus all understanding is always at the same time a not-understanding, all concurrence in thought and feeling at the same time a divergence. The manner in which language is modified in every individual discloses, in contrast to its previously expounded *power*, a dominion of man over it. (*OL*, 63)

As individuals grow, speak, and interact under the influence of their language, the nation takes on a character that is more discernible and fixed than individual character, yet the national imprint also guarantees a degree of variety, both among its members and between itself and other nations. Humboldt linked the national language and character so tightly that he believed that the shrewd observer would be able to derive one from the other. "From every language, therefore, conclusions can be drawn with respect to the national character" (*LVID*, 132). He gave the cause of this fusing as follows: "For *intellectuality* and *language* allow and further only forms that are mutually congenial to one another. Language is, as it were, the outer appearance of the spirit of a people; the language is their spirit and the spirit their language; we can never think of them sufficiently as identical" (*OL*, 46). The coincidence of intellectuality and language means that "there resides in every language a characteristic *world-view*" (*OL*, 60). The indigenous languages of North America illustrate that languages are impregnated with worldviews:

> The languages of the native inhabitants of America are rich in examples of this kind, in bold metaphors, correct—though unexpected—juxtapositions of concepts, cases where inanimate objects are transposed by a fertile, imaginative view of their nature, into the field of the animate, and so on. . . . Their view of the matter results from the practice of their grammar. If they misplace the constellations, grammatically, into the same class with men and animals, they obviously regard the former as beings endowed with personality, moving under their own power, and probably also guiding human destinies from above. (*OL*, 154)

A world outlook implies positioning within and perspective on a given terrain and yielding the distinctive details, proportions, blocked vision, and arrangement of objects that the terrain makes available only from an observer's position. In the illustration above, a worldview also influences grouping and classifying. A given language fixes these and constrains the mind to work along a given track. We should also note the circular thinking in the way Humboldt connects language and the mental lives of nations. Language, the more readily apparent structure, reflects and influences the intellect, another not so apparent structure that must be compatible with it. Humboldt nearly collapses the distinction.

Yet no language and no intellect has, in Humboldt's view, achieved the optimal synthesis between them or between mind-language and experience. That is why humanity still advances. Intellectual strides take place when people exert pressure on their language to reflect more adequately the complexities of their experience. This progress can take place within any language and nation, but not all the structures that nations have fashioned from the resources of language provide equal instruments of thought. In its striving toward "improved language-making" each nation faces limits that are

> prescribed to it by the *original design of the language*. A nation can make a more imperfect language into a tool for the production of ideas to which it would not have given the original incentive, but cannot remove the inner restrictions which have once been deeply embedded therein. To that extent even the highest elaboration remains ineffective. Even what later ages have added from without is appropriated by the original language, and modified according to its laws. (*OL*, 34)

Given Humboldt's thoughts on the varying degrees of limitation and potential within each language form, it was natural for him to state that some languages offered better structures to the striving intellect than others.

> We have spoken at length above of the compounding of the *inner thought-form* with the *sound*, and perceived in it a *synthesis* which—as is possible only through a truly creative act of the mind—engenders from the two elements to be combined a third, in which the particular nature of each vanishes. It is this *synthesis* whose *strength* is at issue here. In the language-making of nations, that race will wrest the palm, which executes this synthesis with the greatest vitality and most unweakened power. In all nations with more imperfect languages, this synthesis is by nature feeble, or is hampered and crippled by some adventitious circumstance. (*OL*, 183–84)

Further, "it is self-evident that the language whose structure is best adapted to the *mind*, and which gives the liveliest incentive to its activity, must also possess the most enduring power of giving birth to all the *new configurations* occasioned by lapse of time and the destinies of nations" (*OL*, 183).

Humboldt felt that he had found the best type of language structure. The inflecting languages, especially those "inflected to a higher degree" (*OL*, 202), clearly engendered new and effective configurations most readily. By contrast, isolating languages lent themselves poorly to the task: "The Chinese structure, however we may explain it, is obviously founded on an imperfection in the making of the language, probably a custom, peculiar to that people, of isolating sounds, coinciding with an insufficient strength of the inner linguistic sense that calls for their combination and mediation" (*OL*, 206–7). Alarmed at his own confidence to pronounce on the intellectual and spiritual quality of nations, Humboldt temporized. To the charge that he might be "singling out certain languages as the only legitimate ones" and thereby branding all others as "more imperfect," Humboldt responded that his judgment applied only to languages abstractly considered and evaluated by norms not fully accessible to us. "But the judgement thereby passed upon the others does not apply in equal measure to *concrete* existing languages, in which no one of these forms prevails exclusively, but a striving towards the correct one is always, on the contrary, visibly at work" (*OL*, 217). He continued:

> To pass sentence of condemnation on any language, even of the rudest savages, is a thing that nobody can be further from doing than myself. I would consider it not merely a disparagement of man in his most individual talent, but also as incompatible with any correct view provided, through reflection and experience, by language itself. For every language always remains a *copy* of that *original talent* for language as such; . . . every language, apart from its already *developed part*, has an incalculable *capacity*, alike for internal flexibility and for the assimilation of ever richer and loftier ideas. (*OL*, 218)

Thus viewing the matter more holistically, Humboldt concluded that every language involves both an unleashing and a constraining. Each aspires along specific paths of thinking and forfeits others. "It is undeniable, however, that languages are guided by the clearer and more definite insight of the inner speech-form to create more varied and sharply delimited nuances, and now make use for this purpose, by *expansion* or *refinement*, of the sound-form they have available" (*OL*, 76).

As people strive to expand and refine their language resources, constrained as they are by the sound-form their language makes available, each person and nation in its own way takes part in the endeavor of the entire race to more adequately conceive of and communicate the world. In this project humanity

> is aided by language, which binds as it individualizes, and beneath the cloak of the most individual expression holds the possibility of universal understanding. The individual, wherever, whenever and however he lives, is a fragment broken off from his whole race, and language demonstrates and sustains this eternal bond which governs the destinies of the individual and the history of the world.[21]

Humboldt thus covered in his theories the limits of both individuality and universality: "For in language the *individualization* within a *general conformity* is so wonderful, that we may say with equal correctness that the whole of mankind has but one language, and that every man has one of his own" (*OL*, 53). Humans share, then, not a common set of ideas or even common structures for relating and communicating them, but the experience of making effable—of conceiving (the inner aspect of language) and expressing (the social aspect) ideas and altering their language to make it more fit to the task of living in and thinking about all that is either internal or external to them.

Humboldt's concept of linguistic form deserves attention because it reveals again both the far-reaching quality of his thought and the circular path by which the far reaches occurred. Of form he wrote, "Since the natural inclination to language is universal to man, and since all men must carry the key to the understanding of all languages in their minds, it follows automatically that the form of all languages must be fundamentally identical and must always achieve a common objective" (*LVID*, 193). But we mistake in thinking this form simply a structural aspect of language. Form is the active harnessing together of language and mental power. Other linguists laid stress on the structures entailed in phonology, grammar, morphology, and syntax. Humboldt considered these necessary but dead artifices if not matched by something far more vital, which was attention to the effort people make as they develop their language to meet their needs. Here the given language, with all it made available to the individual and society, met the mental capacities that had partly been shaped by that language but which yet had powers that exceeded any language. The static forms of word types and grammatical structures Humboldt termed product or *Ergon*; the vital effort to produce language adequate to life he termed activity or *Energeia*. The former type could deal with the mass of details, rules, and exceptions that language contains; only the latter can relate this to the mental power. Form is "the quite individual *urge* whereby a nation gives validity in thought and feeling in language" (*OL*, 50). Without that type of relation, an exhaustive comparison of two languages becomes a fruitless exercise. The ceaseless mental labor, effort, or activity is the essence of form. This type is infinitely more difficult to define, but it is the only type that can make linguistics a living discipline. In language, however much we fix and define, "there always remains something left over in it, and precisely this which escapes treatment is that wherein the unity and breath of a living thing resides" (*OL*, 51).

Linguist as Scout

That is why Humboldt envisioned the linguist performing a vital, even life-giving, role. The linguist grasps the ineffable form and urges humanity forward on its journey. Humboldt wanted linguistics to establish itself on a scientific footing but at the same time to point to and, if possible, encourage and guide humanity in unfolding its full capacities. More than any of his contemporaries who were laying the foundations of modern linguistics, Humboldt saw the field as a dynamic one needing the interplay of two pursuits—the detailed analysis of sounds, grammars, and word forms and the philosophical and even poetic contemplation of the pathways down which language led humanity on its communal journey. Only by attending to both views of language could the linguist find the "path on which he must track the secrets of language" (*OL*, 27). His views of the doctrine of conventionalism illustrate the dual focus of the best linguists. Conventionalism holds that verbal signs are assigned without intrinsic relations to the objects or concepts they name. While Humboldt viewed conventionalism as one of the most valid principles in linguistics, it "kills all mental activity and exiles all life" if applied beyond a certain point (*HWP*, 249). It gave the linguist the needed reminder that words were separate from things and that therefore knowledge of external nature could not be derived from the most careful study of words. At the same time, people often feel as if there were a natural connection between word and thing, and once convention has established and long usage has confirmed the apparent link, language— living, spoken, shared speech—proceeds as if words belonged to the things they named. Structures, too, can be seen as somewhat arbitrary, since they differ from tongue to tongue. But that should not be construed to mean that the structures of language have nothing to do with mind or nature. Rather, linguistic structures mediate between the two other nodes. The feel of the lexical and structural links contributes to the experience of being an intelligent and articulate being. Without attending to both the scientific and the poetic, the formal and the intangible, language study, even comparative linguistics, lost all interest. Linguists must not only lay language beside language to clarify their structures; they must also view structures as they unleash and constrain the mind. They must, in brief, function as poets, linguists, and literary critics.

As a poet, the linguist must sense how the sounds and rhythms of language engage the mind and feelings, even apart from its semantic content, then perceive how the sound-forms and semantics shape each other's contours. As a literary critic, the linguist must be able to view the language and specific discourses as part of a people's joint project, at a given place and time, both to comprehend and shape itself and its world, perceiving how language connects to the "shaping of the nation's mental power." That understanding, together with those connections that pertain to the internal structure of a single language, further depends on "consideration of the overall individuality of mind" (*OL*, 21). This task demanded not only the finest application of logic and formal analysis, it demanded a finely tuned understanding in modes beyond logic:

> The sum of the knowledge, that soil which the human spirit must till, lies between all the languages and independent of them, at their center. But man cannot approach this purely objective realm other than through his own modes of cognition and feeling, in other words: subjectively. Just where study and research touch the highest and deepest point, just there does the mechanical, logical use of reason—whatever in us can most easily be separated from our uniqueness as individual human beings—find itself at the end of its rope. (*HWP*, 246)

The linguist was, ultimately, the only figure who could map the "purely objective realm" that can only be reached without normal logic.

An ignorance of these less tangible aspects of language led some in his lifetime still to wish for a universal language. Humboldt retorted:

> Only a tiny part of that which is thinkable can be designated in that way, because such symbols by their very nature fit only those concepts which can be produced by more synthetic construction. . . . It would be folly and delusion to imagine that such methods might transport one beyond the circumscribed limits of one's own language—not to mention all language. (*HWP*, 245)

In fact, for Humboldt it would be better to multiply languages to the maximum degree than to reduce or, worse, unify them, since no given number of viewpoints can exhaust the possibilities open to humanity.

The philosopher and poet can open up new horizons of thought within a tradition, but only the philosophically astute and poetically inclined linguist can fathom the ways that language impinges upon and constrains the process. Only the linguist is prepared to discern in formal and specifiable ways the linguistic interfaces with intellect and external reality and, in so doing, chart the gaps that separate one nation's route from another's. "To follow and depict this endeavor is the task of the linguist" (Herder, 27). But the linguist not only charts the route leading to the present. He or she grasps the unfolding of the journey forward. "The mutual interdependence of thought and word illuminates clearly the truth that languages are not really means for representing known truths but are rather instruments for discovering previously unrecognized ones" (*HWP*, 246). Humboldt doesn't pretend to dictate what those truths will be, but the discipline of being a linguist makes him a recorder of past and present truths, a participant in the discovery, and a promoter of the process. His enthusiasm for this project leads him occasionally to imply that with a bit more knowledge the linguist will be able to chart the way into the future with far greater certainty than the haphazard groping of humanity had ever achieved in the past.

E. A. Burtt observed in his classic study, *The Metaphysical Foundations of Modern Physical Science*, that with Galileo and the new science, "man begins to appear for the first time in the history of thought as an irrelevant spectator and insignificant effect of the great mathematical system which is the substance of reality."[22] Humboldt studied language, a phenomenon notably on the human side of that divide. However, he studied language in such a way as to make it scientific and, at the same time, make the development of human thought more intriguing and more central than that of the great mathematical spectacle. In Humboldt's vision of humanity's linguistic journey, the spectacle of humanity standing as a spectator would constitute just one stop on the long pilgrimage toward understanding. That moment needs to be followed by another, when humanity recognizes that its task is not simply to pull the veil away from nature, but to perceive its own spiritual and intellectual powers and needs. If the physical universe seemed alien and indifferent, one but had to remember that the image of that universe exists in the mind that grasps it and in the language by which that mind conceives and represents it.

The voyage into language culminated in Humboldt's view of language as humanity's journey across a terrain. The terrain is physical and metaphysical. Physically, it is the locale, as well as the region, continent, earth, and universe. Metaphysically, it is all of reality, together with whatever grasp of it a people have at a given moment in their history. The travelers are individuals and nations; the destination the constant unfolding of possibilities in the tri-fold relations of mind, word, and world; and the travel narrative the history of language and those events, whether the result of genius or ordinary capacity, that trigger change. Options for movement are created, and limited, by where we are and how we got there. Just as the wide-open potential for thought that inheres in human nature can only be realized in a particular form, thought about language must also take a particular form. It is therefore historical and situated, and at the same time it has in it the seeds that, by making thought possible at all, transcend any particular form.

Notes

1 Wilhelm von Humboldt, *On Language: The Diversity of Human Language-Structure and Its Influence on the Mental Development of Mankind*, trans. Peter Heath, with an

introduction by Hans Aarsleff, Texts in German Philosophy (Cambridge: Cambridge University Press, 1988), hereafter cited in parentheses as *OL*.

2 I draw these facts from Dava Sobel, *The Longitude* (London: Fourth Estate, 1995), 2–5.

3 Even without the extracts, it would have been difficult for Herder not to know Maupertuis's ideas on language. As president of the Berlin Academy, Maupertuis had helped set the agenda in language study, an agenda that directed attention not only to the origins of language, but to the influence of language on thought. The prize topic of a decade earlier, for example, led to Johann David Michaelis's *Dissertation on the Influence of Opinions on Language and of Language on Opinions* [1760] (London, 1769), a work I will pass over, however suggestive its title, in favor of the more substantial contributions of Condillac, Maupertuis, and Herder.

4 Johann Gottfried Herder, *Abhandlung über den Ursprung der Sprache* [1772], in *Johann Gottfried Herder: Frühe Schriften, 1764–1772*, ed. Ulrich Gaier, vol. 1, *Johann Gottfried Herder Werke* (Frankfurt: Deutscher Klassiker Verlag, 1985). Here I quote from the translation *Treatise upon the Origin of Language* (London, 1827), 97.

5 Michael Morton, *Herder and the Poetics of Thought: Unity and Diversity in "On Diligence in Several Learned Languages"* (University Park: Pennsylvania State University Press, 1989), 37.

6 Whether Herder misread Condillac is an open question. At any rate, Condillac would later talk about "innate language"—the language of gesture and action which at some point triggered reflection and made possible the language of articulated sounds. Since this innate language presupposes a natural faculty for sign-making, Condillac's account of the rise of language may be closer to Herder's than Herder was willing to allow. See Étienne Bonnot de Condillac, *La logique, ou Les premiers développemens de l'art de penser*, vol. 22, *Œuvres de Condillac* (Paris: Houel, 1798), pt. 2, chap. 2.

7 Johann Gottfried Herder, *On Diligence in Several Learned Languages* (Über den Fleiss in mehreren gelehrten Sprachen) [1764], in *Johann Gottfried Herder: Selected Early Works, 1764–1767*, ed. Ernest A. Menze and Karl Menges, trans. E. Menges with Michael Palma (University Park: Pennsylvania State University Press, 1992), 30, hereafter cited as *On Diligence*.

8 See Condillac's *La logique*, pt. 2, chap. 4.

9 Arno Borst, *Der Turmbau von Babel: Geschichte der Meinungen über Ursprung und Vielfalt der Sprachen und Völker* (Stuttgart: Hiersemann, 1957–1963), 763–64.

10 Giuliano Bonfante, "Ideas on the Kinship of the European Languages from 1200 to 1800," *Journal of World History* 1 (1953): 679–99.

11 Adam Smith to George Baird, 7 Feb. 1763, as quoted in *Adam Smith: Lectures on Rhetoric and Belles Lettres*, ed. J. C. Bryce, vol. 4, *The Glasgow Edition of the Works and Correspondence of Adam Smith* (Oxford: Clarendon, 1983), 24.

12 Don Lorenzo Hervás y Panduro, *Catálogo de las lenguas de las naciones conocidas y numeración, división y clases de éstas según la diversidad de sus idiomas y dialectos* (Madrid, 1800–1805), 1:69–71.

13 Barbara Stafford, "Images of Ambiguity: Eighteenth-Century Microscopy and the Neither/Nor," in *Visions of Empire: Voyages, Botany, and Representations of Nature*, ed. David P. Miller and Hans P. Reill, (Cambridge: Cambridge University Press and University of California Press, 1996), 230.

14 Stafford, "Images of Ambiguity," 254.

15 For an example of this criticism, see Margaret Cavendish, *Observations upon Experimental Philosophy* (London, 1666).

16 Sir William Jones, "On the Hindus," in *The Works of Sir William Jones* (London, 1807), 3:34–35.

17 Friedrich von Schlegel, *Ueber die Sprache und Weisheit der Indier* (On the Language and Wisdom of the Indies) (Heidelberg, 1808), 44–59.

18 James C. O'Flaherty, *The Quarrel of Reason with Itself: Essays on Hamann, Michaelis, Lessing, Nietzsche* (Columbia, SC: Camden House, 1988), 2–9.

19 Wilhelm von Humboldt, *Linguistic Variability and Intellectual Development*, trans. George C. Buck and Frithjof A. Raven (Coral Gables, FL: University of Miami Press, 1971), 24, hereafter cited in parentheses as *LVID*.

20 Wilhelm von Humboldt, *Humanist without Portfolio: An Anthology of the Writings of Wilhelm von Humboldt*, trans. Marianne Cowan (Detroit: Wayne State University Press, 1963), 236, referred to in text as *HWP*.

21 Quoted in Ernst Cassirer, *The Philosophy of Symbolic Forms* (New Haven: Yale University Press, 1953–1957), 1:157.

22 Edwin Arthur Burtt, *The Metaphysical Foundations of Modern Physical Science*, rev. ed. (New York: Humanities Press, 1951), 80.

Conclusion

This book has studied linguistic thought from 1500 to 1800 as it was influenced by encounter with other languages and by spatial experience. I began with the topic of "mapping language" to show that developments in navigation and mapping had telling parallels in language study, including the proposition that grammars are largely spatial. The next few chapters explored the implicit metaphors of early modern language study, the barrier and container. A chapter on rhetoric demonstrated that spatial dislocation—from Old World to New—disrupted the standard doctrines of rhetoric and made irrelevant the topics or commonplaces. The next chapter showed that static hierarchical and tabular correlations between mind and nature informed the attempts to invent a philosophical language. Locke introduced a dynamic ingredient into this by drawing on navigational metaphors and new conceptions of space as he proposed a theory of language that explained differences in ideas from one people to another. I used the phrase "language as the mind's space" to refer to his radical theory. I concluded the historical survey by showing that Locke's ideas led Herder and Humboldt to conceive of language itself as a journey. It is humanity's quest to understand, through the medium of words, the universe and our place within it.

Much of this study has, therefore, implied that metaphors, such as that of space, have a powerful role in two different dimensions, the unfolding of history and our access to that unfolding. It might even be argued, as occasional passages in my study seem to imply, that our knowledge of reality and particularly of history is entirely a matter of metaphors. Someone might question this type of study by asking: Why not just study changes in linguistic thought directly and not view them in terms of spatial experience? The question has several answers that take us to the assumptions behind this study. First of all, it is difficult to know what it means to study linguistic thought directly, since, as I have shown, language thought was persistently cast in terms of other concepts. Second, change makes so-called direct study yet more problematic because change implies some type of continuity by which change can be observed or measured. Once one measures change by continuity, one is essentially forced into metaphor. And perhaps, arbitrariness: What is the continuity, what the change? Third, while we could use many nonlinguistic concepts to explore changes in linguistic thought, space is especially useful. Fourth, language already immerses us in multiple modes of apprehension and experience. As a way of concluding this study, I will discuss these points and then reflect briefly on whether knowledge, and historical understanding in particular, is always so mediated by conceptual metaphors that we have little knowledge outside of them. As strange as it may seem, given the nature of this study, my answer will be that we must be cautious of reducing knowledge to metaphor.

Language Thought as Something Else

First, it is difficult to know what it means to study language thought directly. To think about language is already to think about things other than language. Language, as a topic, is so diffuse and elusive. As long as we talk about specific features of language or their behavior we are talking directly about language, so long as we note that such terms as *feature* and *behavior* actually have metaphorical bases. What if we want to talk more generally about how people have thought about language? The issue here is what we mean by *language*. Language is the aggregation of all linguistic features and their relations, all verbal signs, sound systems, paradigms, grammars, and verbal communication strategies, and we have to use a different strategy to speak about that aggregation in a way that attends to its aggregate nature. We form an abstract term for it—*language*—but that single term masks the composite nature that the term exists to bracket. As soon as we go beyond naming the abstraction, we eventually must talk about it *as* something. For example, in an early chapter I showed that efforts to neutralize the contamination that missionaries perceived in supposedly heathen languages led them to investigate what these languages actually contained. To get at the nature of language they conceived it in one way, as required by their purpose, as a container. Yet they found immediately that languages contained not one order of things, not just terms corresponding to objects and ideas, but many figurative pathways among images, myths, figures, beliefs, social customs, and words. They found so many ways of answering the question that the answers duplicated the problem they set out to solve and invalidated most of the solutions they considered employing.

Michael Polanyi suggested that we can look either *through* or *at* any instrument of knowledge. To look *through* it entails "subsidiary awareness"; to look *at* entails "focal awareness." We have subsidiary awareness of language when we use it to think about the decisions, situations, and problems we confront every day; we have focal awareness of it when we hold our words up for scrutiny. At that point our minds cease to pass "through them unhindered to the things they signify."[1] We can look at written works or attend to the spoken words, but can we really look at language and not just at some sample of it? Many philosophers of language seem to believe that we can. Language philosophers have wanted to look at language as an object or bundle of objects one can separate from oneself and see as if at a distance. Studies of modularity in the brain suggest that we accomplish this task only arbitrarily. Every verbal sign brings with it so many potential neural activations that our brains must sense already in the making or interpreting of the sign its purpose and which of its aspects—image, sound, written form, conceptual structure, symbol, action, state of being, or place in a hierarchy—will be needed to achieve our purposes. We seem to be able to determine such things in the act of conceiving the sign, an indication that our minds, in using language, are accustomed to the efficient management of multiplicity. Language itself requires so many forms of *seeing through* that in trying to look *at* it we are already thinking *through* it.

Ludwig Wittgenstein, who determined that in most cases we can see things *as* something else better than we can see things themselves,[2] came to view language as a patchwork of different strategies and practices, all of them contributing to its nature and function but not capable of being described in a single concept or definition or function. In his view, philosophically rigorous theories of language tend to provide only "an intellectual misconstrual of what we ourselves do with words. We yield to the temptation to assimilate one language-game to another and we make a theoretical mistake which has no effect on our practice but which is very deep and stubborn. We actually see our practice in the wrong way."[3] This is my answer to those who might see the type of study carried out here as merely a casual language-game. My attempt has been to present a history of language study that is, from start to finish, embedded in the world in which that language study occurred.

Stasis and Change

Second, history implies both continuity and change. If a history is more than a series of unconnected events, "event A occurred; later, event Y occurred," there must be starting points, way points, and continuities in the objects under study. Biologists can put bacteria in a petri dish and observe how they grow. The purpose of the petri dish is to control the environment and medium so that any change is produced by the growth of a single type of organism. If language is the patchwork that Wittgenstein held it to be, and we are observing how people thought about it over time, we need something both inside and outside language to allow some coherence to the study. In this book, given my assumptions, there is no way to seal off language and watch it, or thought about it, develop. So I have made a virtue of necessity. I have considered two continuities, both changing and yet both in some strange ways static, and watched them develop together. By *static* I mean something other than the usual sense of "unchanging." I mean that some things remain unchanged even when discursive forces are bringing about new conceptions of them.

I believe I have demonstrated that ideas about space and language changed radically over three centuries. For example, the chapter on rhetoric laid out changes in ideas of space that began to influence ideas in other disciplines. Space had become infinite and centerless, with everything in motion. Objects were understood to be at rest only in relation to other objects moving with them, like masts and rigging on a ship that is moving on the water. To measure motion and stasis required arbitrary axes or reference points. Yet I hold, rather paradoxically as it may seem, that neither language nor spatial experience is comprised wholly by the discourses in which we encounter them. Both of them exist as realities in which discourse takes place and which discourse tries to understand and which discourse does partly shape, but discourse is also shaped by language and space because both exist whether we have discourse of them or not. Both have a nature that is impervious to our ideas and formulations. Both impose great constraints on what we can think and say about them. The easy part of writing a history of language thought as it was conditioned by spatial ideas is to trace and present the train of differing conceptions. The difficult part, always beyond the horizon of this study, is composed of the enduring presence of both space and language. That presence exerts itself not as a clear boundary or track but as the something toward which we can constantly feel discourse moving. The voyage into language is therefore simultaneously only a metaphor and much more than a metaphor. As a metaphor, it has allowed me to tease out strands in the linguistic encounter that might otherwise remain hidden. As a conceptual figure—more than a way of talking about something—the voyage into language constitutes one of the means by which Europe perceived and studied the nature of language. And language and space are such powerful conceptual metaphors because they are also primitives of experience that never yield entirely to mere discursive formulation.

Space as Fundamental

Third, space is an especially useful conceptual metaphor. One reason for this I stated above: space is a product of discourse, but it also exists apart from and before and after any discourse. It is always with us; we can never get away from it. We can say, with Lefebvre in *The Production of Space*, that space is produced by culture, but if we reflect carefully on this provocative over-statement, we understand it to say only that our ideas of space—lived, mapped, spoken, or architecturally arranged—vary in slight ways from cul-ture to culture. I stress "in slight ways." Any person whose ideas of space were wholly "produced" by his or her culture to the degree implied in such studies as Lefebvre's would never be able to exit a room or move from one town to another with the ease of a dog or cat. Space is cultural, but in most ways it transcends culture. Kant considered space an *a priori* mode of per-ception. Space allows us to perceive things external to us *as external to us*. It also allows us to perceive things experienced in the mind as outer to us. Lan-guage, I suspect, functions in the same way. Language resides both in us and yet can be conceived as outside us; therefore, it is no surprise that those who have attempted to investigate it have utilized spatial forms to do so.

My study has been a dual one, treating language as a destination at a distance to which one travels and also as something close and around us by which we locate and represent other things and ideas. Just as in cartogra-phy two techniques complemented each other, the chorographic and the geographic, with the former offering views from a specific location and the latter providing symbolic charts of an entire area, language study moved between types of study that reflect the analyst's position or purpose and types that tried to represent the world systematically and objectively. In exploring the barriers that language erects between the mind and nature, Europe explored the dual experience of being in and part of language and yet separate from it. This dual experience, I argued earlier, constitutes a condition of consciousness and knowledge. Bacon diagnosed as an intellec-tual distemper his era's desire to crack the secrets of nature through lan-guage. The quest had proved, and would always prove, fruitless. To cure the distemper he prescribed separation: view words and things as of entirely different natures; concentrate on matter and not discourse.

Students of language after Bacon continued to employ spatial concepts even though language had been detached from external nature. Locke, with his eye on the enormous variety recorded in travel narratives and his grasp of place and space, may seem to have backtracked from Bacon's proposition when he claimed that to understand knowledge we must understand language. He did not really backtrack. His focus was knowledge itself, not the behavior of external nature. Although nature does not hinge on language, knowledge does. He patterned language upon the moving universe. He mapped the space within the mind, that is, the means by which the mind fixes and locates and relates ideas, and showed that language was integral to that process. Locke replaced universal ideas with a universal process capable of serving every mind in assembling and, just as important, preserving an understanding of nature, even though that process guarantees that separate peoples will arrive at some different ideas. My point is that spatial experience continues to inform the study of language, even when concepts of space have undergone radical transformation. This fecundity reveals how adept people are at relating experience in one realm to that in another, updating their concepts as they go. It also seems to reveal that something remains in spatial experience beyond what a theory or a whole culture is able to represent. In going from earlier students of language to Humboldt, the barrier changed from a negative impediment to a positive mediator, from a punishment and symbol of universal decay to a gift and a symbol of humanity's spirit—indeed, to a symbol of humanity's symbol-making capacity—and from a fairly static to a dynamic nature. The barrier became a set of entities and structures, different for each language-nation, which afforded them a means of grappling with the natural and social world in which they exist. This conception did not, of course, exhaust language's own fecundity.

Language as Entangled

Fourth, language so intertwines with other cognitive faculties that we must be careful when formulating theories about how language interposes between the mind and any reality external to the mind. When Humboldt says that language is a "*world* which the *mind* must insert, by its own inner labour, between itself and *objects*,"[4] we must demur. Language immediately involves many modes of perception and feeling. It involves the self that perceives and experiences, the concepts and perceptions that form in the mind, whether these are sensory or abstract, the operations of the mind that may as yet be unknown to us, the objects and events perceived and experienced, and even the audience for whom thoughts are formulated, whether that audience is an inner one or one external to us. In our representing any facet of experience, language immerses us in the world we live in as accessed and represented by many faculties. Only with difficulty, and often with great distortion, do we shave off enough of the mind and the world that saturate language to be able to speak of it as a separate entity.

When it is the nature of language to provide manifold interfaces between the mind and the world, language deserves to be studied in many ways. In the introduction I referred to the mind's modularity. My view is that language is itself so multimodal that it cannot be divorced from its manifold connections to the mind or to the world we live in. It represents, but it doesn't represent in one way, rather many. It expresses, but in many ways. It communicates, but in many ways. Does language influence thinking? Yes, but it does so partly by offering many different ways to think about the same thing and engaging modes of perception that are separate from language. Does language refer to things in the world? Yes, but by nearly as many means as the mind has for sensing and conceiving them. To talk about language is already to talk about mind and world, and there is no way to detach them except deliberately and for limited purposes. The problems come when we mistake the conclusions drawn from such limited, deliberate separation as valid for thinking about the whole set of relations that language brings with it.

We can talk about noun phrase structures and verb conjugations in an isolated way, but as soon as we use anything but nonsense words in our examples, language drags in the world and the mind along with it. Chomsky's famous and supposedly nonsensical sentence *Colorless green ideas sleep furiously* activates neuronal groups that in ordinary experience process colors, abstract ideas, states of slumber and wakefulness, states of agitated or restful emotions, types of propositional linking, and flurries of figuration. So we might as well face that fact and include the world and the mind in the study whenever we want to reach beyond pure structures, and even then we can't keep all the rest out. That is why I have drawn, however loosely, on cognitive linguistics, which anchors language in the mental processes that create and manipulate language and in many other ways apprehend the objects, persons, actions, and perceptions to which language refers.

An analogy may be helpful here. Physicists can try to approach light as something we can see, or they can study it as something we can't see but can see other things by. A strong argument can be made that we don't see light. When we think we do, we really see only the particles in a light beam or the articles around us that light illuminates. A beam of light is visible when dust particles float in it. Physicists' attempts to study light as an external phenomenon led them to describe light itself first as a particle and, later, as a wave. Language may be similar in that it has altering properties, but what language points to—the objects it illuminates and the particles that float in an otherwise invisible medium—are more akin to what we experience than is the pure medium. We are comfortable with the knowledge that language mediates thought, but language is also mediated to us through what it illuminates: our ideas, thoughts, perceptions, communications to which we add our own meaning as we make them.

Metaphor and History

Does that mean that we must always study a topic such as language through the conceptual metaphors of historical eras? My study may seem to suggest that we cannot avoid it. We will necessarily be seeing ideas *as* something else, yet, even as we do so, we find out more about them in and of themselves. Let me return to a point in the previous section. While it is true that ideas of space and language are constructed in discourse, it is just as true that the discourse is powerfully shaped by the existence, outside discourse, of those facts of existence. When we say we know reality through metaphors, we seem to say that knowledge is not much more than metaphors. We forget that metaphors work only by having a target or source input that is independent of the metaphor. Reality, in the form of the target or source input of metaphorical conceptions, dictates which of all the many possible implications of a figure will be transposed onto itself. If we knew only through metaphor, we would have difficulty separating a figurative input and the object on which we map it. The radical difference between them makes both metaphor and knowledge possible. The gap between metaphor and reality—however complex and inexhaustible that reality is—provides the guarantee that knowledge can progress so that, even though linguists of the 1800s had lost some of the metaphors and thus some of the insights of the 1500s, their net understanding of language had actually increased. This increase would be impossible if knowledge consisted only in changes of metaphor.

When we turn to history we leave the realm of our manifold, complex, inexhaustible reality and face what no longer exists. Can we have knowledge of the past that exceeds a metaphorical contingency? Let me put the question this way, if the gap between metaphor and reality guarantees some certain knowledge in the present, what happens when that reality lives only in our memories and in records which themselves are permeated by metaphors? Even though history is our reconstruction of the past, driven by our present interests and shaped by the tropes and figures through which we view the texts, images, and remains of former days, yet something of the past survives above and beyond our interests and metaphors. With these limitations in mind, we crisscross the terrain along various paths, knowing that by changing perspectives and by paying close attention to the conceptual metaphors of history, we can approximate an understanding of our subject matter as it was conceived in a given place and time. We approximate, in the sense of get closer, because as we switch figures and tropes we at least achieve multiple perspectives on what are ostensibly the same phenomena. That is what language makes us do anyway. Yet any theory of knowledge that denies further access to past objects and their relations than can be mediated by our metaphors keeps excluding the objects and relations themselves. Whatever they are, they exert enormous constraining forces on our knowledge.

Even though I don't believe my book is especially successful at defining without metaphorical filters the history of language thought, and so reveal to us naked space and language, I want to close by noting that many contemporary historical and cultural studies act as if the discourse is everything. History must grant first of all that people of the past lived in a reality that was not merely linguistically or discursively constituted. Insofar as people of the past thought about such things as language, space, social relations, country and city, diet, clothing, domestic architecture—in brief, about anything that is not wholly a fabric of the mind—their lives and thoughts are not just a matter of changing filters and conceptions. Even granting that position, however, the more difficult part remains, which is conceiving of the past as having an independence of its own when most of what had independent existence has vanished or changed so radically that we are driven to history just to recover some of what a past reality was like. Although the parts of knowledge that are easy to specify are those we gain through the filtering and mediating faculties of our minds, our senses, and language, the parts that are less easy to demonstrate are nevertheless still there and make even mediated knowledge possible.

Notes

1 Michael Polanyi, *Personal Knowledge: Towards a Post-Critical Philosophy* (Chicago: University of Chicago Press, 1962), 55–57.
2 Ludwig Wittgenstein, *Philosophical Investigations*, trans. G. E. M. Anscombe (Oxford: Blackwell, 1953), 193–95.
3 Quoted in *Penguin Dictionary of Philosophy*, ed. Thomas Mautner (London: Penguin, 1999), 603.
4 Wilhelm von Humboldt, *On Language: The Diversity of Human Language-Structure and Its Influence on the Mental Development of Mankind*, trans. Peter Heath, with an introduction by Hans Aarsleff, Texts in German Philosophy (Cambridge: Cambridge University Press, 1988), 157.

Bibliography

Aarsleff, Hans. *From Locke to Saussure: Essays on the Study of Language and Intellectual History.* Minneapolis: University of Minnesota Press, 1982.

Acosta, José de. *Natural and Moral History of the Indies* [1590]. Hakluyt Society Publications, 1st ser., no. 60 and 61. London, 1880.

Akhundov, Murad D. *Conceptions of Space and Time: Sources, Evolution, Directions.* Translated by Charles Rougle. Cambridge: MIT Press, 1986.

Albinus, Peter. *A Treatise on Foreign Languages and Unknown Islands.* Translated by Edmund Goldsmid. Edinburgh: Biblioteca Curiosa, 1884.

Albuquerque, Luís de. "Portuguese Navigation: Its Historical Development." In *Circa 1492: Art in the Age of Exploration,* edited by Jay A. Levenson, 35–39. Washington, D.C.: National Gallery of Art, 1991.

Aldrete, Bernardo de. *Del origen y principio de la lengua castellana* [1606]. Edited by L. N. Jiménez. Madrid: Consejo Superior de Investigaciones Científicas, 1972.

Anderson, Arthur O. "Sahagún: Career and Development." In *Florentine Codex: General History of the Things of New Spain,* translated and edited by Arthur O. Anderson and Charles E. Dibble. Introductory Volume. Santa Fe: School of American Research and the University of Utah, 1982.

Andrews, J. Richard, and Ross Hassig. Introduction to *Treatise on the Heathen Superstitions and Customs That Today Live among the Indians Native to This New Spain, 1629,* by Hernando Ruiz de Alarcón. Norman: University of Oklahoma Press, 1984.

Andrewes, Lancelot. "A Sermon" [Christmas Day, 1616]. In *Lancelot Andrewes: Selected Writings.* Manchester: Carcanet, 1995.

Aristotle. *The Rhetoric of Aristotle.* Translated by Lane Cooper. New York: Appleton, Century, Crofts, 1932.

Bacon, Sir Francis. *The Works of Francis Bacon.* Edited by James Spedding, Robert Ellis, and Douglas Heath. 14 vols. London: Longman, 1860.

———. "Advancement of Learning." In *Advancement of Learning and Novum Organum.* New York: Colonial, 1899.

Batz, William. "The Historical Anthropology of John Locke." *Journal of the History of Ideas* 35 (1974): 663–70.

Behn, Aphra. *Oroonoko, or The Royal Slave.* Edited by Lore Metzger. New York: Norton, 1973.

Bennett, J. W. *The Rediscovery of Sir John Mandeville.* New York: Modern Language, 1954.

Bertonio, Ludovico. *Arte y gramática muy copiosa de la lengua aymara.* Rome, 1603.

Besnier, Pierre. *A Philosophical Essay for the Reunion of Languages* [1674]. Translated by Henry Rose. Oxford, 1675.

Bloom, Paul, Mary Peterson, Lynn Nadel, and Merrill Garrett, eds. *Language and Space.* Cambridge: MIT Press, 1996.

Bonfante, Giuliano. "Ideas on the Kinship of the European Languages from 1200 to 1800." *Journal of World History* 1 (1953): 679–99.

Borst, Arno. *Der Turmbau von Babel: Geschichte der Meinungen über Ursprung und Vielfalt der Sprachen und Völker.* 4 vols. Stuttgart: Hiersemann, 1957–1963.

Botero, Giovanni. *The Reason of State*. Translated by P. J. and D. P. Waley. New Haven: Yale University Press, 1956.

Bouwsma, William J. *Concordia Mundi: The Career and Thought of Guillaume Postel (1510–1581)*. Cambridge: Harvard University Press, 1957.

Brehaut, Ernest. *An Encyclopedist of the Dark Ages: Isidore of Seville*. New York: Columbia University Press, 1912. Reprint, New York: Franklin, 1912.

Bruno, Giordano. *De Immenso et Innumerabilibus* [1591]. In *Opera Latine Conscripta* . . . . Vol. 1. Naples: Morano, 1879.

Burnett, James [Lord Monboddo]. *Of the Origin and Progress of Language*. 6 vols. Edinburgh, 1774–1792.

Burtt, Edwin Arthur. *The Metaphysical Foundations of Modern Physical Science*. Rev. ed. New York: Humanities Press, 1951.

Calvin, John. *Commentaries on the First Book of Moses, Called Genesis*. Translated by John King. 2 vols. Grand Rapids, MI: Eerdmans, 1948.

Carreño, Alberto María. *Fray Domingo de Betanzos: Fundador en la Nueva España de la Venerable Orden Dominicana*. Mexico: Victoria, 1924–1934.

Carruthers, Peter. *Language, Thought, and Consciousness*. Cambridge: Cambridge University Press, 1996.

Cassiodorus. *An Introduction to Divine and Human Readings*. Translated by Leslie Webber Jones. New York: Columbia University Press, 1946.

Cassirer, Ernst. *The Philosophy of Symbolic Forms*. 4 vols. New Haven: Yale University Press, 1953–1957.

Cavendish, Margaret. *Observations upon Experimental Philosophy*. London, 1666.

Chirino, Pedro. *Relación de las Islas Filipinas i de lo que in ellas añ trabajado. Los Padres de la Compañia de Jesus*. Rome, 1604.

Chomsky, Noam. *Modular Approaches to the Study of the Mind*. San Diego: San Diego State University Press, 1984.

Coe, Michael D. *Breaking the Maya Code*. New York: Thames and Hudson, 1992.

Columbus, Christopher. *The Diario of Christopher Columbus's First Voyage to America, 1492–1493*. Translated by Oliver Dunn and James E. Kelley, Jr. Norman: University of Oklahoma Press, 1989.

Comenius [J. H. Komensky]. *The Way of Light*. Translated by E. T. Campagnac. Liverpool: University Press, 1938.

Condillac, Étienne Bonnot de. *Essay on the Origin of Human Knowledge* [1746]. Translated by Thomas Nugent. London, 1756.

———. *La logique, ou Les premiers développemens de l'art de penser*. Vol. 22, *Œuvres de Condillac*. Paris: Houel, 1798.

Cook, James. *The Journals of Captain James Cook*. Edited by J. C. Beaglehole. 4 vols. Cambridge: Cambridge University Press, 1955–1967.

Cooper, Michael. *They Came to Japan: An Anthology of European Reports on Japan, 1543–1640*. London: Thames and Hudson, 1965.

Cornford, F. M. "The Invention of Space." In *Essays in Honour of Gilbert Murray*. London: Allen & Unwin, 1936.

Court de Gébelin, Antoine. *Monde primitif, analysé et comparé avec le monde moderne*. 9 vols. Paris, 1774–1796.

Covarrubias, Sebastián de. *Tesoro de la lengua castellana o española*. 1611.

Cuevas, Mariano, comp. *Documentos inéditos del siglo XVI para la historia de México*. Mexico: Editorial Porrúa, 1975.

Cummins, J. S., ed. *The Travels and Controversies of Friar Domingo Navarrete 1616–1686*. Cambridge: Hakluyt Society, 1962.

Dalgarno, George. *Ars Signorum*. London, 1661.

Daniel, Samuel. *Musophilus: Containing a General Defense of All Learning* [1599]. Edited by Raymond Himelick. West Lafayette, IN: Purdue Research Foundation, 1965.

Descartes, René. *Discourse on the Method*. In *The Philosophical Writings of Descartes*, translated by J. Cottingham, R. Stoothoff, and D. Murdoch. Vol. 1. Cambridge: Cambridge University Press, 1985.

———. *Principles of Philosophy*. In *The Philosophical Writings of Descartes*. Vol. 1. Cambridge: Cambridge University Press, 1985.

———. *Philosophical Letters*. Translated and edited by Anthony Kenney. Oxford: Clarendon, 1970.

Dietrich, Eric. "Analogy and Conceptual Change, or You Can't Step into the Same Mind Twice." In *Cognitive Dynamics: Conceptual and Representational Change in Humans and Machines*, edited by Eric Dietrich and Arthur B. Markman, 265–294. Mahwah, NJ: Lawrence Erlbaum, 2000.

Doi, Tadoa. "Researches in the Japanese Language Made by the Jesuit Missionaries in the Sixteenth and Seventeenth Centuries." *Proceedings of the Imperial Academy of Japan* 13 (1937): 232–36.

Durán, Diego de. *The History of the Indies of New Spain* [1581]. Translated by Doris Heyden and Fernando Horcasitas. New York: Orion, 1964.

Duret, Claude. *Discours de la vérité des causes et effets des décadences, mutations, changements, conversions et ruines de monarchies, empires, royaumes, et républiques*. Paris, 1595.

———. *Discours de la vérité des causes et effets des divers course, mouvements . . . et saleure de la Mer Océane*. Paris, 1600.

———. *Histoire admirable des plantes et herbes esmerveillables et miraculeruse en nature*. 1605.

———. *Thresor de l'histoire des langues de cest univers, contenant les origines, beautez, perfections, decadences, mutations, changements, conversions, & ruines des langues . . . .* Cologne, 1613.

Dyck, Joachim. "The First German Treatise on Homiletics: Erasmus Sarcer's *Pastorale* and Classical Rhetoric." In *Renaissance Eloquence: Studies in the Theory and Practice of Renaissance Rhetoric*, edited by James J. Murphy, 221–37. Berkeley: University of California Press, 1983.

Eco, Umberto. *The Search for the Perfect Language*. Translated by James Fentress. Oxford: Blackwell, 1995.

Eisely, Loren. *The Man Who Saw through Time*. New York: Charles Scribner's Sons, 1973.

Elliott, J. H. *The Old World and the New, 1492–1650*. Cambridge: Cambridge University Press, 1970.

Elliott, Ralph W. V. "Isaac Newton's 'Of an Universall Language.'" *Modern Language Review* 52 (1957): 1–18.

Fauconnier, Gilles. *Mappings in Thought and Language*. Cambridge: Cambridge University Press, 1997.

Fauconnier, Gilles, and Mark Turner. *The Way We Think: Conceptual Blending and the Mind's Hidden Complexities*. New York: Basic Books, 2002.

Fenton, William, and Elizabeth Moore. Introduction to *Customs of the American Indians Compared with the Customs of Primitive Times*, by Joseph François Lafitau. Vol. 1. Toronto: Champlain Society, 1974.

Fernandez de Oviedo, Gonzalo. *Historia general y natural de las Indias* [1535]. 4 vols. Madrid: Real Academia de la Historia, 1851.

Fodor, Jerry. *The Modularity of Mind*. Cambridge: MIT Press, 1983.

------. *The Mind Doesn't Work That Way: The Scope and Limits of Computational Psychology*. Cambridge: MIT Press, 2000.

Formigari, Lia. *Language and Experience in Seventeenth-Century British Philosophy*. Amsterdam Studies in the Theory and History of Linguistic Science, vol. 48. Amsterdam: John Benjamins, 1988.

Forster, J. R. *Observations Made during a Voyage round the World*. London, 1778.

Foucault, Michel. *The Order of Things: An Archaeology of the Human Sciences*. New York: Vintage Books, 1970.

------. "Of Other Spaces." *Diacritics* 16, no. 1 (1986): 22–27.

Fuller, Mary. *Voyages in Print: English Travel to America, 1576–1624*. New York: Cambridge University Press, 1995.

García, Gregorio. *Origen de los Indios de el Nuevo Mundo, e Indias Occidentales* [1607]. 2d ed. Madrid: Abad, 1729.

García Icazbalceta, Joaquín, ed. *Annales del Meseo Michoacano*. Morales, 1888.

Garcilaso de la Vega. *Royal Commentaries of the Incas and General History of Peru*. Translated by Harold V. Livermore. Austin: University of Texas Press, 1966.

Gentner, Dedre, and Phillip Wolff. "Metaphor and Knowledge Change." In *Cognitive Dynamics: Conceptual and Representational Change in Humans and Machines*, edited by Eric Dietrich and Arthur B. Markman, 295–342. Mahwah, NJ: Lawrence Erlbaum, 2000.

Gómara, Francisco López de. *Historia general de las Indias*. Saragosa, 1554.

Goodman, Godfrey. *The Fall of Man, or The Corruption of Nature, Proved by the Light of our Naturall Reason*. London, 1616.

Grafton, Anthony. *New Worlds, Ancient Texts: The Power of Tradition and the Shock of Discovery*. Cambridge: Belknap Press of Harvard University Press, 1992.

Granberry, Julian. *A Grammar and Dictionary of the Timucua Language*. 3d ed. Tuscaloosa: University of Alabama Press, 1993.

Greenblatt, Stephen. "Learning to Curse: Aspects of Linguistic Colonialism in the Sixteenth Century." In *First Images of America: The Impact of the New World on the Old*, edited by Fredi Chiapelli. Vol. 2. Berkeley: University of California Press, 1976.

------. *Marvelous Possessions: The Wonder of the New World*. Chicago: University of Chicago Press, 1991.

Guitarte, Guillermo L. "La dimensión imperial del español en la obra de Aldrete: Sobre la aparición del español de América en la lingüística hispánica." In *The History of Linguistics in Spain*, edited by Antonio Quilis and Hans-J. Niederehe, 129–87. Amsterdam Studies in the Theory and History of Linguistic Science, 3d ser. Amsterdam: John Benjamins, 1986.

Guzman, Luis de. *Historia de las missiones*. 1601.

Hale, John. *The Civilization of Europe in the Renaissance*. New York: Simon & Schuster, 1995.

Hampden-Turner, Charles. *Maps of the Mind*. New York: Macmillan, 1981.

Hanke, Lewis. "Pope Paul III and the American Indians." *Harvard Theological Review* 30, no. 2 (1937): 65–102.

------. *All Mankind Is One: A Study of the Disputation between Bartolomé de Las Casas and Juan Ginés de Sepúlveda in 1550 on the Intellectual and Religious Capacity of the American Indians*. DeKalb: Northern Illinois University Press, 1974.

Hanzeli, Victor. *Missionary Linguistics in New France: A Study of Seventeenth- and Eighteenth-Century Descriptions of American Indian Languages*. The Hague: Mouton, 1969.

Harrison, John, and Peter Laslett. *The Library of John Locke*. Oxford: Oxford Bibliographical Society, 1965.

Heidegger, Martin. "Building, Dwelling, Thinking." In *Poetry, Language, Thought*, translated by Albert Hofstadter. New York: Harper & Row, 1975.

Herbert, Thomas. *A Relation of Some Yeares Travaile into Afrique, Asia, Indies*. London, 1634.

Herder, Johann Gottfried. *Abhandlung über den Ursprung der Sprache* (Treatise upon the Origin of Language) [1772]. In *Johann Gottfried Herder: Frühe Schriften, 1764–1772*, edited by Ulrich Gaier. Vol. 1, *Johann Gottfried Herder Werke*. Frankfurt: Deutscher Klassiker Verlag, 1985.

———. *On Diligence in Several Learned Languages* (Über den Fleiss in mehreren gelehrten Sprachen) [1764]. In *Johann Gottfried Herder: Selected Early Works, 1764–1767*, edited by Ernest A. Menze and Karl Menges and translated by E. Menges with Michael Palma. University Park: Pennsylvania State University Press, 1992.

———. *Treatise upon the Origin of Language* [1772]. London, 1827.

Hervás y Panduro, Don Lorenzo. *Catálogo de las lenguas de las naciones conocidas y numeración, división y clases de éstas según la diversidad de sus idiomas y dialectos*. 5 vols. Madrid, 1800–1805.

Hirschfield, Lawrence, and Susan Gelman. *Mapping the Mind: Domain Specificity in Cognition and Culture*. New York: Cambridge University Press, 1994.

Hodgen, Margaret T. *Early Anthropology in the Sixteenth and Seventeenth Centuries*. Philadelphia: University of Pennsylvania Press, 1964.

Holguín, Diego González. *Arte de la lengua general del Perú, llamada quichua* [1586]. Lima, 1607.

Howell, Wilbur Samuel. *Logic and Rhetoric in England, 1500–1700*. Princeton: Princeton University Press, 1956.

Humboldt, Wilhelm von. *On Language: The Diversity of Human Language-Structure and Its Influence on the Mental Development of Mankind*. Translated by Peter Heath, with an introduction by Hans Aarsleff. Texts in German Philosophy. Cambridge: Cambridge University Press, 1988.

———. *Linguistic Variability and Intellectual Development*. Translated by George C. Buck and Frithjof A. Raven. Coral Gables, FL: University of Miami Press, 1971.

———. *Humanist without Portfolio: An Anthology of the Writings of Wilhelm von Humboldt*. Translated by Marianne Cowan. Detroit: Wayne State University Press, 1963.

Jackendoff, Ray. *Consciousness and the Computational Mind*. Cambridge: MIT Press, 1987.

———. "On Beyond Zebra: The Relation of Linguistic and Visual Information." *Cognition* 26 (1987): 89–114.

John of Salisbury. *The Metalogicon of John of Salisbury: A Twelfth-Century Defense of the Verbal and Logical Arts of the Trivium*. Translated by Daniel D. McGarry. Berkeley: University of California Press, 1955.

Johnson-Laird, Philip N. "Space to Think." In *Language and Space*, edited by Paul Bloom, Mary Peterson, Lynn Nadel, and Merrill Garrett. Cambridge: Bradford Books of MIT Press, 1996.

Jones, Sir William. "On the Hindus." In *The Works of Sir William Jones*. Vol. 3. London, 1807.

Kain, Roger J. P., and Elizabeth Baigent. *The Cadastral Map in the Service of the State: A History of Property Mapping*. Chicago: University of Chicago Press, 1992.

Lach, Donald. *Asia in the Making of Europe*. Vol. 2, *A Century of Wonder*. Chicago: University of Chicago Press, 1977.

La Condamine, Charles Marie de. *Relation abrégée d'un voyage fait dans l'intérieur de l'Amérique méridionale* [1745]. In *A General Collection of the Best and Most Interesting*

Voyages and Travels in All Parts of the World, edited by John Pinkerton. Vol. 14. London, 1808–1814.

Lafitau, Joseph François. *Customs of the American Indians Compared with the Customs of Primitive Times* [1724]. Translated and edited by William Fenton and Elizabeth Moore. 2 vols. Toronto: Champlain Society, 1974.

Lakoff, George. *Women, Fire, and Dangerous Things: What Categories Reveal about the Mind.* Chicago: University of Chicago Press, 1987.

———. "The Invariance Hypothesis: Is Abstract Reason Based on Image-Schemas?" *Cognitive Linguistics* 1 (1990): 39–74.

Lakoff, George, and Mark Johnson. *Metaphors We Live By.* Chicago: University of Chicago Press, 1980.

Lamy, Bernard. *The Art of Speaking, written in French by Messieurs Du Port Royal, in pursuance of a former treatise intituled The Art of Thinking, and rendered into English* [French 1675]. London, 1696.

Lancelot, Claude, and Antoine Arnauld. *A General and Rational Grammar* (Grammaire générale et raisonnée) [1660]. Menston: Scholar, 1968.

Landa, Diego de. *Relación de las cosas de Yucatán.* Edited by Alfred M. Tozzer. Papers of the Peabody Museum, vol. 18. Cambridge, MA, 1941.

Landau, Barbara, and Ray Jackendoff. "'What' and 'Where' in Spatial Language and Spatial Cognition." *Behavioral and Brain Sciences* 16 (1993): 217–65.

Langacker, Ronald. *Foundations of Cognitive Grammar.* 2 vols. Stanford: Stanford University Press, 1987–1991.

Las Casas, Bartolomé de. *History of the Indies.* Translated and edited by Andrée Collard. New York: Harper & Row, 1971.

———. *In Defense of the Indians: The Defense of the Most Reverend Lord, Don Fray Bartolomé de Las Casas, of the Order of Preachers, Late Bishop of Chiapas, Against the Persecutors and Slanderers of the Peoples of the New World Discovered Across the Seas.* Translated and edited by Stafford Poole. DeKalb: Northern Illinois University Press, 1974.

Laslett, Peter. Introduction to *Two Treatises of Government*, by John Locke. Cambridge: Cambridge University Press, 1960.

Latimer, Hugh. *Selected Sermons of Hugh Latimer.* Edited by Allan G. Chester. Charlottesville: Folger Library and the University of Virginia Press, 1968.

Lechner, Joan Marie. *Renaissance Concepts of the Commonplaces.* New York: Pageant, 1962.

Lefebvre, Henri. *The Production of Space.* Translated by Donald Nicholson-Smith. Oxford: Blackwell, 1991.

Leibniz, G. W. *New Essays on Human Understanding* [1703]. Translated and edited by Peter Remnant and Jonathan Bennett. Cambridge: Cambridge University Press, 1981.

———. *De Scientia Universalis seu Calculo Philosophico.* In *Die philosophischen Schriften von G. W. Leibniz.* Vol. 7. Berlin, 1875.

Léry, Jean de. *History of a Voyage to the Land of Brazil, Otherwise Called America* [1578]. Translated by Janet Whatley. Berkeley: University of California Press, 1990.

Locke, John. *An Essay concerning Human Understanding.* Edited by Peter H. Nidditch. Oxford: Clarendon, 1975.

———. *Drafts for the Essay concerning Human Understanding, and Other Philosophical Writings.* Edited by Peter H. Nidditch and G. A. J. Rogers. Oxford: Oxford University Press, 1990.

———. "Of the Conduct of the Understanding." In *Posthumous Works of Mr. John Locke.* London, 1706.

Lope Blanch, Juan. "Los Indoamericanismos en el *Tesoro* de Covarrubias." *Nueva revista de filología hispánica* 26 (1977): 296–315.

Lucy, John A. *Language Diversity and Thought: A Reformulation of the Linguistic Relativity Hypothesis.* Cambridge: Cambridge University Press, 1992.

———. *Grammatical Categories and Cognition: A Case Study of the Linguistic Relativity Hypothesis.* Cambridge: Cambridge University Press, 1992.

Magalhães, Gabriel de. *A New History of China.* Translated by Bernou. London, 1688.

Marshall, P. J., and Glyndwr Williams. *The Great Map of Mankind: British Perceptions of the World in the Age of the Enlightenment.* London: Dent, 1982.

Martyr, Peter. *The Decades of the Newe World* (De Orbe Novo). In *The First Three English Books on America,* translated by Richard Eden and edited by Edward Arber. Birmingham, 1885.

Maupertuis, Pierre-Louis Moreau de. *Réflexions philosophiques sur l'origine des langues et la signification des mots* [1748]. In *Maupertuis, Turgot et Maine de Biran sur l'origine du langage,* edited by Ronald Grimsley and translated into English by Marie-Henriette Day. Geneva: Droz, 1971.

McKeon, Richard. "Creativity and Commonplace." In *Rhetoric: Essays in Invention and Discovery.* Woodbridge, CT: Ox Bow, 1987.

Melby, Alan, and C. Terry Warner. *The Possibility of Language: A Discussion of the Nature of Language, with Implications for Human and Machine Translation.* Amsterdam: John Benjamins, 1995.

Mendieta, Gerónimo de. *Historia eclesiástica indiana.* Edited by Joaquín G. Icazbalceta. Mexico City: Editorial Porrua, 1971.

Mendoza, Antonio de. "Relación, Apuntamientos y Avisos que por Mandado de S. M. Dió D. Antonio de Mendoza á D. Luis de Velasco, Nombrado Sucerderle in este Cargo." In *Colección de documentos inéditos relativos al descubrimiento, conquista y organización de las antiguas posesiones españolas de América y Oceania.* Vol. 6. Madrid: Quirós, 1864–1884.

Mentner, Edgar. "Topos und Commonplace." In *Strena Anglica: Fetschrift für Otto Ritter,* edited by G. Dietrich and F. W. Shulze. Halle: Niemeyer, 1956.

Michaelis, Johann David. *Dissertation on the Influence of Opinions on Language and of Language on Opinions* [1760]. London, 1769.

Mignolo, Walter. "Literacy and Colonization: The New World Experience." In *1492–1992: Re/Discovering Colonial Writing,* edited by René Jara and Nicholas Spadaccini. Hispanic Issues, vol. 4. Minneapolis: Prisma Institute, 1989.

Molina, Alonso de. "Epistle Nuncupatoria." In *Vocabulario en lengua castellana y mexicana y mexicana y castellana.* Mexico, 1571. Reprint, Leipzig: Teubner, 1880.

Montaigne, Michel de. "Of Cannibals." In *The Complete Works of Montaigne: Essays, Travel Journal, Letters,* translated by Donald M. Frame. Stanford: Stanford University Press, 1958.

Morton, Michael. *Herder and the Poetics of Thought: Unity and Diversity in "On Diligence in Several Learned Languages."* University Park: Pennsylvania State University Press, 1989.

Mundy, Barbara E. *The Mapping of New Spain: Indigenous Cartography and the Maps of the Relaciones Geográficas.* Chicago: University of Chicago Press, 1996.

Mungello, D. E. *Curious Land: Jesuit Accommodation and the Origins of Sinology.* Honolulu: University of Hawaii Press, 1989.

Murra, John V. "Waman Puma, etnógrafo del mundo Andino." Introduction to *El primer nueva corónica y buen gobierno por Felipe Guaman Poma de Ayala,* edited by John V. Murra and Rolena Adorno. Vol. 1. Mexico City: Siglo Veintiuno, 1980.

Navarrete, Domingo de. *An Account of the Empire of China: Historical, Political, Moral and Religious.* In *A Collection of Voyages and Travels,* compiled by Awnsham Churchill. Vol. 1. London, 1704.

Nerlich, Graham. *The Shape of Space*. 2d ed. Cambridge: Cambridge University Press, 1994.

Newton, Isaac. "On the Gravity and Equilibrium of Liquids." In *Unpublished Scientific Papers of Isaac Newton*, edited and translated by A. R. Hall and M. B. Hall. Cambridge: Cambridge University Press, 1962.

Nicolau d'Olwer, Luis. *Fray Bernardino de Sahagún, 1499–1590*. Translated by Mauricio J. Mixco. Salt Lake City: University of Utah Press, 1987.

O'Flaherty, James C. *The Quarrel of Reason with Itself: Essays on Hamann, Michaelis, Lessing, Nietzsche*. Columbia, SC: Camden House, 1988.

Ong, Walter J. "Peter Ramus." In *The Encyclopedia of Philosophy*. Vol. 7. New York: Macmillan, 1967.

Padley, G. A. *Grammatical Theory in Western Europe, 1500–1700: Trends in Vernacular Grammar*. Vol. 1. Cambridge: Cambridge University Press, 1985.

Pagden, Anthony. *Spanish Imperialism and the Political Imagination*. New Haven: Yale University Press, 1990.

Pariente, Jean-Claude. *L'analyse du langage à Port-Royal*. Paris: Éditions de Minuit, 1985.

Paxman, David. "'Adam in a Strange Country': Locke's Language Theory and Travel Literature." *Modern Philology* 92 (May 1995): 460–81.

———. "Language and Difference: The Problem of Abstraction in Eighteenth-Century Language Study." *Journal of the History of Ideas* 54 (1993): 19–36.

Payne, Edward J. *The History of the New World Called America*. 2 vols. Oxford: Oxford University Press, 1892–1899.

Peacham, Henry. *The Garden of Eloquence* [1577]. London, 1593.

Penguin Dictionary of Philosophy. Edited by Thomas Mautner. London: Penguin, 1999.

Percival, W. K. "Renaissance Linguistics: General Survey." In *Encyclopedia of Language and Linguistics*, edited by R. E. Asher and J. M. Y. Simpson. Oxford: Pergamon, 1994.

Pinker, Steven. *How the Mind Works*. New York: Norton, 1997.

Polanyi, Michael. *Personal Knowledge: Towards a Post-Critical Philosophy*. Chicago: University of Chicago Press, 1962.

Quintilian. *Institutes of Oratory, or Education of an Orator*. Translated by John Selby Watson. London: George Bell and Sons, 1909.

Ramus, Peter. *The Logike of the most excellent Philosopher P. Ramus Martyr*. Translated by R. MacIlmaine. London, 1574.

Rawlinson, H. G. "India in European Literature and Thought." In *The Legacy of India*, edited by G. T. Garratt. Oxford: Oxford University Press, 1938.

Ricard, Robert. *The Spiritual Conquest of Mexico: An Essay on the Apostolate and the Evangelizing Methods of the Mendicant Orders in New Spain, 1523–1572*. Translated by Lesley Byrd Simpson. Berkeley: University of California Press, 1966.

Rincón, Antonio del. *Arte mexicana* [1595]. Mexico: Secretaría de fomento, 1885.

Rousseau, Jean-Jacques. "Rousseau's Notes." In *The First and Second Discourses*, translated and edited by Victor Gourevitch. New York: Harper & Row, 1986.

Rowe, John H. "Sixteenth- and Seventeenth-Century Grammars." In *Studies in the History of Linguistics: Traditions and Paradigms*, edited by Dell Hymes, 361–79. Bloomington: Indiana University Press, 1974.

Rubio, Angel. *De la obra cultural de la antigua españa: Trabajos filológicos en Indias durante los siglos XVI, XVII, y XVIII*. Panama, 1939.

Ruiz de Alarcón, Hernando. *Treatise on the Heathen Superstitions and Customs That Today Live among the Indians Native to This New Spain, 1629*. Translated and edited by J. Richard Andrews and Ross Hassig. Norman: University of Oklahoma Press, 1984.

Sagard, Gabriel. *The Long Journey to the Country of the Hurons* (Grand voyage du pais des Hurons). Translated by W. H. Langton. Toronto: Champlain Society, 1939.

Sahagún, Bernardino de. "Introductions and Indices." In *Florentine Codex: General History of the Things of New Spain*, translated and edited by Arthur O. Anderson and Charles E. Dibble. Santa Fe: School of American Research and the University of Utah, 1950–1982.

———. *Colloquios y doctrina christiana con que los doze frailes de San Francisco embiados por el papa Adriano sesto y por el emperador Carlos quinto convirtieron a los Indios de la Nueva España*. Edited by Vargas Rea. Mexico: Biblioteca Aportación Histórica, 1944.

Salmon, Vivian. *The Works of Francis Lodwick: A Study of His Writings in the Intellectual Context of the Seventeenth Century*. London: Longman, 1972.

Salust, Guillaume de [Seigneur du Bartas]. *The Divine Weeks* (Les semaines) [1578]. Translated by William L'Ilse. London, 1596.

Santo Tomás, Domingo de. "Prólogo del Autor, al Christiano Lector." In *Grammatica, o Arte de la lengua general de los indios de los reynos del Perú* [1560]. Edited by Raúl P. Barrenechea. Lima: Universidad Nacional de San Marcos, 1951.

Sassetti, Filippo. *Lettere edite e inedite de Filippo Sassetti*. Edited by E. Marcucci. Florence: Monnier, 1855.

Schlegel, Friedrich von. *Ueber die Sprache und Weisheit der Indier* (On the Language and Wisdom of the Indies). Heidelberg, 1808.

Schreyer, Rudiger. "The Language of Nature: Inquiries into a Concept of Eighteenth-Century British Linguistics." In *Progress in Linguistic Historiography*, edited by Konrad Koerner, 153–73. Amsterdam Studies in the Theory and History of Linguistic Science. Amsterdam: John Benjamins, 1980.

Shaftesbury, Earl of [Anthony Ashley Cooper]. "Advice to an Author." In *Characteristics of Men, Manners, Opinions, Times*, edited by John M. Robertson. Vol. 1. Gloucester, MA: Peter Smith, 1963.

Shuger, Debora. *Sacred Rhetoric: The Christian Grand Style in the English Renaissance*. Princeton: Princeton University Press, 1988.

Simpson, J. M. Y. "Writing Systems: Principles and Typology." In *Encyclopedia of Language and Linguistics*, edited by R. E. Asher. Vol. 9. Oxford: Pergamon, 1994.

Slaughter, Mary. *Universal Languages and Scientific Taxonomy in the Seventeenth Century*. Cambridge: Cambridge University Press, 1982.

Smith, Adam. *Considerations concerning the First Formation of Languages*. In *The Theory of Moral Sentiments*. 1853. Reprint, New York: Kelley, 1966.

———. *Adam Smith: Lectures on Rhetoric and Belles Lettres*. Edited by J. C. Bryce. Vol. 4, *The Glasgow Edition of the Works and Correspondence of Adam Smith*. Oxford: Clarendon, 1983.

Sobel, Dava. *The Longitude*. London: Fourth Estate, 1995.

Sprat, Thomas. *History of the Royal Society of London, for Improving of Natural Knowledge* [1667]. Edited by Jackson I. Cope and Harold W. Jones. St. Louis: Washington University Press, 1958.

Stafford, Barbara. "Images of Ambiguity: Eighteenth-Century Microscopy and the Neither/Nor." In *Visions of Empire: Voyages, Botany, and Representations of Nature*, edited by David P. Miller and Hans P. Reill. Cambridge: Cambridge University Press and University of California Press, 1996.

Stillman, Robert E. *The New Philosophy and Universal Languages in Seventeenth-Century England: Bacon, Hobbes, and Wilkins*. Lewisburg, PA: Bucknell University Press, 1995.

Streit, Robert. *Bibliotheca Missionum*. 30 vols. Münster and Aachen, 1916–1959.

Talmy, Leonard. "How Language Structures Space." In *Spatial Orientation: Theory, Research, and Application*, edited by H. Pick and L. Acredolo, 225–82. New York: Plenum, 1983.

———. *Toward a Cognitive Semantics*. 2 vols. Cambridge: MIT Press, 2000.

Temple, Sir William. *Memoirs of What Past in Christendom from the War Begun 1672 to the Peace Concluded 1679*. London, 1692.

Todorov, Tzvetan. *On Human Diversity: Nationalism, Racism, and Exoticism in French Thought*. Translated by Catherine Porter. Cambridge: Harvard University Press, 1993.

Tooke, John Horne. *The Diversions of Purley*. 2d ed. 2 vols. Menston: Scholar, 1968.

Torreti, Roberto. "Space." In *Routledge Encyclopedia of Philosophy*, edited by Edward Craig. Vol. 9. London: Routledge, 1998.

Tsiapera, Maria, and Garon Wheeler. *The Port-Royal Grammar: Sources and Influences*. Münster: Nodus, 1993.

Turner, Mark. "Aspects of the Invariance Hypothesis." *Cognitive Linguistics* 1 (1990).

———. *The Literary Mind*. New York: Oxford University Press, 1996.

Urquhart, Thomas. *Logopandecteision, or An Introduction to the Universal Language* [1653]. In *The Admirable Urquhart: Selected Writings*, edited by Richard Boston. London: Fraser, 1975.

Valadés, Diego. *Rhetorica Christiana* [1579]. Edited and translated by Esteban J. Palomera, Alfonso Castro Pallares, and Tarsicio Herrera Zapién. Mexico: Universidad Nacional Autónoma de México, Fondo de Cultura Económica, 1989.

Vico, Giambattista. *On the Study Methods of Our Time* [1709]. Translated by Elio Gianturco. Ithaca: Cornell University Press, 1990.

Voltaire. *Le philosophe ignorant*. In *Œuvres complètes de Voltaire*. Vol. 26. Paris: Garnier, 1879.

———. *La philosophie de l'histoire*. In *Œuvres complètes de Voltaire*. Vol. 59. Toronto: University of Toronto Press, 1969.

Waite, Joseph. "To my intimate and ingenious Friend, Mr. Beck, upon his Universal Character, serving for all languages." In *Cave Beck, The Universal Character By which all the Nations in the World may understand one anothers Conceptions, Reading out of one Common Writing their own Mother Tongues*. London, 1657.

Wardy, Robert. "Chinese Whispers: The Jesuit Policy of Accommodation and Western Philosophy in China." *Proceedings of the Cambridge Philosophical Society* 38 (1992): 149–70.

Webster, John. *Academiarum Examen . . . .* London: Calvert, 1654.

Wells, G. A. "Herder's Resistance to Language as Invention." *JEGP* 86 (1986): 167–90.

Whately, William. *Prototypes*. 1640.

Wheeler, Garon. "Port Royal Tradition of Grammar." In *Encyclopedia of Language and Linguistics*, edited by R. E. Asher. Vol. 6. Oxford: Pergamon, 1994.

Whorf, Benjamin Lee. "Science and Linguistics." In *Language, Thought and Reality: Selected Writings of Benjamin Lee Whorf*, edited by John B. Carroll, 207–19. Boston: MIT Press, 1956.

Wilkins, John. *An Essay towards a Real Character and a Philosophical Language*. London: Gellibrand, 1668.

Wittgenstein, Ludwig. *Philosophical Investigations*. Translated by G. E. M. Anscombe. Oxford: Blackwell, 1953.

Wood, Neal. *The Politics of Locke's Philosophy: A Social Study of "An Essay concerning Human Understanding."* Berkeley: University of California Press, 1983.

Woodward, David. "Maps and the Rationalization of Geographic Space." In *Circa 1492: Art in the Age of Exploration*, edited by Jay A. Levenson. Washington, D.C.: National Gallery of Art, 1991.

Woodward, David, and G. Malcolm Lewis. Introduction to *The History of Cartography*. Vol. 2, bk. 3. Chicago: University of Chicago Press, 1998.

Index

A

Aarsleff, Hans, 184
abstraction: problem of, 195–200, 207; in reports from abroad, 200–203; required for language, 198; vital role of, 206
Acosta, José de, 43, 103
Adamic tongue, 70, 89–90
Adelung, J. C., 119, 228, 231
Aegidus of Viterbo, 23
Aelius Antonius (Frances Ximenes), 23–24
agglutinating languages, 46
Agricola, Rudolph, 166
Akhundov, Murad, 32, 34, 173
Alarcón, Ruiz de, 73, 75
Albinus, Peter, 23–26, 36, 40–41
Aldrete, Bernardo de, 79–80
Alembert, Jean le Rond d', 233
alphabetic writing, 45
ambiguity, fundamental, 149
analog languages, 231
analogies, 15
Andrewes, Lancelot, 89
Andrews, Richard, 73
Aquinas, Thomas, 38
Aristotle, 83; organized knowledge on a spatial model, 165; place theory, 166;
Arnauld, Antoine, 58, 61, 62; *Grammaire générale et raisonnée* by, 58, 60–64
awareness, focal and subsidiary, 248
Ayala, Guaman Pomo de, 105
Aztec language and culture, 109

B

Babel, 36–38, 69–71, 89
Bacon, Francis, 3, 14, 41, 167; New Atlantis and control of communication, 76–77; need for philosophical grammar, 54–57; proper language study, 90–94; on rhetoric, 155
Baigent, Elizabeth, 28

Bartas, Salust du, 70
Beck, Cave, 131, 133, 134
Behn, Aphra, 125–26
Bertonio, Luis de, 105
Besnier, Pierre, 58–59
Bibliander, Theodore, 40–41, 42
blended spaces, 11, 13–15
Boehme, Jacob, 89
Bonfante, Giuliano, 227
borrowed words, 116–17, 224
Borst, Arno, 36, 226–27
Brazil, 121–26
Breydenbach, Bernard von, 119
Bruno, Giordano, 51–52, 174
Burtt, E. A., 243

C

cabalists, 39
Calepino, Ambrogio, 119
Calvin, John, 71
Campanella, Tommaso, 83
Cano, Melchior, 84
Cassiodorus, 166
Cassirer, Ernst, 3
Charles V, 81
China, 77
Chinese: characters, 40, 133; Humboldt's view of, 238; language, 74, 97, 118
Chirino, Pedro, 117
Chomsky, Noam, 1, 36, 62, 253
Cicero, 158, 166
classifications, challenges of, 229, 234
cognition, 4–5, 119; intertwined with language, 252
cognitive linguists, 7
Columbus, Christopher, 24–25, 28, 36, 101–2
Comenius, 132, 133
compass, 28
Condillac, Etienne Bonnot de, 196, 203–7, 225; chains of ideas, 205, 207; *Essay on the Origin of Human*

language: absolute — , 17–18; abstract relational — , 17, 183; agglutinating type, 232; American, 232; Asian, 232; checks on, 198; Chinese, 232; as conceptual metaphor, 250; as cognitive map, 183; as related to cognition, 220; other cognitive faculties intertwined with, 252; connection of to logic and nature, 91–93; context-free vs. context-dependent, 18; creative by nature, 143; and culture, 113–14; families, 226; figurative language, 12; history of, 217, 220; and ideas, 201; inflecting and non-inflecting, 232; as inseparable from reason, 233; isolating type, 232; as journey, 217–43, 247; limits nations, 238; Locke on, 183, 220; and longitude, 219; maps space, 9–10; as mind's space, 190; no mind without, 221; multimodal view of, 253; not one thing, 8, 248; as outer appearance of a people's spirit, 237; and peoples' rights, 86–88; philosophical, 90; posed dangers, 72; power to shape thinking, 234; as primitive of experience, 250–51; as private, 198; and relationship among mind, Other, and external world, 196; removes us from experience, 211; requires generalization and abstraction, 198; self-reflection made possible by, 222; and separation, 90–91, 93; spatial structures in, 7; as theology, 102; typologies of, 220; as true world, 235; and violence, 99; world views in, 237

language barriers, 69–76; aggravated by the devil, 71–76; between the mind and the world, 88–94; and ethics, 78, 81

language policy, Spanish, 80–81, 85

language study: effects of, 105, 116; and ideology, 52–53; medieval, 36–44, 49–50, 60; motives for, 97–99; as sign of divine era, 23–24

Las Casas, Bartolomé de, 85–88, 98

Laslett, Peter, 184

Latimer, Hugh, 153–54

Latin grammar, 35, 46–47; as imperialism, 49–51; as linguistic cosmology, 51; Nebrija's, 49–50

Latin language, 232

Lechner, Joan Marie, 168

Lefebvre, Henri, 8–9, 32–34, 251

Leibniz, Gottfried Wilhelm, 10, 133, 144–48; encyclopedia, 146; point of view in knowledge, 144; relational view of space, 176; universal character, 145

Léry, Jean de, 121–23, 191–92

ligne ideale, 230

linguist, role of, 4, 240–43

linguistic collections, 3–4, 41, 57

linguistic determinism, 125–27

linguistic diversity, 4–5, 99, 149

linguistic imperialism, 78–80, 83

linguistic purity, leads to stagnation, 225

linguistic relativism, 15, 97, 126–27

Locke, John, 146, 147; association of ideas, 199, 204–6; centrality of comparison, 188; Condillac on deficiency, 204; language the mind's space, 190; language theory of, 183; on limits to relativism, 199; mixed-mode ideas, 199; need for multiple viewpoints, 186; place as relative position, 190; spatial conceptions of, 176, 247; spatial metaphors, 183; travel literature used by, 184–87; no universal morality, 187

Lodwick, Francis, 133, 134

logographic writing systems, 46, 133

longitude, 30, 35, 56; as a language-like problem, 218–26; longitude prize, 219

Lord's Prayer, 119

Lucy, John, 126

Lull, Raymond, 39

Luther, Martin, 24

Lyonet, Pierre, 230

M

Magalhães, Garbriel, 118

Magellan, Fernando, 25, 119

Malayālam language, 119

Mandeville, John, 119

mapping, 7, 22, 26–32; of language, 21; as model, 26; and navigation, 22; parallels with language study, 34–35